FREDERICK THE GREAT
AND HIS OFFICIALS

FREDERICK THE GREAT
AND HIS OFFICIALS

HUBERT C. JOHNSON

NEW HAVEN AND LONDON, YALE UNIVERSITY PRESS, 1975

Published with assistance from the Principal's Publication
Fund Committee, University of Saskatchewan

Library of Congress catalog card number: 74-84085
International standard book number: 0-300-01755-3

Designed by Sally Sullivan
and set in Times Roman type.
Printed in the United States of America by
The Murray Printing Co., Forge Village, Mass.

Published in Great Britain, Europe, and Africa by
Yale University Press, Ltd., London.
Distributed in Latin America by Kaiman & Polon,
Inc., New York City; in Australasia and Southeast
Asia by John Wiley & Sons Australasia Pty. Ltd.,
Sydney; in India by UBS Publishers' Distributors Pvt.,
Ltd., Delhi; in Japan by John Weatherhill, Inc., Tokyo.

CONTENTS

KEY TO ABBREVIATIONS

The following sources are usually listed in abbreviated form in the notes:

AB: Acta Borussica, die Behördenorganisation und allgemeine Staatsverwaltung Preussens im 18. Jahrhundert. Editors: Gustav Schmoller et al. 15 vols. (Berlin, 1894–1935). This documentary collection is the most valuable source of material on the administrative history of Prussia up to 1772. Many of the documents included in it are no longer in existence due to destruction of the Breslau and other archives during World War II.

CCM: Corpus Constitutionum Marchicarum. Constitutionum Marchicarum-Continuationes und Supplement. Editor, C.O. Mylius (Berlin, 1744–51). This, together with later supplements under the title of *Novum Corpus Constitutionum* constitute a contemporary collection of public edicts.

FBPG: Forschungen zur brandenburgischen und preussischen Geschichte (Leipzig).

PKPA: Puolikationen aus den preussischen Staatsarchiven (Leipzig).

VSWG: Vierteljahrschrift für Sozial- und Wirtschaftsgeschichte (Wiesbaden).

Merseburg: indicates files to be found in the *Deutsches Zentralarchiv* Merseburg, German Democratic Republic.

Potsdam: indicates files to be found in the *Staatsarchiv Potsdam,* "Orangerie," Potsdam, German Democratic Republic.

INTRODUCTION

Frederick II of Prussia, called "Frederick the Great" in his own lifetime and thereafter, was a remarkable monarch. His long reign, from 1740 to 1786, was filled with wars: the War of the Austrian Succession from 1740 to 1748, the Seven Years' War from 1756 to 1763, and the War of the Bavarian Succession of 1778 to 1779. Through military action Frederick added the province of Silesia to his realm. Through diplomatic negotiations he added the province of East Frisia in 1744 and part of Poland in 1772. His remarkable leadership of a minor state in war and peace[1] was paralleled by a quite extraordinary participation in the intellectual life of Europe. Frederick wrote hundreds of letters and several score of historical, philosophical, and literary works: his total output fills forty volumes. In his own day he achieved a kind of legendary status as Prussian admirers circulated anecdotes about him. To foreigners he appeared to be one of the greatest men of the age. But Frederick was an enigmatic personality. Early exposed to heavy psychological pressures, he armored himself against the world. As Mirabeau, the great tribune of the French Revolution, said as early as 1788: Frederick "was born sensitive" but learned through adversity to steel himself and to present to others an impenetrable facade.[2] Overshadowed by his

1. The best survey of German history before 1740 remains Bernhard Erdmannsdörffer, *Deutsche Geschichte* (Leipzig, 1932), vol. 2. He portrays the gradual rise of Prussia and concludes his work with a discussion of the reign of King Frederick William I, stating that the failure of the Holy Roman Empire had left Austria and Prussia as the rivals for future leadership in the German nation (p. 469). Otto Hintze, *Die Hohenzollern und ihr Werk* (Berlin, 1915), is the best survey of Prussian history. He built on foundations laid by Leopold von Ranke, *Zwölf Bücher Preussischer Geschichte*, 2nd ed. (Leipzig, 1878); and by J. G. Droysen, *Geschichte der preussischen Politik,* 2nd ed. (Leipzig, 1872).

2. Honore G. V. Riquetti, Comte de Mirabeau, *De La Monarchie Prussienne sous Frédéric le Grand*, 4 vols. (London, 1788), was the most famous of the early

military and literary exploits, the importance of his role in the day-to-day administration of the state has remained obscure.

As the head of the Prussian state Frederick supposedly made all important decisions. In common with all other statesmen, however, he required the assistance of numerous officials. When a ruler is surrounded by able ministers one always wonders who in fact governed. Some historians have claimed that Frederick ruled absolutely, others that his officials ruled, still others that the landed nobility or the army ruled.[3] In truth Frederick governed in cooperation with his senior officials: he and they provided ideas, programs, guides, and legislation for Prussia.

A great deal has been written about the government of Prussia during the eighteenth century, but much of it has been derived from certain basic assumptions: that the authority of the king was "absolute," that the corps of officials composed themselves into a monolithic "bureaucracy," or that the army (with or without the help of the officials) reduced the populace to unquestioning military disci-

---

critics of Frederick. Nevertheless, he was fascinated by the personality of Frederick. See 1:63.

3. The role of Frederick is emphasized in Hintze, *Die Hohenzollern und ihr Werk*; and by Reinhold Koser, *Geschichte Friedrichs des Grossen*, 4 vols. (Stuttgart, 1912). Gustav Schmoller was the most celebrated of the advocates of the bureaucracy. See his excellent survey of the rise of bureaucratic institutions in Europe and Prussia in *Acta Borussica. Die Behördenorganisation und die allgemeine Staatsverwaltung Preussens im 18. Jahrhundert* vol. 1 (Berlin, 1892); and in idem, *Preussische Verfassungs-, Verwaltungs- und Finanzgeschichte* (Berlin, 1921). Hintze also devised an interpretation which tried to spell out the importance of the army in "Der preussische Militär- und Beamtenstaat im 18. Jahrhundert," *Geist und Epochen der preussischen Geschichte* (Leipzig, 1943). Ludwig Tümpel, *Die Entstehung des brandenburgisch-preussischen Einheitsstaats im Zeitalter des Absolutismus (1609–1806)*, (Breslau, 1915), provides the most exaggerated interpretation of the "military–bureaucratic" State and its evolution. Marxist writers tend to focus on the nobility as the presumed ruling class of Prussia: Franz Mehring, *Historische Aufsätze zur preussisch-deutschen Geschichte* (Berlin, 1946), pp. 62–63 ff. Horst Krüger, *Zur Geschichte der Manufakturen und der Manufakturarbeiter in Preussen* (Berlin, 1958), pp. 278–84. The most radical interpretation of the role of the army is found in Otto Büsch, *Militärsystem und Sozialleben im alten Preussen* (Berlin, 1958), pp. 278–84. Sidney B. Fay, *The Rise of Brandenburg–Prussia* (New York, 1964) provides an interpretation similar to that of Hintze. Gustav Schmoller, *The Mercantile System and its Historical Significance* (London, 1897), introduces English readers to his interpretation.

pline. The central aim of this work is to set aside the concept of the "military–bureaucratic" state and associated descriptive words: "bureaucracy," "militarism," "autocracy," and "absolutism," and to try to evaluate the governmental policies of Frederick the Great in an eighteenth–century context. What was the nature of the Prussian government between 1740 and 1786, what was its scope, what were its functions, and how were decisions made?[4]

Frederick's role as an administrator was usually restricted to the approval of proposals submitted by others. At times he initiated programs, while at other times senior officials were responsible. The relationship between king and minister was one of cooperation rather than one of master and servant. Regardless of who made the decisions or initiated the policies, everything depended upon the cooperation, or lack of it, of subordinate officials and of the people of Prussia. Some royal commands were never translated into practice because they were universally unpopular. In a state with a population of five million persons scattered in far-flung provinces with diverse cultures and economies, the Prussian government had great difficulty in establishing a uniform rule. The whole of local government cannot be examined here because of the vastness and complexity of the documentary sources. Local government has been analysed only when it seemed to exert an influence on higher levels of government.

Frederick II inherited a civil service, a particular kind of society, and worked within a particular political context. He soon discovered that the administrative machinery of the state he had inherited was inadequate to maintain the role of a great power. Little did he suspect that he would spend a great deal of his time trying to adapt the modest government he inherited to the new Prussian state which he caused

---

4. Certain modern analyses of bureaucracy are important aids to the understanding of administrative history. Max Weber, *Essays from Max Weber*, ed. and trans. H. Gerth and C. Wright Mills (Glencoe, 1950), pp. 196–218, has had great influence on modern theory. His views of the Prussian government were heavily influenced by those of Gustav Schmoller. Weber described the nature of "modern" bureaucracy, which he claimed arose first in the Prussia of Frederick II, as the result of the rationalization of offices and techniques and as due to the growth of a trained and supposedly loyal administrative corps of officials (loyal to the king at all times).

to come into being when he invaded Silesia. Frederick William I could afford to be the conservative custodian of the old Prussia, but Frederick II was the radical promoter of a new state. In Old Regime Europe, however, old institutions were not easily discarded, and Frederick found, in fact, that he had to preserve them while trying to introduce new governmental forms.

Naturally Frederick did not do everything himself and had to rely on selected individuals to devise new programs and approaches to government. This work attempts to explain how leadership within the Prussian state was shared between the king and other individuals, including officials, businessmen, and jurists. At no time is it assumed that bureaucratic institutions inevitably grow or decline, or that the opinions of king and officials remain the same over a course of time.

In common with many others, this manuscript has been changed, expanded, and revised in detail and in interpretation since its beginnings as a doctoral dissertation. The dissertation was prepared under the direction of professors Hans Rosenberg, Werner T. Angress, and Dwight Waldo in 1962 at the University of California at Berkeley. Since that time others have read the manuscript in various stages of revision: my colleagues at the University of Saskatchewan at Saskatoon, professors Ivo Lambi and Michael Hayden. It must be emphasized that none of these persons can be held responsible for errors in fact or in interpretation, or for any other fault now present. Much of the research incorporated in this work was made possible by grants in 1965 and 1967 from the Principal's Research Fund, University of Saskatchewan, Saskatoon, and by a travelling grant from the Canada Council in 1967. My wife, Suzanne Pasche Johnson, deserves to be rewarded by my dedication of this work to her, however inadequately this dedication may reflect my dependence upon her.

I

THE SHAPE OF PRUSSIAN
GOVERNMENT BY 1740

Frederick II inherited a particular kind of leadership, a type of government, and an existing society with its economic strengths and weaknesses. The Prussian state had been constructed over the course of several centuries and could be considered to be at a stage of mature development by 1740, when Frederick William I died and Frederick II came to the throne. The son inherited not only the crown, he inherited the whole complex of laws, customs, and ways of doing things which had been elaborated by rulers and their subjects alike over a long period. Before one can understand the administrative role of the son after 1740, one must briefly look at that of the father.

Frederick William I reigned from 1713 to 1740, and his rule was distinguished by notable accomplishments. While keeping Prussia free from involvement in war, he, built an army of formidable size for defensive purposes. He established a military conscription system which drew into the reserve force of the army many Prussians of all social ranks and made them aware of a common membership in the State and a common allegiance to a sovereign. He supervised the complete reconstruction of the machinery of government in order to centralize political power in the hands of an extraordinary permanent committee called the General Directory of War and Finance. At the same time his government rested more lightly upon the populace than the governments of many other states during the century.

Frederick William I should not escape criticism for the less laud-able aspects of his reign. He was possessed by a military obsession, for example, which influenced his whole career.[1] He was quite narrow-minded and immune to the intellectual influences of his day, except for his concern for a recently developed strain of evangelical Christianity called Pietism. His role of parent earned criticism in an age where parental authority was almost universally celebrated and filial obedience and subjugation expected. Rather than becoming excessively preoccupied with previous opinions of Frederick William I, one might adopt the famous concept of Herbert Butterfield, which he used to explain the emergence of modern science: one must put on a different thinking cap. Frederick William I was no martinet nor was he a progenitor of totalitarian despots of the twentieth century. He was the chief executive of a state attempting to work on routine and not-so-routine problems within the eighteenth-century context. Frederick the Great reviewed his accomplishments, adopted some of his policies, and abandoned others after his accession to the throne in 1740.

General Governmental Policies of Frederick William I

The general and guiding principles of Prussian government had been steadily constructed by a series of rulers and their officials beginning with the legislation of the Great Elector (1643–1688) and ending with the *Political Testament* of Frederick William I (1722). These principles were most clearly summarized in the *Instructions* which Frederick William I prepared for the establishment of the General Directory and the provincial war and domains boards in

1. Reinhold Dorwart, *The Administrative Reforms of Frederick William I* (Cambridge, Mass., 1953), describes the foundation of the General Directory. His view that the foundation of the General Directory was the start of a monolithic bureaucracy is not reflected in the work of Fritz Hartung, "Studien zur Geschichte der preussischen Verwaltung," in his collected essays, *Staatsbildende Kräfte der Neuzeit* (Berlin, 1961), pp. 178–345. Otto Hintze, *Die Hohenzollern und ihr Werk* (Berlin, 1915), entitles his chapter on King Frederick William I "The Military and Bureaucratic State of Frederick William I," and states: "Frederick William I is the single founder of the old Prussian state organization with its harsh discipline and its narrow but magnificent direction, which served as the foundation for military–political power." See the bibliographical essay for further discussion.

1722.[2] These instructions served as a prelude to a wholesale reconstruction and centralization of government from the lowest to the highest levels. According to this document, Frederick William I had three governmental aims: to increase public revenues, to maintain peace and order, and to provide auxiliary support for the army. These aims were connected to one another and stemmed from two fundamental assumptions. First, the State must be made as powerful as possible in order to protect itself from neighbouring and rival states, and second, such increase in power could only come about if the inhabitants of the Prussian realm cooperated. Firm direction from the top must be matched by willing obedience from below. Despite his obsession with his army, Frederick William I had really tried to maintain peace with his neighbours and had tried, according to his own beliefs, to make his government fair and just insofar as the people of Prussia were concerned. His was a government small in size and limited in scope.

He tried from 1722 to the end of his reign to develop means to increase the revenues of this government. In common with many other rulers, ancient and modern, he found it much easier to streamline the machinery of the bureaucracy in the hope of creating cheaper and more efficient operation than to increase existing taxes or to create new ones. Part of this "economy drive" involving governmental operations proved successful when a handful of competitive state treasuries were consolidated under the umbrella of his new committee of four ministers, the General Directory, in 1722. Unfortunately, such administrative reshuffling resulted in rather short-term and meager accomplishments. He also hoped to create more affluent tax payers by sponsoring a long-term mercantilistic policy: internal trade and manufacturing were to be increased and the importation of foreign goods curtailed. This plan of economic development was never elaborated clearly in theory and emerged only in fragmentary programs. Frederick William, for example, directed his officials to undertake a closer supervision of trade, a closer enquiry into the

2. See the comment by the editors in *AB*, 3: 532–36, and the text of the instructions of 1722 which follows, pp. 540 ff.

requests of entrepreneurs for privileges and monopolies, a greater effort to recruit foreign workmen and to inspect manufactured products, and, finally, to establish workhouses for the indigent. None of these policies were in the least remarkable: all had been popularized earlier by Colbert. But all were part of one aim: to increase taxes.

The second great aim of government was to maintain peace and order. Frederick William I was not so naive as to think that he could achieve this aim simply by increasing the size of the army and the police forces, or by devising more criminal laws. He knew that the bulk of the population must at least passively accept his leadership and his efforts to keep order. Perhaps he remembered James II, who suffered from lack of a political consensus, although no evidence exists to suggest that he knew of the fate of that king. Needless to say, he apparently remained ignorant of Locke. Instinctively perhaps, Frederick William I based his decisions on what he estimated it was possible to enforce within his realm. Most likely, he simply tried to imitate the techniques of his grandfather, the Great Elector. His officials were even more aware than he was of the difficulties which might be encountered if unpopular or unrealistic decrees were thrust on a sullen society. The officials had to negotiate with landlords, domain contractors, and with businessmen. Occasionally they recognized that they had to listen to the voice of the peasants.

Frederick William considered the third aim of his government to be the provision of auxiliary support to the army. Military garrisons had served as supports for the government in towns and countryside since the time of the Great Elector; the state thus had an obligation to provide food, forage, and other material needs to its military guard. Recognizing the interlocking nature of civil–military operations, Frederick William I devoted the greater part of his instructions of December, 1722, to descriptions of the quartering of troops, securing of forage, recruitment, payment of the army, and related problems. He thought that military administration was an integral part of the work of the General Directory and of the boards in the provinces. General Grumbkow, who was the senior minister of the General

Directory, opposed the joining of such apparently disparate functions as domain administration and the supervision of forage collection under one directing body.

Rule by Consent of the Governed

Prussian society in 1740 reflected pervading economic conditions. Since the population was predominately agrarian (perhaps 80 percent or more), it was obvious to all that the social structure included two major classes: the class of landowners, which was aristocratic for the most part, and the class of peasants, which was primarily made up of serfs of varying status. The remaining 20 percent were designated by contemporaries as the urban professional and business group, the artisans, and the urban (and rural) unemployed and indigent. The last, large, minority could be considered *declassée* since the indigent of city and country were outside of the system, except if they were recipients of some kind of charity, were pressed into military service, or were the natural prey of the police. In this heterogenous society only the landowning aristocracy could be considered members of an upper class. Obviously the relationship between the government and this class was a more important one than any relationship developed with any other class.

Of all the classes of Prussian society the landed aristocracy was the most difficult to lead. Prior to the reign of the Great Elector the noble-dominated estates still possessed considerable power in the various provinces, and the representatives of the ruler had to bargain with them long and hard at each session. The prohibition of the meetings of some of these estates and the reduction of rights and privileges of others after 1648 did not mean that henceforth the aristocrats of the realm were helpless and servile followers of the ruler. They petitioned the king to grant them favorable tariffs and to allow them to ship their grain abroad without duty. They continued to insist on the right to elect their own officials, which the Hohenzollern rulers usually allowed them in regard to *Landräte*, the county administrators, but not provincial governmental officials. The nobles

also wished to maintain their own local treasuries for local governmental expenditures.[3] The Great Elector and his successors took away
some political independence from the aristocracy, but had to grant
privileges in return.

The *Junker* landlords were powerful after 1713, but they were
forced to work with the officials of the ruler to an increasing extent.
Only a relatively small percentage of aristocratic families were really
wealthy, and the rest were only too willing to accept jobs from the
king. Frederick William I harnessed his vassals with a number of
silken threads. Many posts in the civil service, and virtually all in the
army officer corps except those in the engineers and artillery, were
reserved for those of noble blood. The minority of aristocrats who
actually owned seigneurial property were encouraged to take command over the serfs. These landlords became, in effect, "little kings"
on their own estates, even if successive rulers frequently attempted to
check their abuses and to remind their vassals of the rights of the
peasants. Some vassals, of course, failed to see that conditions had
changed and remained sullen and rebellious: in East Prussia the
provincial governmental agencies had great difficulty in rounding up
aristocratic youths for the compulsory cadet schools of the army
after 1730, and the periodic meetings of the provincial estates remained stormy forums.[4] Nevertheless, the active rule of aristocrats
on their own property and their participation in local and central

3. F. L. Carsten, *The Origins of Prussia* (Oxford, 1954), discusses this history.
E. Spiro, *Die Gravamina der ostpreussischen Stände auf die Huldigungstägen des
18 Jr.* (Breslau, 1929), pp. 1–34, discusses the negotiations between Frederick
William I and the East Prussian estates.
4. The provincial estates long continued to pose problems to the king and his
civil service. Spiro, *Die Gravamina*, pp. 12–19, indicates that the East Prussian
estates protested the establishment of a militia, the quartering of troops, their
inability to nominate provincial and local officials, and their inability to agree to
tax levies. The Pomeranian estates were more moderate, but still resisted the loss
of their right to approve taxes, taking their cue partly from their East prussian
counterparts. *AB*, 3:229, 349. Since, however, the nobility of one province did
not usually cooperate with that of other provinces, it was possible for the king to
deal with them in turn. E. Schwenke, *Friedrich der Grosse und der Adel* (Berlin,
1911), claimed that the disorganization of the aristocracy as a class under Frederick William I was followed by their amalgamation: "The nobility first perceived
the feeling of belonging to one group," under Frederick II (pp. 6–7).

government made them partners of the king in the governance of Prussia.

The peasants throughout the realm did not possess any obvious role in the consensus that underlay the real authority of the state. Nevertheless, even contemporary natural law jurists recognized that the mostly illiterate serfs formed a necessary portion of society and of the State. Indeed, the Baron von Bielfeld claimed that the peasants formed an order separate from but equal to the aristocratic and bourgeois orders—each order had its rights and obligations. The peasants expected little of life: a share of land and of the produce from it, a place to live, and a secure environment. If they obeyed the orders of their landlord, they obeyed within limits established by themselves within the village society. Much of the time peasants were left alone by recruiting agents, landlords, and officials. The routine of agrarian life was old and was ingrained in the minds of peasants throughout the eighteenth century. To the despair of agrarian reformers such as Süssmilch, the peasants preferred to follow their old methods of cultivation. Prussia had its "Turnip Townsends," but they were not able to persuade many of these crafty, if conservative, farmers of the necessity of change.[5] Officials and landlords by and large did not try to force them into new paths. Indeed, the officials recognized that little could be done regarding the peasant, and the peasant in turn avoided people of quality whenever possible. In times of bad crops, famine, and extreme rural distress, peasant revolts did occur, but fortunately for the State, not everywhere at the same time.[6] The State could crush such sporadic uprisings with comparative ease.

5. J. P. Süssmilch, *Die Göttliche Ordnung in den Veränderungen des menschlichen Geschlechts* . . . (Berlin, 1765–1777), Pt. 1., 90–91, 521–22, 428 ff., gives a very compassionate analysis of the problems of the peasantry: "A complete release from all services and burdens would greatly aid the countryman who is robbed by the present *Frondienst* of his time, health, and energy"(p. 428). The high mortality rate, coupled with the feudal burdens, kept the peasants in a perpetual state of apathy according to this reform-minded pastor. Nevertheless, as Skalweit states (*AB Getreidepolitik*, 3:22–23), the entire agrarian economy was not very compatible with commercial and industrial development in Prussia, and Süssmilch and other theorists never decided how it could be made compatible.

6. Stadelmann, PKPA, 11: 101–18.

The lives of the vast majority of the subjects of the king of Prussia were confined to the routine of farming within the rural social order. Because of the aristocratic landlord's legal authority over these peasants as police chief and as magistrate, as well as organizer of work and collector of rents and fees, the bureaucracy did not often come into contact with individual serfs. Even on the royal domains the land was contracted out to private overseers. The only official who had any kind of regular firsthand contact with a large portion of the rural population was the *Landrat*, who resembled the English justice of the peace. But in most cases the *Landrat* was a land-owning aristocrat and was more apt to identify his interests with those of his friends and neighbors rather than with those of the provincial board. He was an ambiguous figure in the public service.[7]

In urban centers the Hohenzollern rulers had likewise tried to subordinate the local governmental bodies to central control. The influential classes of these cities were composed of merchants, lawyers and other professionals, and certain guild masters. This leading element of the *Bürgerschaft* or bourgeoisie, had previously dominated local administration. A few families had often monopolized public offices for generations. The Great Elector introduced his own officials, called *Commissarii Loci*, and tried to seize control of municipalities.[8] In cities where the local economy was stagnant, the boards

7. Rudolph Stadelmann, *Preussens Könige in ihrer Thätigkei für die Landescultur*, pt. 2, *Friedrich der Grosse PKPA* 11 (Berlin, 1882): 1–64, gives a review of Frederick's agrarian policies. The most thoughtful analysis of these policies is by Otto Hintze in *FBPG*, X: 293–94. For further sources see the notes to chapter 8 below. A vast number of monographs have been written on the social and economic conditions of the peasantry in Prussia. Consult B. Gebhardt, *Handbuch der Deutschen Geschichte* II 8th ed. (Stuttgart, 1955), pp. 419 ff.; and Dahlmann-Waitz, *Quellenkunde der Deutschen Geschichte* (Berlin, 1931), for lists of the most prominent.

8. Gustav Schmoller, *Deutsches Städtewesen in älterer Zeit* (Bonn, 1922), p. 272, develops the thesis that the cities fell under the control of a few families which monopolized public office and passed this control on in hereditary succession. This oligarchy in each city was usually corrupt and ignored the plight of the lower classes. But the Hohenzollern rulers sent their *Commissarii Loci* into the cities to assume the reigns of local government: "The reforms are democratic and favourable to the citizens; they are fully directed to the interest of the lower, exploited, classes and most of the time secure the approval of these classes."

of aldermen (such a board was called a *Magistrat*), were quite willing to sacrifice their political liberties if the ruler agreed to help support local budgets and to assist in bringing about an economic revival. These smaller towns had experienced a period of decline from the greatness of the Hanseatic League times. In the larger municipalities, however, the bourgeois clique which dominated local affairs resisted the officials of the Elector because it was satisfied with existing conditions. Particular economic conditions in each of the chartered towns and cities ultimately determined whether the *Commissarii Loci* would be favorably received or not by the bourgeois oligarchs.

The Great Elector and his successors ultimately developed a method which was used to subjugate the municipalities. Concurrently with the introduction of the *Commissarii Loci* they established military garrisons. The Prussian army was quartered in private homes as well as in barracks. This military part of the local population frequently amounted to 20 percent or more of the total inhabitants of such large cities as Berlin, Königsberg, Magdeburg, and Halle by 1740. This garrison included the families of soldiers, and they were placed in private homes. Naturally the presence of this military contingent constituted an onerous burden on the municipal economy and created public order problems. All cities were subjected to two foreign influences: the *Commissarii Loci* and the military garrisons. Gustav Schmoller characterized this loss of local municipal self-government as a triumph of the countryside over the city.[9]

Elsewhere, Schmoller claimed that the long economic decline of the cities also prepared the way for the intervention of the central government (pp. 248–49), Kurt Schrader, "Die Verwaltung Berlins" (D. Phil. diss., Humboldt University, Berlin, 1963), p. 49, emphasizes this belief that the aim of the municipal policies of King Frederick William was "not so much the improvement and administration of the Prussian cities, but primarily the raising of the income of the State." Ziekursch, *Ergebnis der friderizianischen Städteverwaltung* (Jena, 1909), pp. 79–111, describes the introduction of "Prussian" techniques of municipal government in Silesia.

9. Schmoller, *Städtewesen*, pp. 248 ff., 272. Fritz Gause, *Die Geschichte der Stadt Königsberg* (Cologne, 1968), 2: 48–62. Friedrich Holtze, *Geschichte der Stadt Berlin* (Tübingen, 1906), gives a brief history of the city; this and other sources agree that Berlin was not an important metropolis in 1700. Due to the growth of industry and to the growth of the military garrison, Berlin grew in

The Great Elector built his army using aristocratic officers and a combination of peasants and mercenaries to constitute the soldiery. This motley force was dominated by country squires and (partly), by their peasant–serfs. In any event, the army had been developed to a size of 80,000 men by 1740 and was connected to the life of the municipalities.

Because local governmental councils remained in force and the Hohenzollern rulers up to 1740 had superimposed a central bureaucratic control on them, it quickly became obvious that city dwellers would have to come to terms with the government. King Frederick William I replaced the *Commissarii Loci* with new officials, called *Steuerräte*, who were supposed to be members of the new provincial governmental boards (*Kriegs- und Domänen Kammern*) which he established in 1722.[10] The *Steuerräte* were required to supervise a number of chartered towns and cities within specified geographical areas within the provinces. Afterward, Frederick William I tried to make the municipal councils obey the orders of the *Steuerräte*. He did not think, however, that the intimidating presence of the army and the *Steuerräte* was sufficient to insure the cooperation of town dwellers.[11] The "stick" was accompanied by a "carrot" in the form of governmental plans to rejuvenate municipal economies. These plans entailed the infusion of monetary and other investments, and proved highly desirable to local bourgeois oligarchs. The king en-

---

population from 58,122 in 1730, to 121,873 in 1780. See Horst Krüger, *Zur Geschichte der Manufakturen und die Manufakturarbeiter in Preussen* (Berlin, 1958), p. 33. For purposes of comparison and contrast of Prussian cities with west European and English cities of the eighteenth century, see Johannes Ziekursch, *Das Ergebnis der friederizianischen Städteverwaltung und der Städteordnung Steins* (Jena, 1909); M. Dorothy George, *London Life in the Eighteenth Century* (New York, 1964), pp. 1–21, 155–215, especially; and for France, F. Furet, "Structures sociales Parisiennes au XVIII Siècle," *Annales: Economies, Sociétés, Civilizations* (1961), pp. 939–58; and the articles of Lemoigne and Trenard conveniently translated in Jeffry Kaplow, ed., *New Perspectives on the French Revolution* (New York, 1965), pp. 47–100.

10. Bruno Gloger, "Der Potsdamer Steuerrat" (Dr. Phil. diss., Humboldt University, Berlin, 1957), pp. 15 ff., describes the introduction of *Steuerräte* throughout the realm in general before concentrating on the Potsdam example. Gause, *Königsberg*, 2: 76 ff., describes loss of local authority in Königsberg.

11. Gloger, "Steuerrat," pp. 15–22, 62 ff.; Schrader, "Berlins," pp. 60–71.

couraged business growth because he considered it part of the foundation of his political power. Because of his interest in sponsoring armaments manufacturing in Berlin, he encouraged such down-at-the-heel merchants as David Splitgerber and Gottfried Daum when the old-line craft guilds refused to admit them. As a result Splitgerber and Daum and other entrepreneurs came to prosper under his patronage. Another factor contributing to cooperation was the spread of Pietism in the ranks of the civil service and in the army, which produced a new spirit of toleration between aristocrat and *Bürger* and between the common soldier and the household in which he was quartered. Rules laid down for the behavior of soldiers and tax collectors by the king and his officials also had their effect, so that gradually the influential families of the towns came to accept the Prussian government. The town dweller and the official recognized that they could live together and that differences could be negotiated. As in the case of the aristocracy, the king, especially Frederick William I, encouraged sons of prominent bourgeois families to enter his civil service and his judiciary. By 1740 many bourgeois had risen to important positions in the civil and military establishments and some had been ennobled.[12] Underneath the surface of what appeared to be despotism and absolutism a kind of consensus reigned: the king ruled, but he ruled within limits and because he could obtain the silent assent of the ruled. Perhaps he more often guided than decreed.

A Small Bureaucracy with Limited Goals

The civil service, excluding the judiciary, was small in 1740. At

12. Hans Rosenberg, *Bureaucracy, Aristocracy, and Autocracy* (Cambridge, Mass., 1958), pp. 1–88 discusses the rise of commoners in the civil service until 1740 and includes some perceptive comments on Frederick William I, but his claim that that monarch was a bureaucratic reformer interested in efficiency in the modern sense does not agree with the interpretation presented in this study (see pp. 75 ff. of Rosenberg). See Carl Hinrichs "Der hallische Pietismus als politische-soziale Reformbewegung des 18. Jahrhunderts," *Jahrbuch für die Geschichte Mittel- und Ostdeutschlands* 2(1953): 177–89. Friedrich Lenz and Otto Unholtz, *Die Geschichte des Bankhauses Gebrüder Schickler* (Berlin, 1912), pp. 3–46, describes the career of David Splitgerber, prominent Berlin banker and entrepreneur, up to the death of Frederick William I.

the top the General Directory was composed of four departments and each of the ministerial chiefs of these departments supervised the work of three to five privy finance councillors. The executive personnel of the General Directory, including in addition to the departments a Central Accounting Bureau and the Central Registry of Documents, numbered about twenty-four.[13] Nine provincial war and domains boards were patterned after the General Directory. The total number of executive personnel in the boards, counting presidents, directors, and councillors, did not exceed one hundred and seventy persons. At the most, then, the Prussian bureaucracy, or precisely that executive part of it which has been the subject of most studies, was no larger than two hundred persons.[14] In 1722 Frederick William I had allowed

13. Otto Hintze, "Einleitende Darstellung der Behördenorganisation und allgemeinen Verwaltung in Preussen beim Regierungsantritt Friedrichs II," *AB*, 6:1. 152–59 and passim. The sources for the numerical size of the Prussian civil service are few: Hintze tabulates the force of executive level officials and the efficiency reports of the period after 1750 (*AB*, 10:4–12, 155–62, 178–82, 202–10), give further information of these officials. But it is impossible to determine precisely how many subaltern clerks, messengers, tax collectors, toll gate keepers, etc., were employed at any time in the civil service. No records survive in the central archives at Merseburg as far as this author or the archivists know. However, the overall costs of administration were kept rather low until after 1763, so it is reasonable to suppose that the number of subalterns never amounted to more than two thousand at any time before the Seven Years' War. See the first table in appendix 1.

14. See note 13 above. In the fiscal year 1747–48 the General Directory in Berlin included 6 ministers, 7 Privy finance councillors, 4 privy finance councillors in the fifth department, 7 privy councillors and secretaries, 13 chancellery clerks, 2 copyists, 6 registry clerks, 5 chancellery messengers, 23 treasury clerks: a total of 73 persons of all ranks in the headquarters. Out of this number some 27 were executive personnel. To this must be added 21 persons in the newly established *Oberrechnungskammer* (Central Accounting Office), which did not exist before 1740. In the efficiency reports cited in note 13 above, and in the archival sources, the proportion of one executive rank official to two subalterns seemed to prevail. See Merseburg. Gen. Dir. Gen. Kassen Dept. No. 24, pp. 65–89. The Electoral Mark board, the largest of the boards, included about 22 executive rank officials including president, directors, councillors, and *Steuerräte*. In addition, in 1754 some 29 secretaries, copyists, and clerks of various types worked in Berlin. Potsdam. Rep. II. A. Allgemeine Kammer A 367, pp. 2 ff. To these must be added the number of local officials, for which the information is difficult if not impossible to obtain. Circa 1750, the entourage maintained by Frederick II at both the Potsdam and Berlin residences totalled 151: 5 privy secretaries including the famous Eichel, 15 clerks, 8 royal pages, 12 other pages, 8 lackeys in

the General Directory to hire nine copyists and clerks to serve this body. It is possible that similar ceilings were placed on the size of the clerical staff in the various boards, but published evidence is lacking. If one makes a generous estimate to include a clerical and work staff twice the size of the executive group of the boards, and adds local officials, it is still possible that no more than three thousand persons composed the entire Prussian civil service in 1750.[15] The smallness of the clerical staffs made it necessary for ministers and councillors to open correspondence, prepare replies, and supervise record-keeping for their respective work areas.[16] If the total population of Prussia in 1740 was about three million, the proportion of administrators to the total was remarkably small.[17] The army, of course, could be considered a part of the bureaucratic system, but it was not so considered by Frederick II in the *Political Testament* of 1752, for example.[18] In terms of size alone it is obvious that the civil service played a minor role in the lives of most people.

Throughout the eighteenth century the civil service was organized around the principle of collegiality.[19] Even the king did not view

Potsdam, 12 lackeys in Berlin, 1 barber, 21 other servants, 4 royal huntsmen, 7 other pages and the master of the household, 5 pages and lackeys in Berlin, 1 maître d'hotel (a French chef, Fazard), 11 cooks, 12 "champagne cooks", 3 lesser cooks, 11 kitchen helpers, 3 bakers, 6 wine cellar servants, and 5 silverware servants. Of these only ten or so were of executive importance. Although this number appears high, one must remember that Frederick lived in Sans Souci practically all the time, and his wife remained in the Charlottenburg palace; entourages had to be maintained at both places. As many have remarked, a glittering court life did not exist in Prussia during the reign of Frederick II. Courtiers became secretaries, assistants, or intellectual foils for the king while the queen attracted an entourage of sympathizers of little consequence. (Merseburg. Gen. Dir. Gen. Kassen Dept., No 49, pp. 4 ff). See appendix 1.

15. That is, one thousand executive level officials and about two thousand subalterns of various degrees. Dorwart, *Reforms*, p. 174.

16. See the General Directory *Instructions* of 1722, *AB*, 3; 575 ff.

17. Krüger, *Manufakturen*, pp. 31–32, discusses Prussian population and its changing distribution in countryside and in the towns.

18. Frederick divided the *Political Testament* of 1752 into two parts, one pertaining to civil government and the other to the army. The editors of the *Acta Borussica* left out the second part because it has little or nothing to do with administration. See *AB*, 9: 372 ff.; and G. Küntzel and M. Hass, *Die Politischen Testamente der Hohenzollern* (Berlin, 1920), 2: 1–84.

19. Haussherr, *Verwaltungseinheit*, pp. 1–54, discusses the collegial system.

himself as the pinnacle of a formal hierarchy of officials. When
Frederick William I planned the amalgamation of his civil service in
1722, he announced that he would serve as the president of the board
of ministers that composed the General Directory, "so that it will
have more lustre, authority, and vigor."[20] But the first five ministers
were called "vice presidents" and characteristically possessed complete theoretical equality with one another in the discussion of plans,
decisions, reports, and recommendations. They were ranked around
the conference table in order of seniority, as established by the king,
and he himself was obviously always more than *primus inter pares.*
Each minister supervised affairs in a particular group of provinces,
and some ministers were, in addition, in charge of the work of the
General Registry, the Accounting Bureau, and the Post Office. But
the minister did not "control" the work of the provincial war and
domains boards and other agencies that came under his purview. He
collected reports from the provincial presidents and other officials,
prepared recommendations on the basis of these reports, and attended
the sessions of the General Directory. In the thrice-weekly meetings
of the ministers administrative matters were discussed and collective
decisions made. Frederick William I stipulated that the senior
minister, or "first vice president" (originally Grumbkow), and the
"second vice president" would countersign all decrees. Even though
the king decreed that the sessions would be held on particular days
and at particular times each week,[21] it is wrong to say that the General
War and Domains Directory, the supreme *Collegium* of the civil

---

See also Henry F. Schwarz, *The Imperial Privy Council in the Seventeenth Century* (Cambridge, Mass., 1943), pp. 187–89, who describes the Austrian Privy
Council as a committee of ministers interested in pursuing "the maintenance and
extension of the Emperor's power in the Empire, rather than the creation, for its
own sake, of a Hapsburg territorial state." But the reform-minded bureaucrats of
Leopold I succeeded in stripping it of authority by 1705. Becher and his as-
sociates *were* interested in the creation of a territorial state and were among the
first to denounce collegialism because it did not seem to make for strong and
efficient administration.

20. *AB*, 3: 575.

21. See Dorwart, *Reforms*, pp. 161–81, and his convenient, if abbreviated,
translation of the instructions, pp. 199–211.

service, was hierarchically ordered and placed under a rigid, quasi-military command system.

Frederick William I directed the original ministers of the General Directory in 1723 to prepare instructions for the nine provincial war and domains boards. These general instructions were subsequently modelled on those of the General Directory, a major part being taken verbatim from the instructions of the superior agency. The principle of collegiality again prevailed in the provincial boards. Functioning in place of the king at the level of the board was a senior official termed the president. Each board consisted of a president, several "directors," and a number of war and domains councillors and *Steuerräte*. The board possessed a great deal of authority because it was close to local conditions, and the councillors travelled about the province frequently, inspecting the work of the domain contractors, municipal governments, and the rural *Landräte*. Routine provincial matters were handled by collective action in the board sessions.[22]

The collegial system prevailed throughout the civil service. The corps of clerks, messengers, and porters employed by the General Directory and by the Boards were seldom assigned directly to one supervisor. Frederick William I stated flatly in the *General Instructions* that seven to nine privy finance councillors would be supervised by five ministers, but presumably some of these officials might work most of the time for a particular minister, while others worked for several superiors at the same time.[23] Outside this framework the collegial system reigned supreme in the judiciary (a board of judges composed a court) and in the municipalities, where *Bürgermeister* responsible for police, fire protection, and taxes worked together.[24]

What, then, was the *Collegium*? It was an administrative system based upon the interrelated work of a number of different committees. The committee, not the individual, ruled at every stage. The origin of the system is difficult to trace; certainly it was highly evident in the

22. *AB*, 3: 682–721.
23. Ibid., pp. 538–75.
24. Ibid., pp. 682–721.

organization of the medieval church. The college of cardinals, the curial organization, the cathedral and monastic chapters, all were collegial in nature. The privy councils and the very structure of the central German estates in the early modern period were collegial. An examination of the work of a *Collegium* is necessary at this point. It was conducted on the basis of the consensus of the participants in particular sessions; the "seat and voice" an official possessed determined his importance.[25] Authority was kept vested in the collective, and the cooperation of colleagues was absolutely necessary if a particular official wished to act. Since the corps of executive officials, that body of the civil service that included the directing ministers of the General Directory and the presidents and councillors of the boards was composed of both aristocrats and bourgeois, each session became, in fact, a minor meeting of minds of the two great upper classes of Prussian society. Ordinarily the work of a provincial board was entirely devoted to the three aims of the civil service: maintenance of peace and order, provision for auxiliary support for the army, and the collection of taxes. These problems never ceased to exist, or to diminish in importance.

Exceptional projects, such as land reclamation, settlement of artisans, and the subsidizing of entrepreneurs, would inevitably be carried out after 1722 by the strenuous efforts of select individuals. The great limiting factor of the collegial system was its conservative character. It aimed to maintain previous administrative projects rather than to introduce new ones. The careers of Councillor Hille before 1740, and of many others during the reign of Frederick II, were stormy because these men had to fight the jealousies and inherent lethargy of their colleagues.[26]

25. Patents issued to officials by Frederick William I and Frederick II usually included the statement that the appointee had the right to vote in whatever board he was appointed to.

26. Hille, for many years board director in Cüstrin, was a cosmopolitan and was very much aware of English and Dutch commercial success in the early eighteenth century. He tried to reorient the Prussian bureaucracy towards these western models and influenced his most famous pupil, the future Frederick II. As early as January, 1725, he complained that "the merchant group (*Kaufmannschaft*) does not, most of the time, obtain enough respect and attention in this

Unlike the civil service of various other German states, the Prussian bureaucracy did not hire large numbers of officials from outside the realm. Throughout the eighteenth century, about one-half of all officials in the small principalities of Thuringia were consistently drawn from other parts of Germany. The Austrian bureaucracy had always attracted professional jurists and administrators from elsewhere.[27] In Prussia, the civil service was relatively provincial in background. As long as these Germanic bureaucracies were dominated by university-educated jurists, they all had much in common, but in Prussia the jurists had been identified with the cause of the landed aristocracy for many years. They were distrusted by Frederick William I and his bureaucrats, who recruited into the executive ranks in-service apprentices in preference to university graduates. The very reorganization of the higher administrative agencies was quite obviously a fruit of the indigenous political and bureaucratic history of Prussia and was not noticeably or directly conditioned by the works of the Cameralists or the jurists.[28] Ingrown, small in size,

country." He realized the social and economic conservatism of the king and people in Prussia and formulated plans to combat this lethargy. But he was successfully opposed by the old line bureaucrats led by Privy Councillor Reinhardt; the tax collectors emerged victorious over the promoters of economic development. See Carl Hinrichs, "Hille und Reinhardt, Zwei Wirtschafts-und Sozialpolitiker des preussischen Absolutismus," *Preussen als historisches Problem* (Berlin, 1964), pp. 161–71.

27. Ulrich Hess, *Geheimer Rat und Kabinett in den Ernestinischen Staaten Thüringens* (Weimar, 1962), pp. 419–22. Goethe was an outstanding example of the "migrant" corps of officials of the eighteenth century. The presence of foreign officials in the Austrian service did not, of course, insure that that service was more efficient or better organized than others. Austria had problems of a magnitude undreamed of in Prussia: ethnic and religious diversity, powerful and independent-minded provincial estates, and the necessity since the Middle Ages to act as a great power in European politics. The best of the cameralists probably went to Vienna after 1648, because employment in the service of the foremost prince of central Europe was more desirable than in the service of the various imperial electors. This preference persisted at least until 1740. Excellent accounts and discussions of the similarities and differences between Prussian and Austrian absolutism can be found in "Der österreichische und der preussische Beamtenstaat im 17. und 18. Jahrhundert," by Otto Hintze in *Staat und Verfassung* (Leipsig, 1941), pp. 311–48; and, in more general form, Fritz Hartung, *Das Reich und Europa* (Leipzig, 1941), pp. 75–91.

28. Rosenberg, *Bureaucracy*, pp. 46–75, discusses the gradual decline of the

and provincial in approach, the Prussian civil service before 1740 revealed little professional élan.

Officials as Class Representatives

The most important generalization that can be made concerning the aims of Prussian bureaucrats at this time is that they were infinitely more modest and less ambitious than those of the civil service in a modern state. These officials had emerged from both the noble and the bourgeois classes, but they could not forget their origins. Life was localized, steeped in tradition, and based upon a commonly understood class differentiation. There was not one project initiated by either official or ruler in Prussia during the eighteenth century which was designed to eliminate the old social order. Economic projects were strictly limited in conception, and if successful, modest in execution. Even the famous decrees of Frederick II concerning the emancipation of the serfs on the royal domains were not executed very successfully, and the king never tried to force the private landowners to free their peasants.[29]

Because the bureaucrats had never abandoned their social origins, the government they staffed became congruent with the structure of private life. The government had grown out of East Elbian conditions and fitted a society of country squires, serfs, and a small class of urban bourgeois and artisans. The proof of this contention can be

judicial bureaucracy and its replacement by a fiscally oriented bureaucracy. See also Gustav Schmoller, *Über Behördenorganisation* . . . , *AB*, 1, for a far-ranging discussion of the development of civil service in Europe, including the Prussian example. A similar split between the jurists and the newer bureaucracy was mirrored in the literature of cameralism; jurists cease to speak for bureaucrats as a whole after 1648. See H. C. Johnson "Theory of Bureaucracy in Cameralism," *Political Science Quarterly* 79 (1964): 378 ff. Leading cameralists such as Becher, Schröder, and Sonnenfels were also prominent figures in the Austrian bureaucracy between 1690 and 1790. They were consulted on a multitude of specialized problems. See Louise Sommer, *Die österreichischen Kameralisten* (Vienna, 1920–25), 2: 354–369. Not until the reign of Frederick II does one find examples of public officials in Prussia influenced by certain cameralists. See chapter 9 below.

29. Otto Hintze, "Agrarpolitik Friedrichs der Grossen," *FBPG*, X: 290 ff.; and August Skalweit's very shrewd comments in *AB Getreidepolitik*, 3: 31–49.

discovered in the relationship of this government with the provinces that did not have the social characteristics of the heartland of the realm. Prussian rule had been extended to various enclaves in western Germany, of which Cleves and the County of Mark in the Rhineland were probably of most importance. As Carsten suggested, the Prussian government never became popular with the inhabitants of these provinces. Until Napoleonic times Prussian officials as well as successive kings could never force these people to accept their government without protest, resentment, and passive and open opposition. Frederick II was later to hold the Cleves nobility in contempt[30] and failed, perhaps, to understand that the social compact which seemed to work in East Elbia failed completely in Cleves. As a viable governmental system the Prussian government failed in the Rhineland. It succeeded in the heartland of the realm, east of the Elbe, because it fitted certain social patterns in that area.

The assumptions of the different social classes of Prussia before 1740 were shared by bureaucrats of various ranks. Officials imbibed the same opinions as nonofficials. The aristocracy produced its share of bureaucrats, the bourgeoisie its share, and the peasantry produced the menial hirelings.

Conservative-minded civil servants persuaded Frederick William I and his ministers to balance the requirements of statecraft against the concrete social and economic realities of the realm. As long as official

---

30. F. L. Carsten, *Origins of Prussia* (Oxford, 1954). The final test of the effectiveness of any government is its ability to collect taxes, and taxes will not be paid if taxpayers do not cooperate. The history of the Prussian occupation of Cleves reveals that the regime always had trouble collecting taxes because the *Clevois* detested it. See Fritz Hartung, *Staatsbildende Kräfte der Neuzeit,* "Der preussische Staat und seine westlichen Provinzen," (Berlin, 1961), pp. 420 ff. Reinhold Dorwart, *Reforms,* pp. 16–46, describes the government of Frederick William I as having "run the gamut of functional or institutional forms which appeared in the other states of Europe" (p. 17), but the ministers of the Hohenzollern rulers up to the time of Frederick II had little connection with their Austrian counterparts, for example. They were not cosmopolitan in outlook or professional in the sense that the radical Austrian cameralists such as Becher were under Leopold I. See a brief discussion, together with citations in Johnson, "Theory of Bureaucracy," pp. 384 ff. On the difficult question of the existence of a bureaucratic ethos see ibid., pp. 378–402, and the provocative remarks of Rosenberg, *Bureaucracy,* pp. 137 ff.

edicts did not clash very much with the values of society, they would be obeyed by the people. Local officials knew that they could not secure the enforcement of an unpopular decree: those who command must have willing followers. As perhaps in all governments, the range of decision making was quite restricted in Prussia. When Frederick William I decreed the establishment of the military cantonal recruitment system the peasants cooperated because it was developed as an outgrowth of the agrarian social order. The aristocracy, for the most part, accepted the abolition of many provincial estates because they and their sons were brought into the government as junior partners. They did not accept this change because they were cowed into submission. The businessmen cooperated instead of leaving the realm because the government provided opportunities for profit making, even if it also tried to weaken municipal political self-government. Surely the government functioned because it seldom required of its subjects things which they were unwilling to give? Inescapably, the Prussian government existed in a pluralistic society, and it ruled through consent of the governed. In an age prior to the emergence of the modern urbanized and industrialized State, governments all too often had no choice but to submit to the requirements of the societies they presumed to govern.

The Army and the Government

No central European state other than Prussia tried to tie military functions closely to purely administrative functions. The Electorate of Saxony, comparable in size and population to the Prussian realm before the acquisition of Silesia, never attempted to field a large army and made no efforts to build an elaborate auxiliary service. Its main army consisted of 9,000 men at the time of its surrender to the Prussians at Pirna in 1756. In Austria, military administration was kept separate until the reforms of 1750, and even after that time only by the most strenuous efforts on the part of its officials could this large and wealthy state support an army equivalent in size to that of Prussia during the Seven Years' War.[31] Since the beginning of the reign of the Great Elector, the army in Prussia had been closely connected to the fortunes of the civil service. Prominent generals frequently passed over to ministerial jobs, and a significant percentage of the councillors, board presidents, and ministers had begun their careers as military clerks (*Auditeure*). There was no significant departure from this pattern of civilian and military executive cooperation throughout the eighteenth century.[32] But one must avoid drawing the conclusion that Prussia in fact was a "military state" in which the civil service was a humble supplier of men and material to an ever-growing war machine. Generals and civilian ministers were not confused about their respective roles; they presided over different institutions with different purposes. They cooperated with one another most of the time, but quarrelled occasionally over jurisdictional problems. Frederick William I, the "Soldier King," did not, in fact, force his officials to accept military discipline. He had stern conceptions of bureaucratic duty, but these conceptions did not stem from a military monomania. He understood thoroughly the collegial nature of the bureaucracy, but did not for a minute administer his army in other than a strictly hierarchial, superior, and subordinate command relationship.[33]

31. Durichen, "Geheimes Kabinett und Geheimer Rat unter der Regierung Augusts des Starken in den Jahren 1704–1720," *Neues Archiv für sächsische Geschichte und Altertumskunde* 51 (1930): 72–88, describes the establishment of the Saxon Privy Council of 1706 by August the Strong. The army administration was not even incorporated in one of the portfolios of the three ministers, but was left as a modest additional duty for a subordinate official. August was, of course, deeply involved in his Polish ambitions at this time. In Austrian administration, as Hintze explained, the various estates of the realm continued to maintain great control over taxes, military troop levies, and other matters throughout the eighteenth century. Despite the much greater size of that state it could not send more than 177,144 men to fight in 1756; this amounted to scarcely more than the Prussian troop strength. Hintze, "Der österreichsche und der preussische Beamtenstaat," *Historische Zeitschrift* 86 (1901): 402–44. A good analysis of the strength and effectiveness of the Prussian, Saxon, and Austrian armies in 1756 will be found in Der Grosse Generalstab, *Die Kreige Friedrichs des Grossen* (Berlin, 1900) 3:1. 152, 134 ff.

32. Rosenberg, *Bureaucracy*, pp. 137 ff.

33. Otto Büsch, *Militärsystem und Sozialleben im alten Preussen, 1713–1807* (Berlin, 1962), pp. 167 ff., concludes his discussion with the claim that "the end

With the introduction of the cantonal system by Frederick William I in 1733, an increasing proportion of peasant youths faced periodic service in the army. They apparently accepted this stoically as part of the price one paid to exist. It is fundamentally wrong to suggest that the peasant was brainwashed into becoming a thoughtless automaton of Prussian despotism through his service in the army. Certainly the collapse of the Prussian army in 1806 was partly attributable to the fact that basically unwilling conscripts serving under conditions of ruthless discipline were no match for French troops. Everything we know of the life of soldiers in eighteenth century Europe, the wholesale desertions, the doglike existence, and the abysmal social position of the common soldier, inclines us to believe that the peasant soldier did his job reluctantly. But military life was to some extent an extension of life at home. As Büsch shrewdly remarked, the peasant worked under the aristocrat on the *Rittergut* in peace and followed him to war when he himself became a soldier and his landlord his commanding officer.[34] But Büsch also claims that both aristocrat and serf were indoctrinated with a spirit of militarism through service in the army. Quite the reverse may have been the case; the long-standing, symbiotic, rural social relationship that tied peasant to *Junker* may have, in the long run, drastically altered the Prussian army for the

---

result was the militarization of the agrarian society" of the realm and that "the official, like the officer, was a deliverer and a carrier of orders for the monarch." He then concludes, too rashly perhaps, that the bureaucracy was militarized from top to bottom. Nevertheless, King Frederick William I, in his instructions to the crown prince, stated that the army was needed to preserve Prussia's foreign and international diplomatic position, and warned that "the ministers will say that your treasury cannot support such a formidable army" and "your ministers will intrigue all the time in order to prevent the increase of the army" (*AB*, 3: 446–47).

34. Büsch, *Militärsystem*, pp. 27 ff. An important percentage of the army was made up of peasant conscripts after 1733. The realm was divided into districts or cantons and the names of men between the ages of 18 and 45 were entered on lists in each canton. Periodically many of these persons were called to active service for short periods. Many artisans and practically all of the middle and upper class men were exempted from the lists. In each canton a paper organization, or "regiment" was created and the conscripts were considered part of this unit. As late as 1750, however, some 50 percent of the total was still composed of mercenaries. The land owned and farmed by an aristocrat was called a "*Rittergut*."

worse. With the introduction of the cantonal system, the influx of peasants increased with each passing decade, although the foreign mercenaries remained a large minority in the army throughout the eighteenth century. King Frederick William I and his successors took pains to provide lowly jobs in the civil service for invalided soldiers. Many of these veterans had started life as peasants. Frederick William I emphasized in the *General Instructions* of 1722 that only disabled veterans would be appointed porters, messengers, rural policemen, and receptionists,[35] Instead of the army molding the peasants, the peasant steadily molded the army and the lower ranks of the civil service. The bluff invalided soldier and former peasant stood at the door of the General Directory in the role of porter. The peasant inhibited the freedom of action of the upper classes and of the bureaucracy. Ignorant but shrewd, he determined the mode of cultivation of the land and resisted, with his well-known inertia, the attempts initiated by others to complicate his existence. In the restrictive sense of stubborn adherence to the practices of his ancestors he was a conservative influence in the passive political consensus that allowed the King to live in Potsdam.

Frederick William I

The bones of Frederick William's government are now laid bare. He accepted the society as he found it. He accepted the collegial system of administration as well as the collegial system of social organization of which it was an outgrowth. He did not accept the political organization of the aristocrats and the bourgeoisie in the forms of provincial estates or municipal boards of *Bürgermeister*, since they existed outside of the administrative structure which formed the Prussian civil service. Frederick William I tried to persuade and to coerce his subjects to abandon corporative associations with political aims which existed outside of his purview and to work instead to achieve their aims through participation as individuals in the collegia of the civil service or in the army.

35. *General Instructions* of 1722, *AB*, 3: 575 ff.

Of course the king and his officials could not eliminate the entrenched institutions of society. He attempted to subordinate the municipal boards of aldermen to domination by his officials, the *Steuerräte*. From 1722 to 1740 the *Steuerräte* encountered much opposition and foot-dragging on the part of the local boards of *Bürgermeister*—even from individual *Bürgermeister* the king had selected. Inevitably the conflict seemed to center on attempts of the provincial board and its *Steuerrat* to increase tax revenue over the limits which the municipal governments thought they could, or would pay. The *Steuerrat*, if he travelled often to visit his cities, would readily appreciate local problems, but he was subjected to pressure from above. Also, the estates of the provinces of Pomerania and East Prussia, for example, resented the appointment of royal officials from outside their provinces to govern them in the boards. They also resisted increased tax levies; the provincial boards in those provinces which continued to have estates were often involved in thorny negotiations with the aristocratic landlords. In the Electoral Mark, on the other hand, where provincial estates had been abolished, the king still found it necessary to permit the development of a *Landschaft* or associations of landlords, as well as the growth of small estates in the various counties.[36] The central government tried, at the same time, to subordinate or even to eliminate the old institutions and to work with the same institutions in order to govern. It was a perplexing problem.

Frederick William I also made support of the army the primary aim of bureaucratic effort instead of diverting the energies of his officials into a multitude of diverse channels. The core of the Prussian bureaucracy, as it existed before 1806, was developed in accordance with the plans of Frederick William I, but this does not mean that it became increasingly professional in approach or that it achieved the status of government for itself alone, reducing the successive kings to the position of figureheads. If Frederick William I strengthened the civil service by means of his 1722 reforms and through the partial abolition of *Ständesstaat* government, he also insured that the future

36. *AB*, 3: 229, 349; Gloger, "Steuerrat," pp. 15–99. Schrader, "Berlins," pp. 144–48; Spiro, "Gravamina," pp. 20–34.

history of this organization was tied to the most conservative and traditional social forces existent in East Elbia. From the beginning, the civil service was connected, for better or for worse, to the agrarian, semifeudal, society. The interlocking system of collegia that connected the inhabitants of Prussia to the king served as the most durable of ties. Through arduous wrangling in these many committees the aims of the king were modified and partially translated into action. The process of consensus ensured that little of an innovative nature could be introduced. Of course, another secret of the success of this most able ruler was the conservative and acquiescent frame of mind he usually possessed. He could be, and was, ruthless in his quest for bureaucratic honesty and for the punishment of individuals or groups that resisted too overtly his policies. But he exercised the right to punish individual officials, aristocrats, and other persons; it was too dangerous to launch crusades against large social groups. Usually Frederick William treated his ministers and generals as near equals in the luncheon meetings of the General Directory as well as in the "tobacco salons." He had no intellectual pretensions, but he was amazingly honest in his approach to ideas as well as to people. To him the state existed as a concrete embodiment of his religious ideal.[37] Most men were self-seeking and were prone to live in discord with one another. The political saving grace of this potential anarchical tendency was the contrary impulse of men to cooperate with one another. The ruler had to repress the first human tendency and to encourage the second, provided that the second was expressed in working arrangements that revolved around the primary authority of the king. Of course, these ideas were very old and very ordinary, but they formed part of the teachings of German Pietism. The good man prepared for salvation through an upright life as an individual and as part of a collective such as a *Collegium*. Frederick William I did not express his views in writing very effectively, and no one can ascribe to him any "philosophy." In common with most of his contemporaries he probably would deny that he possessed any

37. Hinrichs, "Der Hallische Pietismus," *Preussen als historisches Problem*, pp. 171–85.

intellectual rationalization of his own life and actions. He found himself in a particular society and tried to fortify his position as ruler within this society.

The natural conservatism of Frederick William I and of his officials was reflected in administrative policies. But the king and his lieutenants were influenced, in turn, by the traditionally collegial organization of society and by Pietism. The civil service was small in size and provincial in outlook and its aims were frankly housekeeping or custodial in nature rather than innovative.

One final question remains, the geographical limitations of government in the Prussian realm and how this might have affected the administrative system. It is often forgotten that East Elbian society was extremely particularistic in composition before the nineteenth century. People lived in groups of villages or in rather small cities. As far as 90 percent of the population was concerned, life was very largely confined to the small circle in which individuals identified themselves and their activities. There were differences in the conditions of servitude, in dialects, and in the ethnic composition of the peasantry. Because the population of Prussia, unlike that of a modern industrialized state, was not very mobile, either socially or occupationally,[38] it is obvious that very little knowledge of or belief in a political abstract called "the State" existed in the minds of Prussians of all classes. To believe in an abstract political institution, a "State",

---

38. This question is, of course, difficult. A large migration of persons from the Prussian realm occurred during the Seven Years' War, perhaps as many as 500,000 according to Frederick II in *Oeuvres*, 6: 74–5. The population of Berlin grew rapidly as Krüger, above, pointed out, p. 33. But some figures from the archives are interesting. The civilian and military population of Berlin between 1750 and 1753:

	1750	1751	1752	1753
Civilians	89,523	92,446	94,688	97,040
Military	23,766	24,035	24,536	25,169
Total	113,289	116,481	119,224	122,209

This illustrates an important point: the military population was kept stable and only gradually increased over the years cited. But the civilian population was growing at a considerable rate, mainly through absorption of ex-peasants from the Prussian countryside (Merseberg. Rep. 96, 412c, p. 18).

one must believe oneself to be a constituent of a vast and highly organized and interdependent community of persons. Even Frederick II, for example, ordered officials to be diligent "in *my* service," and the royal "We" seemed all to often to overshadow his other concept of the "State" as expressed in "I am the first servant of the State."

The civil service functioned most effectively at the provincial level, where officials could come to know each community through frequent travel and consultation with local inhabitants. The War and Domains Board was always the most important cog in the machinery of the State, not the General Directory, because the technological and geographical limitations of the time militated against the effectiveness of a far-removed administrative direction. Except in the province of the Electoral Mark communication between the provincial boards and the General Directory took at the least several days, and sometimes several weeks. It is true to say that part of the difficulties the Hohenzollern rulers encountered with the Rhenish provinces was due to their defective communication with the isolated officials they had dispatched to these areas. These natural limitations on governmental influence certainly affected the policies of Frederick William I, and to a greater extent, those of his successor.

Finally, it can be said that Frederick William I only fostered governmental centralization through his efforts to combine the top level and provincial agencies under the General Directory and War and Domains Board. This was a modest achievement because the collegial system remained, as did the other social and political attitudes of East Elbia. The *Ständesstaat* did not disappear, it merely merged into the civil service proper so that a greater harmony came to exist between the aims of the ruler and the desires of the aristocratic landlords. Prussian absolutism, then, was the product of collective effort; it was a successful merging of diverse interests under one banner.

II

EMERGENCE OF THE
ADMINISTRATIVE STALEMATE

When Frederick II came to the throne in May 1740 he was faced with a diverse collection of bureaucratic agencies: the General Directory and the provincial boards, the Department of Justice, the Department of Foreign Affairs, and a number of minor ecclesiastical consistories and other small agencies. Some of these organizations were well established and adequately financed, while others, including the consistories and the judiciary, existed in rudimentary forms. Since no central parliamentary body equivalent to the French Estates General or the English Parliament existed in Prussia, the autocratic aspect of the government seemed, on the surface, to be unchallenged. Nevertheless, provincial *Stände* or estates still met on occasion in some provinces and the central governmental agencies in Berlin had to negotiate with such bodies. Similarly, the military services of the realm had not yet been organized into a cohesive and all-embracing system. On the purely military side, as expressed in the actual command of serving units, the army was under the direct supervision of the king and of a changing coterie of generals, a collegium which could not yet be dignified with the appellation of "general staff" even if it could be called the "tobacco salon" of Frederick William I. Auxiliary military services were handled as additional duties by the officials of the General Directory and of the boards. Of these various agencies only those concerned with fiscal affairs, namely the General Directory and the boards in the provinces, had been reorganized under the instructions of 1722.[1] Since these agencies constituted the key elements of

1. Otto Hintze, "Einleitende Darstellung der Behördenorganisation und

the entire Prussian administrative system they can be collectively described as the core bureaucracy.

Frederick II and the General Directory

After his accession in 1740 Frederick found himself in frequent conflict with the officials of the General Directory, who constituted, *en bloc*, the leadership of the core bureaucracy. He announced ominously in 1740 that it was better to have energetic and capable people in the General Directory than "noble *Dummköpfe*."[2] Unfortunately, neither he nor his advisers seemed to know where or how to effect reforms. He did not intend to allow ministers to govern him, but expected, conversely, that they would move more quickly to solve the problems of the day as they arose. Frederick naturally hoped to direct all major policy formulations and to obtain an intelligent response from the core bureaucracy when it was given new duties and changes in policy.

Because the king vaguely felt that his ministers ought to be more flexible, but did not know precisely how they should respond, his whole relationship with them was fraught with ambiguity. He announced, for example, that "the ornamentation of a building can be changed without altering the foundations and the masonry,"[3] and this comment was interpreted by many frightened officials as heralding their dismissals. But the "noble *Dummköpfe*" who he claimed infested the General Directory were not, in fact, replaced, and no ambitious reshuffling of officials ensued. "Ornamentation" in the form of veteran officials and modes of operation remained untouched.

Frederick began to wage a constant and subtle campaign against what he thought were the unwarranted pretensions of the officials of

allgemeinen Verwaltung in Preussen beim Regierungsantritt Friedrichs II," *AB*, 6: 1. 152–58, a very detailed description of the bureaucracy in 1740, including sketches of the officials in each board and in the General Directory. Gordon A. Craig, *The Politics of the Prussian Army* (Oxford, 1956), p. 30.

2. Hans Haussherr, *Verwaltungseinheit und Ressorttrennung* (Berlin, 1953), p. 121.

3. Ibid.

the General Directory. From the first he refused, for example, to sit as chairman of the biweekly sessions of the ministers of the General Directory. This act isolated the *Collegium* from collective contact with him. Instead, he summoned individual ministers to audience whenever he pleased. He may have hoped to make each one of them feel that he was working independently of his colleagues, or, possibly, he may have been trying to discover which of them *could* work for his monarch even if this meant that his colleagues would be upset.[4] This early attempt to combat the ministerial collective had unforseen results. Instead of destroying the cosy division of responsibility that characterized the old core bureaucracy, it reinforced it. Henceforth the ministers could work out plans jointly with greater freedom and could concert their efforts and excuses, if the latter became necessary. They could present a united front to their monarch. Such a natural development soon aroused the suspicions of Frederick. He felt that his ministers were conspiring behind his back. "Intrigue" and "chicanery" became customary epithets in his frequent written admonitions to them.

The estranged relationship that developed so early in the reign of Frederick II between that monarch and his ministers continued and became in time an accepted fact of bureaucratic life. It is quite possible that the ministers enjoyed a more intimate relationship with the violently abusive Frederick William I than with his more polite son. Frederick William, for example, had combined business with pleasure in his meetings with the directing ministers. He had provided excellent lunches for them. He had allowed them to rule their bailiwicks with a minimum of petty interference as long as they followed certain broad policies. His promotion system was liberal to some extent, and he distributed titles of nobility to his faithful subordinates upon occasion. If he sometimes castigated them in unprintable terms, the bureaucrats learned not to take such outbursts too seriously. Quite obviously Frederick II did not feel confident that these officials would

4. Walter Dorn, "The Prussian Bureaucracy in the Eighteenth Century," *Political Science Quarterly* 46 (1931): 403–23, and ibid., 47 (1932): 75–94, 259–73; see especially pp. 75–77.

respond to his direction as well as they had responded to that of his father. The ministers of the General Directory had worked for Frederick William I for many years; he knew them and he knew their habits of work. Frederick II not only did not know many of them, but since he had been effectively excluded from the main stream of public life for some years, he, perhaps, was inclined to see in them the intimidating presence of his father. Frederick had at least two alternatives in this situation: he could have imitated his father in the expectation that his subordinates would grant him the same obedience they had granted to Frederick William I, or he could have tried to impress upon them his belief that conditions of work had now changed and that other responses were now required, responses which would be the appropriate administrative measures occasioned by his new administrative direction. If he followed the latter course, and the ministers proved unable or unwilling to change their habits, he could have replaced them with others. But such clear-cut alternatives seldom present themselves as logical possibilities to a statesman under daily pressure to act, to decide, and to govern.

During this early period of encounter between an intelligent and wilful monarch and an experienced, if somewhat unimaginative corps of executive officials, Frederick alternated between each of the above approaches. Although he feared and disliked his father, he nevertheless aped his grotesque and barbaric German prose style as well as his choice invective. He also adopted a harsh and formal approach in his communications with his officials. In fact, the Frederick of the office would have dismayed those used to the cultured Frederick of the salon. The young king was a far more complex person than his father, however, and his efforts to present a stern and uncompromising facade to the world appeared precisely stern and uncompromising since he lacked the bluff, but often humane and even generous personality of Frederick William I. The father could curse, dismiss officials, hang embezzlers, browbeat and intimidate, but he had redeeming human failings. He was a soulmate of the provincial, ignorant, crude coterie of barracks habitués of his tobacco salon. He shared many of their simplistic and earthy attitudes. When Frederick William I bc-

came enraged, a shrewd old friend and official such as Grumbkow
would believe that his monarch was merely involved in a temper
tantrum and would eventually emerge from it.[5] The son was subtle,
quiet, and soon revealed an incapacity to appreciate illogical or
ignorant human actions.

Frederick II was an intellectual, a product of bookish seclusion at
Rheinsberg, a dabbler at poetry and at philosophy, but he was probably an innocent in regard to the intricacies of human relationships.[6]
Ministerial discretion, obfuscation, and collective harmony soon began to seem to him to be nothing more than obstinate disobedience,
inefficiency, or stupidity. He began to suspect that his officials were
guilty of the most petty misdemeanors. Throughout the entire period
from 1740 to 1748 the ministers of the General Directory came to
realize that Frederick viewed them contemptuously as rather incompetent custodians of "bagatelles." In reality, however, Frederick
was probably no more severe or critical of his subordinates than had
been his father; he simply could not project any feeling of empathy in
his relationships with others.

Frederick fostered the esprit de corps of his directing ministers by
declaring that each of them had to coordinate with the others all
matters not strictly germane to his own province.[7] Perhaps he hoped

5. Reinhold Koser, ed., *Briefwechsel Friedrichs des Grossen mit Grumbkow und
Maupertuis, PKPA* (Leipzig, 1898), pp. 39 ff., should be examined for insight
into the difficult role of guardian and protector that Grumbkow filled. See also
the correspondence between councillor Hille and Grumbkow between 1730 and
1732, which reveals how adroitly these two worked to keep the crown prince
safe from the wrath of the king following the court martial. This exchange is
conveniently included in Gustav Volz, *Friedrich der Grosse im Spiegel seiner
Zeit* (Berlin, 1901), 1: 12–59.

6. Koser, *Geschichte Friedrichs des Grossen* (Stuttgart, 1912) 1: 101–30,
discusses the Reinsberg days. See also Koser's illuminating remarks, pp. 174
ff., concerning Frederick's education as a crown prince. Frederick believed, late
in life, that his tutoring had stressed the learning of Latin and ancient Greek and
Roman history rather than modern history since the time of the Emperor Charles
V. In fact, in almost every educational area, Frederick felt that he had been
cheated. Frederick William I prescribed for his son the same curriculum that he
had himself received in the last decade of the seventeenth century.

7. Dorn, "Prussian Bureaucracy," pp. 75–77.

to curtail undue influence wielded by a particular minister as well as to insure more efficient and unified administrative services. Regardless of his motives, a result of his attitude was the reinforcement of ministerial solidarity. The ministers of the General Directory sought refuge from the king's wrath in consultation and cooperation with one another.

Several important administrative changes occurred primarily because the ministers grouped together in a mutual protective association and because Frederick decided quite early to change the "public image" of the directing ministers. He knew that these chiefs imagined themselves to be important cogs in the administrative machinery and that they enjoyed an elevated position in public esteem throughout the realm. They were not underpaid hirelings. Many received salaries in excess of 3,000 talers a year, which was a substantial income not equaled by most aristocrats from their estates. As a consequence they built fine houses and were lionized by Berlin society. Frederick chose, however, to believe that they were no more than humble custodians of the routine duties he chose to delegate to them. An example of the disparity between the ideas the bureaucrats formed of themselves and those Frederick formed of them was the horse and buggy controversy of 1747. In that year Frederick became alarmed with the mode of travel adopted by ministers on their inspection trips through the realm. They often traveled in the style of potentates with substantial equipages and trains of clerks, servants and toadies. He attacked this prestigious display by declaring that no minister could take with him more than four horses. The ministers of the General Directory protested this edict, which gave them precisely the same traveling privileges as any provincial board president. Frederick sarcastically replied that they must be "bogged in sand" to desire more horses. Frederick also declared in another instance that such inspection trips should be rare and enjoined both ministers and humble clerks to obey this rule. He broke from time-honoured tradition in yet another instance: he refused to allow the bureaucrats to distribute grandiloquent but meaningless titles such as *Hofrat* to their favored friends outside the civil service. In a veto of such a title he remarked: "such people will not be richer."[8] Perhaps he failed to realize that a most important and attractive aspect of an executive position was the intangible one of superior prestige manifested in countless small ways. A man of importance, and a minister of the General Directory was obviously such, appreciated the outward symbols and trappings of power.

Frederick developed a poor relationship with his ministers during these early years in yet other ways. In line with his consistent attempts to denigrate ministerial prestige, he preferred to let his ministers know that he believed them capable of the most petty chicanery in the malperformance of their duties. When the minister of the second department reported the initiation of criminal prosecution against a councillor in one of his boards, Frederick accused him of collusion with the board with intent to foster some unnamed but criminal conspiracy.[9] He may have possessed inside information which has not survived in the archives, but such sarcastic sallies could not encourage even the most sophisticated and self-confident official to do more than avoid trouble.

Even during the first few months of his reign he revealed his poor opinion of the ministers with distressing regularity. In criticizing the progress of land settlement programs, for example, he remarked: "The Directory should draw people into the land and not send them out." Subordinate officials, he averred, use every pretext to "ruin" peasants and "to hunt them from house and home."[10] When told that a shortage of 6,871 talers had been discovered in the salt accounts of the Halle office, he cynically ordered an investigation: "The investigation should be diligently undertaken so that the negligence of the Directory is not apparent and the *Herren* ministers show up well in the outcome of the affair." A few days later, in November, 1740, the General Directory asked if a previously reported financial balance

8. *AB*, 7: 10–12, 329, 418.
9. Ibid., 7: 80, 572.
10. Ibid., 6: 2. 141. *PKPA*, 11: 253–54.

could be corrected in the light of new reports, and he replied that he had already ordered the correction "but the *Herren* have perhaps not yet observed this." When a minister mentioned the placement of an elderly misfit in the *Oberrechnungskammer* Frederick angrily remarked: "Such people are already working here" and should be replaced by young, energetic, and competent officials.[11] In the years from 1740 to 1748 he consistently abused his ministers with similar remarks.

Perhaps the most important case that arose during these years to fortify Frederick's already low opinion of his ministers of the General Directory was the so-called Liebeherr Affair. Liebeherr, a councillor in the Pomeranian board, had taken advantage of the loose accounting system of that board to embezzle about 50,000 talers. Cocceji, the chancellor of justice, had held an investigation in May, 1748, and had subsequently recommended prosecution of some officials.[12] Frederick first directed a stinging rebuke to the minister of the first department for his negligence in failing to "keep a watchful eye" on the treasuries entrusted to his care. Coincident with the revelation of this sensational embezzlement, or because of it, Frederick began to study the regulations establishing the General Directory and to think about possible ways to improve its operations. The chief edict concerning the General Directory was of course the *General Instructions* of 1722. By far the most sarcastic of Frederick's marginal notes to that document was one concerning the preparation and submission of financial reports. The General Directory should investigate the boards constantly and completely to see "whether any more Liebeherren can be found" by stirring up the "old yeast" in the provinces. Going further, he declared that he would not tolerate incorrect or falsified financial reports: officials remiss in this duty merited "hanging." "Such a person sits at present in the Directory" he mysteriously declared,

11. *AB*, 6: 2. 167, 169; 7: 422.
12. The judiciary was then in the process of reorganization under Cocceji; from 1748 onward it was to serve as a useful watchdog on the core bureaucracy. See chapter 4 below.

but he failed to name the culprit. Drastic punishment, Frederick concluded, would be meted out to such malefactors regardless of their positions.[13]

In 1748 Frederick decided to issue revised *General Instructions* for the conduct of the core bureaucracy. In the preamble to this document he remarked that he had found three areas of weakness in the operations of the General Directory, which "must be absolutely changed and replaced in the future". First, the ministers were guilty of superficial reporting of taxes; they were lax in overseeing settlement programs; and they failed to provide direction in these matters. Second, "His Majesty has discovered with the greatest displeasure that a kind of hate, animosity, and *esprit de parti* exists among the ministers." Persons guilty in this regard stood in danger of being cashiered if they did not cease their "intrigues." Third, he accused the ministers of gross negligence and indifference concerning the maintenance of financial records. He intimated that officials who shielded embezzlers stood in danger of extreme punishment. He thus summed up his feelings of resentment and anger, feelings which had been steadily intensified by the ministerial protective alliance as it had operated smoothly through the years.[14] Frederick felt, quite rightly, that his ministers conspired behind his back. He did not realize of course that his own attitude had fostered the continuance of "intrigues" on the part of his subordinates.

By removing himself from the position of chairman of their sessions, Frederick had brought about a substantial change in the relationships of the ministers with one another and with him. Yet he continued to insist that they coordinate their efforts with one another and refused to give preference to any of them. They were thus forced to work together and to prepare common reports for his perusal.[15]

13. *AB*, 7: 525 ff., 569.
14. Ibid., pp. 573–75.
15. This interpretation holds only for the period up to 1756 and does not take into account the judicial administration or the Silesian ministry; Frederick obviously felt, in 1748, that he could not trust the ministers of the General Directory. Naturally the Silesian ministry was a special arrangement established to administer a new province. Similarly the judicial administration was outside

Frederick's suspicious attitude undoubtedly made them extremely cautious in referring matters to his attention; consequently, they tried to ward off his easily aroused wrath with vague reports. Frederick had insulated himself from administrative reality. He easily discovered the various and mostly harmless deceptions his ministers prepared for him. Sensitive to an extraordinary degree and obsessed with jealousy over the prospect that any official knew more about a certain affair than he did, Frederick reviled his ministers all the more as fresh evidence of their conduct came to his attention.

Two of the three points of criticism Frederick stressed at the time of the rewriting of the *General Instructions* in 1748 reflected his concern with proper financial reporting and auditing. Frederick caused the ministers of the General Directory to take more precautions in the preparation of such reports, but failed to establish any efficient and centrally directed accounting system. The *Oberrechnungskammer* possessed authority, according to the revised *General Instructions* of 1748, to review most financial reports from the boards and to make these agencies correct their reports to agree with the treasury balance in Berlin. But the actual auditing of the two general treasuries remained the responsibility of the directing ministers; the *Oberrechnungskammer* was to have "nothing to do with it."[16] A central auditing system could not be established until the numerous treasuries had been subordinated to one overall direction. Frederick preferred to make all the ministers jointly responsible for the total auditing each year rather than to single out a single supervisor. As a consequence, each year the king had to review a number of independent reports concerning these treasuries, reports which were submitted from different departments as well as from the boards. Such a system, he rightly believed, created numerous opportunities for potential embezzlers. But he had no real solution to the problem of financial direction. He simply chastised his officials and exhorted them to more faithful

of the core bureaucracy. If Frederick trusted Cocceji as chancellor of justice and Münchow as Silesian minister in 1748, he did not trust the ministers of the General Directory.

16. *AB*, 7: 641. See Dorn, "Prussian Bureaucracy," for discussion of the *Oberrechnungskammer*.

performance of duty. The *Oberrechnungskammer* was gradually to increase its scope of authority in succeeding years as some of the mediocre councillors within it were replaced, but Frederick apparently had little to do with the improvement. The ministers themselves came to desire better accounting procedures and regular audits.

Frederick thus failed to change either the basic structure of the first four departments of the General Directory or the patterns of power within them to any substantial extent. If the top level departments of the core bureaucracy were to be made more efficient, some alteration in the method of operation was necessary. But because he could not devise any other method of administration which would not change the *Collegium* into a collection of independent ministers—a course which would of necessity have increased the authority and power of the individual officials—Frederick failed to do anything constructive in this line. Because of his disgust and distrust, Frederick was unable to contemplate any scheme which would result in giving the ministers more effective authority, and before 1763 he could devise no solution superior to periodic insults, jibes, and exhortations. Instead of adopting a cabinet system, he chose to devise ways to separate certain functions from the control of the General Directory and to limit to some extent the authority that that body could exercise over the boards. As he proceeded along these lines, he forced the directing ministers to draw ever closer to one another and to present an ever stronger front to him. His attempts to disperse authority resulted in aggravating the impasse that already existed between him and his ministers.

The Passive Resistance of the Provincial Boards

On the provincial level of administration the war and domains boards (*Kammern*) constituted the most important links in the chain of command and communication within the core bureaucracy. Like the General Directory, these agencies were organized in collegial fashion: the provincial president was a local equivalent of the king, his directors and councillors the local equivalents of the ministers and privy finance councillors, and finally, administrative authority was invested in the collective membership. Because the boards constituted a kind of "buffer zone" between the policy makers and Prussian society at large, they were never quiet backwaters and their members could never feel that their efforts were automatically agreeable to both their superiors and provincial society. Instead, the councillors were expected to be experts in domain management, excise collection, military provisioning, livestock diseases, and a multitude of other subjects. These *Räte* managed to divide the collective labor to some extent; some concentrated on the domains while others supervised the counties and cities.[17] Naturally the work of these overburdened officials was not, in contrast to modern organizational theory, neatly divided between command and expertise functions; only eight *Räte* of the Electoral Mark board in 1755 were assigned to specific technical functions such as the supervision of dikes, canals, and other construction matters. Eight others held geographical responsibilities. One, for example, was responsible for the domain units (*Ämter*) of Cottbus, Beeshau, and Stahnsdorf. The remaining six councillors performed mixed expertise and command functions. The *Steuerräte*, who numbered seven, all held responsibilities for the supervision of a number of towns and cities.[18] Nevertheless, fiscal duties claimed the attention of most of the officials most of the time; the periodic treasury accounts were obvious and tangible signs of progress or retrogression as far as the king and the General Directory were concerned.

The complex and interlocking system of board administration did not function smoothly because individual councillors possessed little or no authority and had to bargain with one another constantly in order to arrive at an administrative decision. Ultimately only the collective agreement of the *Räte* provided the necessary strength needed for effective administrative action. The councillors tended to operate in an extremely conservative fashion because they found that any departure from routine was difficult to instigate. In addition, overall

17. *AB*, 8: 562–63; 10: 568; Dorwart, *Reforms*, p. 177.
18. *AB*, 13: 403 ff.; 10: 202–10.

performance tended to obliterate individual differences. The exceptionally able councillor could not be readily identified nor the incompetent one eliminated. Responsibility under the collegial system was shared by so many that the incompetence or dishonesty of one person implicated all.[19] As a result of such internal enervating devices the boards tended to erect a defensive facade against outsiders.

Frederick II, isolated except for a short period in 1731 from contact with provincial administration, could not immediately recognize the inflexible and conservative nature of the boards. He had served as a youth on the Electoral Mark board under the famous councillor Hille and others. But this experience had been merely a case of the son of the boss familiarizing himself with the duties of lowly subordinates. Hille had reported shrewdly at the time that "the involvement in state affairs is considered by him to be nobler and more important than in finance."[20] He probably meant that his pupil was bored by the colorless routine of the board and yearned for participation in the more exciting world of war and diplomacy. At any rate, in 1740 Frederick approached the boards with the same suspicious and cynical attitude he displayed toward the General Directory.

In the eight years preceding the issuance of the revised *General Instructions* to the General Directory in 1748, Frederick came to believe that the officials composing the provincial boards throughout the realm were "idiots" and that their work was marked by "indolence" and "carelessness." In addition, these functionaries appeared to him to engage in the same sort of intrigues and chicanery that characterized the General Directory. He violently reprimanded a director and a board president at different times for submission of deceptive reports and for intrigues against superiors. By 1748 he had come to believe that the boards were nothing more than institutionalized conspiracies against him. Councillors were too often pretentious, lazy, lax, and dishonest. In the revised instructions of 1748 he emphasized that he wanted "energetic, knowledgeable, and honest"[21] persons re-

19. See chapter 6 for examples of efficient collegial administration.
20. Quoted in Reinhold Koser, *Geschichte Friedrichs des Grossen* (Berlin 1912), 1: 77.
21. *AB*, 7: 264–65, 532 ff., 579.

commended for board presidencies and councillorships by the General Directory. Frederick devised a number of methods to insure that the conspiracy of the incompetent and the dishonest would be eliminated within each of the boards. He tried to develop in addition methods to select the "right" kind of official for these agencies. The ministers of the General Directory and some of the more intelligent and ambitious officials in other positions also tried to raise the level of performance of the boards.

The king's methods and objectives were not those of an official working within the system to make it more efficient. He distrusted the organization itself, including its ingrained rules and customs, and tried to devise means to control it and to circumvent the unwritten alliances between officials. Frederick gave considerable attention to the problem of elimination of the bureaucratic defensive barriers that hamstrung the boards. He hated the fact that the board presented a united front to him and protected its members. One interesting solution he concocted was an edict which placed two different officials in charge of the same set of duties.[22] He hoped that one of them would counterbalance the other and that each would be inspired to be more energetic and honest than the other. Frederick cynically believed that the greed and dishonesty of each would make him doubly suspicious of the other. Frederick also ordered the superior courts to place a spy called the *Fiscal* in the ranks of the board. The *Fiscal* thus became a pariah among suspicious and watchful bureaucrats. He was from the ranks of the enemy, the judiciary, and could be counted upon to cause trouble if given sufficient provocation. Finally, the king instituted elaborate methods of gaining information concerning the performance of each councillor and *Steuerrat*. All of these efforts were directed primarily against the massive and inscrutable facade which the officials of the boards had erected to protect themselves. He needed independent sources of information and control to achieve personal domination over the boards.

22. Rosenberg, *Bureaucracy*, p. 177, describes the social ramifications of this bureaucratic defensive barrier construction. For sources and a different interpretation of these measures see Dorn, "Prussian Bureaucracy," pp. 87, 91–92. Also see *AB*, 10: 202–10, 4–12, 178–82, 155–62.

The outcome of these efforts inevitably proved frustrating to Frederick. Far from being potential spies on each other, board members were more likely to become fellow conspirators. The solidarity of the board operated against the ambitious maverick who wished to make an impression on superiors at the expense of his colleagues. Group opinion forced all to toe the line. The *Fiscal* in turn had to live among the core bureaucrats and to depend upon them for information and support. No one wanted to be despised as a pariah. As a consequence, the *Fiscal* frequently did nothing of importance and the whole system of espionage of which he was a key part failed to function. By 1750 Frederick decided to make the *Fiscal-General* responsible for seeing that both the courts and the boards kept aristocrats from leaving Prussia for employment abroad. He had obviously given up hope of making the *Fiscals* efficiency experts and spies within the boards. Frederick also had no reason to believe that the system of cooptation had resultated in increased efficiency or honesty on the part of the provincial councillors. He still continued to berate the boards for "chicanery."[23] The protective facade of the boards was not destroyed.

The results obtained from the efficiency reports were likewise disappointing to Frederick. Although these were supposed to give the king information concerning the competence of councillors they actually proved of little value. The reports became perfunctory exercises. The board president usually described a councillor as "an able and industrious man" without venturing to discuss possible embarrassing details.[24] Sometimes the misconduct of a subordinate was so obvious that the president had difficulty in avoiding frankness; in Halberstadt

---

23. *AB*, 7: 220–22; 459, 460–63. The *Fiscals* were originally established in Prussian and Austrian administration to keep a check on the collections and dispersal of funds by officials of different levels. See Eberhard Schmidt, *Fiskalat und Strafprozess* (Munich, 1929), pp. 149 ff. for discussion of the Prussian *Fiscals*. Schmidt quotes a disgruntled *Fiscal* who said, in 1751, that his office "is nothing more than an overwhelming burden" and makes "an enemy for everybody" (p. 149). See *AB*, 3: 522–23; and Walter, *Österreichische Zentralverwaltung* 2: 1. 305. The latter deals with Kaunitz's attempt to centralize all financial and judicial affairs under one directorate. *AB*, 8: 754; 9: 486.

24. Dorn "Prussian Bureaucracy," pp. 87–92. See also note 22 above. *AB*, 9: 285.

a councillor described by his president as a "very inferior and confused person" given to drunkenness was dismissed. However, *Steuerrat* Voss of Potsdam was described as "capable . . . but his reports are very late," two years before his death. In 1757 investigators discovered that Voss had mixed his public finances with his private finances to such an extent that it was impossible to determine how much he had transferred from the former to the latter in the course of seven years.[25] The structure of power within the board imposed certain limits on the scope of the president's actions. Subordinates soon knew via informal sources if a superior had submitted an unfavorable report. If the report was too harsh, the higher authority had to take punitive action that might arouse the resentment of the councillors. Subordinates began to distrust their own president and to refuse to cooperate with him. Soon the president found that he no longer knew what was going on. His subordinates did not tell him. Eventually he found that his effective authority over them had virtually evaporated. The delicate and complex machinery of the *Collegium* began to break down. At this point the internal difficulties of the board could no longer be kept secret from the king and the General Directory. Frederick's attitude in such cases was usually consistent. He held the president responsible for keeping his councillors in line. He cashiered a number of presidents for failure to accomplish this task. Unless the president possessed an unusually strong will, as well as considerable intelligence, he was forced to depend upon his councillors for support. Sometimes the councillors would sabotage an unwary president, such as von Wegern of the East Frisian board in 1769. During the course of an audience with the king, Wegern, who was kept uninformed by his councillors, revealed such ignorance concerning the progress of reconstruction work that Frederick cashiered him.[26]

The board president had to maintain good relations with the king,

25. Gloger, "Der Potsdamer Steurrat" (Dr. Phil. diss., Berlin, 1957), pp. 110–29.
26. *AB*, 14:492–93. See the chapter on the Silesian ministry for support of these generalizations. The removal of von Wegern had important ramifications during the *Rétablissement*. See chapter 9.

with the General Directory, with his councillors, and also with local pressure groups. All subjects of the king of Prussia possessed the right of *Gravamina*, petitioning the king for redress of wrongs. Frederick often received written complaints and anonymous charges. He listened eagerly to such dubious communications and used them to harry his officials all the more. Martin Hass has shown[27] that Frederick cashiered 11 out of his 41 presidents between 1740 and 1786. The board president could feel safe from royal displeasure if he could show that the provincial revenues increased from year to year. At the end of the fiscal year he anxiously awaited the comments of the king concerning his financial reports. During the first week of June, Frederick usually called together the ministers of the General Directory to discuss these reports. He took the opportunity afforded him by these conferences to threaten punishment or to apportion praise. The ministers in turn, or the king directly, communicated these impressions to the board presidents.[28]

The status of the board president was changed by Frederick after 1740. From the first he chose to deal with the presidents directly rather than through their nominal superiors in the General Directory. This created an embarrassing situation for the directing ministers, since all too often they were forced to take action on a matter which the king had previously and unsuccessfully entrusted to a board president. Frederick obtained increased control over the boards through this shrewdly conceived policy. One could question whether the direct relationship so established actually resulted in increased efficiency on the part of the provincial officials. The very attempt of Frederick to deal with them directly forced them to take an even more defensive attitude and made them more cautious and less willing to embark on challenging projects of one kind or another. Frederick did not choose to use his considerable charm in his dealings with the "idiots" in the boards and habitually dealt with them contemptuous-

---

27. Martin Hass, "Friedrich der Grosse und seine Kammerpräsidenten," *Beiträge zur brandenburgischen und preussischen Geschichte: Festschrift zu Gustav Schmollers 70. Geburtstag* (Leipzig, 1908), pp. 210–19.
28. *AB*, 14: 63, 84.

ly. It took the accumulated disappointments of twenty years to convince him of his error but, after 1763, "Old Fritz" did mellow somewhat and even enquired politely about the personal problems of the presidents.[29] This latter day exhibition of charm did not fail to improve his relationship with these custodians of the "bagatelles."

Prospects for Reform of Provincial Administration before 1763

Because of his consistent attitude of distrust, Frederick did not encourage reform movements among the core bureaucrats. Some of them desired to make the civil service more professional in orientation and more efficient in operation. The history of these thwarted reforms goes back to the founding of the core bureaucracy in 1722. Some officials soon realized after that date that a system of recruitment and training should be instituted in the boards to furnish more capable councillors. But all such attempts failed to come to fruition until after 1763. If one studies the efficiency reports submitted to the king in 1756, it is at once apparent that the boards did not possess any standardized recruitment system. The boards of Pomerania, Magdeburg, Minden, New Mark, the Electoral Mark, and Lituania included 24 councillors of noble origin and 62 from the bourgeoisie. Socially the boards were a conglomeration. Of the *Steuerräte* of the whole realm outside of Silesia, 33 were of bourgeois origin and only 9 from the nobility. Out of the 86 councillors of these boards, 18 had been appointed directly from posts in the army such as that of regimental quartermaster or *Auditeur*. Some of them had even held commissions in the line. Only 17 had served as *Auscultatoren* or administrative interns in the boards, though the administrative intern system had been in effect for several decades. The remaining 51 had formerly been excise collectors, domain contractors, merchants, building and dike inspectors, minor board clerks, or officials in the diplomatic corps.[30]

29. Hass, "Kammerpräsidenten," pp. 210–20. Koser, *Geschichte Friedrichs des Grossen*, 3: 185 ff.

30. *AB*, 10: 202–8, 4–12, 178–82, 155–62. Johannes Ziekursch, *Beiträge zur Charakteristik der preussischen Verwaltungsbeamten in Schlesien bis zum Untergange des friderizianischen Staates* (Breslau, 1909), pp. 32–40. *AB*, 9: 559–62.

Although Frederick had initially supported the *Auscultator* system in 1742, when he decreed that promising young men should be placed as apprentices in the various boards to study their operations in the expectation of future promotion to councillor positions, he tended to ignore the program later in making appointments.

From the vantage point of the king the problems of bureaucratic recruitment appeared to be somewhat different from those envisaged by both veteran and novice officials. Frederick inherited a corps of bureaucrats recruited by his father, or perhaps by an even earlier monarch. Left alone, these officials would probably tend to recruit persons like themselves. Frederick continued the recruitment policies of his father because these policies placed a minimum amount of responsibility for selection of novice officials upon the shoulders of high ranking bureaucrats. After 1740 Frederick, for example, appointed a number of former *Auditeure* and regimental quartermasters to councillor posts in the various boards. A few other recruits were appointed *Auscultatoren*, but the total number of these positions was strictly limited, despite the fact that these interns served without pay and were no expense to the State.[31] He obviously did not intend to allow his own senior officials to recruit even the most humble apprentices without consulting him.

The ministers of the General Directory followed a different type of hiring policy; they were not fond of *Auditeure*. They believed that entrance into the ranks of the civil service could be facilitated in several ways. The lowest clerical and custodial ranks were filled with veteran noncommissioned soldiers as a matter of policy. In order to obtain a coveted appointment to the executive ranks one usually had first to serve as an unpaid intern or *Auscultator* for several years in one of the boards. These youths were placed most often when their relatives secured the support and patronage of a prominent official such as president of a board or a minister in the General Directory. This official then sought to obtain the permission of the king to place the youth in a particular board. Many examples survive of letters prepared by such patrons outlining the qualifications of the would-be

31. *AB*, 8: 327, 665; 9: 339–40, 190.

apprentice.[32] Once an *Auscultator*, the recruit still needed the influential patronage of a veteran official so that his patron could look for a councillor opening in one of the boards and endeavor to persuade the king to appoint his protégé. Not surprisingly, the whole civil service consisted of congeries of influence-wielders and their aspiring clients. Minister von Blumenthal, for example, began his career in the East Prussian board at Königsberg. As president he fostered the career of an able *Bürgher*, Joachim Domhardt, and was able to help his favorite become first director of the board by 1757. When Blumenthal went to the General Directory as a minister, he still forwarded the career of Domhardt so that the latter ultimately became president of the Königsberg board.[33] Careful study of the structure of the executive ranks of the service at any particular time would reveal the nature of this informal hierarchy of patrons and clients. This system did not appeal to either Frederick William I or to Frederick II for obvious reasons: inefficient and even corrupt officials could be quite efficient in building up personal followings of admiring subordinates. The vital control of patronage, which underlay recruitment, promotion, and all important stages in the career of a bureaucrat, would pass into the hands of a few senior ministers since no

32. The usual pattern in all branches of the civil service, including the foreign service, began when the prospective employee either wrote to the king or to some prominent minister outlining his desires. Frederick II then either ordered the placement of the person or referred the letter to a subordinate to find out if a position could be found. This lack of a systematic approach to recruitment obviously gave officials a great deal of opportunity to build their own bureaucratic empires. See the references in note 31 above and the application of Georg Wediger in 1743 to the king for an *Auscultator* post. Frederick sent this letter together with a supporting order to the Electoral Mark board· "The . . . Board is to discover whether the person is solid in background and whether he applies himself." This correspondence, now in Potsdam, Rep. 2, I, Dom. Reg., All, pp. 29–30, is similar to many others in the *Acta Borussica*, but the marginalia of the king and, various officials, together with the formal correspondence, illustrate quite clearly how the process worked.

33. Erich Joachim, *Johann Friedrich von Domhardt* (Berlin, 1899), chapter 1; and Merseburg, Rep. 96, 411D, p. 49, letter of von Blumenthal of May 11, 1754, in which he praises Domhardt as "an able and laborious man" who could be expected to forward "His Majesty's service and highest interests." This recommendation obtained the post of first director in the Gumbinnen board for Domhardt.

monarch could know first hand the capabilities of all the councillors in the nine boards.

Frederick, as well as his father, determined to minimize the undesirable effects of the recruiting system by first attempting to introduce into the service prospective councillors who had received training outside and would presumably continue to consider the king, rather than some high-ranking official, as their permanent patron. The military clerks (*Auditeure* and regimental quartermasters) were obvious choices since they had spent years in the cast-iron administrative system of the army with virtually no contact with the civil bureaucracy.

Yet the selection policies that Frederick employed in connection with the boards were influenced by other than purely administrative and political considerations. He determined to name only aristocrats to the post of board president. Obviously the president had to meet three important criteria: he had to obtain the leadership of the corps of the officials in the board; he had to maintain the trust of the king; and he had to possess sufficient prestige to assume leadership in the province at large. In the Prussian realm the aristocracy had long possessed, as a class, leadership in the predominately rural society. Frederick thought that provincial aristocrats would be more willing to follow a fellow aristocrat who was also president than to follow a commoner who had been temporarily raised to this important bureaucratic post. The king himself automatically esteemed members of the aristocracy, particularly if they had distinguished themselves in military service before entering the civil service. Such a preference for the highborn may seem irrational, especially in a supposed "enlightened despot." In reality it was a shrewd policy because the king realized that the bureaucracy mirrored the society it presumed to administer: the *Junker* ruled his estate; he ruled the common soldiers as a military officer; and he ruled within the provincial service. Frederick admitted that he preferred to appoint retired military officers, aristocratic veterans, directly to presidential posts because they "obey and are obeyed" and show more "solidity" than civilians. In 1753 Frederick stated that presidents should come from "good, old, noble families that have the natural industry and capacity for such presidential positions." Out of a total of 41 presidents appointed by 1786, only 23 had obtained previous experience as councillors and only 3 had been commoners.[34]

One policy concerning the assignment of officials was usually followed by both Frederick William I and Frederick II. Councillors were not appointed to provinces where they had extensive personal or property ties because, if they were, they could easily become embezzlers or make alliances with local interest groups. Naturally this policy did not stop officials from conniving with the local merchants or from lining their own pockets, especially since most officials remained in a particular board for the duration of their careers in the capacities of councillor or director. For obvious reasons Frederick could not make intensive investigations of the past careers of such officials before he made appointments. He did attempt to rotate presidents from time to time, but had no systematic plan in operation to accomplish this.[35] When presidents were transferred they often took along with them their favorite subordinates, or friends, and reestablished a ruling clique in the new board. A new president could claim, of course, that certain individuals knew his ways and could help him establish his authority quickly in the new assignment. Such practices had particularly serious ramifications in the history of the Silesian boards, which will be examined later.

The contemporary cameralists, especially Justi, recommended the establishment of uniform systems of recruitment and training for both councillors and board presidents. But in practice, in the East Elbian states, particularly Prussia, Saxony, and the Austrian monarchy, these bureaucratic reforms were not introduced very quickly, nor implemented very well in the eighteenth century.[36] Any true reform in

34. *AB*, 9: 339, 726–27, 171. Appointment of Lenz. Also, see Hass "*Kammer Präsidenten*" p. 201.

35. Dorn "Prussian Bureaucracy," pp. 86; 87, 91–92.

36. Haugwitz, the great Austrian administrative reformer, was impressed by the need to overhaul the civil service so that expert officials could be hired to administer it more efficiently. He was influenced by the older German Cameralists such as von Schröder, and by the example set by the Prussian administration in Silesia after 1749. But Haugwitz was more interested in establishing the

the direction of selecting better personnel would have required the institution of some kind of examination system, regular courses of instruction (either in universities or on the job), and boards of selection made up of senior bureaucrats. In short, such a "modern" selection system presupposes that one hunts out personnel strictly upon the basis of merit rather than social class or friendships with important officials. The clublike atmosphere of the *Collegia* required that officials with "seat and voice" accept into their midst new colleagues with whom they would have to work intimately and constantly. Selection processes could not be impersonal and automatic under such practical conditions. In addition, an innovation of this kind would be bound to find a poor reception in the socially conservative minds of officials. Viewed in this light it is truly remarkable to note that attempts were actually made, first in the judiciary under Cocceji after 1746 and later, in the core bureaucracy itself, by certain Silesian ministers and by Minister von Hagen after 1767, to institute a rationalized selection system.[37] High-ranking bureaucrats remained dubious about the recommendations of the cameralists, and most eighteenth-century rulers, including Frederick II, showed little more interest.

Prior to the Seven Years' War Frederick was never able to work out a real relationship of trust with his officials in the General Directory. Most of these officials as well as the provincial councillors and presidents had already reached positions of eminence in the civil service before 1740. Perhaps Frederick felt that they still owed allegiance to his father rather than to him. The long catalog of imprecations, insults, and deprecating remarks that one can collect

---

agencies themselves than in setting up a new recruiting program; the most he said was that officials should be employed by the central government and not by the estates. See Friedrich Walter, *Die österreichische Zentralverwaltung* (Vienna, 1938), pt. 2, 1: 110 ff. As for the Saxon bureaucracy, the efforts of August the Strong and of Count Brühl were not directed particularly towards administrative reform of this type. In 1768, however, bureaucratic reform began. See Werner Hahlweg, "Die Grundzüge der Verfassung des sächsischen Geheimen Kabinetts 1763–1831," *Zeitschrift für die gesamte Staatswissenschaft* (Tübingen, 1943), pp. 1–37.

37. See chapters 4 and 9 below.

from marginalia to decrees as well as from Frederick's attitude toward his officials as manifested in various matters such as the Liebeherr scandal, reveal that the king was wary of entrusting too much authority to his officials. This distrust extended to the selection of provincial councillors by senior officials. The king should have the authority to accept or reject any candidates for any office without having to justify his selection on the basis of merit or any other criteria. An examination system might well take real selection authority out of the hands of the ruler and entrust it to those who prepared and judged the examinations and the candidates, the ministers of the General Directory. Frederick might have thought, in addition, that it was much safer to appoint military clerks and inexperienced aristocrats to councillorships and other posts. What one lost in efficiency one might recoup in loyalty and gratitude to the king since the appointees were supposedly under no personal obligation to the senior bureaucrats. Unfortunately, both Frederick and his lieutenants were proven wrong, and by 1770 the cameralists were justified.

A condition of perpetual misunderstanding existed between the king and the boards. The first, albeit unwritten, duty of the board was to reconcile official policy with local conditions. Sometimes those in Berlin and Potsdam had only the faintest idea of the conditions in a given province. Frederick at one time ordered the Minden and Halberstadt boards to ascertain the number of serfs, their labor services, and their relationship to the landed nobility. Both board presidents had to reply with lengthy descriptions of the local condition of agriculture in order to show that labor burdens and serfdom in the East German sense did not exist in their provinces. The Cleves board tried for years to explain the nature of the Rhine trade and the reasons for the decline of revenues due to slumping trade, but failed to convince its suspicious superiors. Confronted with such ignorant obstinacy, board presidents often falsified reports. In 1751 when the president of the Electoral Mark board reported the colonization of 100 foreign families, Frederick caustically replied that he had counted only 25 on a recent trip. Sometimes the reports revealed a flagrant violation of a royal order such as in the report, also from the Electoral

Mark president, which mentioned that 379,000 talers worth of sugar had been imported into the province in 1753. Frederick asked him to explain this fact in view of the official prohibition of such importation.[38] This mutual suspicion was a by-product of the "buffer zone" operations of the board. It constantly had to adjust royal edicts to fit local conditions.

Certain built-in impediments in the structure of the boards kept these agencies from instituting internal administrative reforms. Frederick fostered the continuance of these limiting devices. Most bureaucrats viewed an official position as a collection of perquisites possessed by a particular individual independently of his actual functions. If a vacancy occurred among the councillors his colleagues would sometimes divide the salary among themselves.[39] All councillors did not receive the same salaries; some were paid 400, some 600, some 800 talers a year. No overall salary schedule existed. Some had to pay the "office charge" or tax upon assumption of a position, while others were exempted, according to royal whim. Taking advantage of the upset created by the Seven Years' War, the Cleve board raised its collective salaries with the excuse that debased currency had decreased the value of their old ones.[40] These practices tended to create the impression in the mind of Frederick that the boards were collections of conspirators. In fact, the councillors were conspiring together in order to protect themselves. Both councillors and presidents preferred to operate in the most conservative manner. They collected taxes and attempted to conciliate the unhappy populace and the king. A spirit of routine performance, of mediocrity, pervaded the boards and made them incapable of adaptation or innovation. Nothing could be done to disturb the status quo.

The nature of the provincial board organization made it a "defensive" rather than "offensive" bureaucracy. Only the presence of common problems and dangers kept some degree of cohesion within the ranks. Internal strength came with the formation of bureaucratic

38. *AB*, 9: 650–64, 199, 627–28.
39. Ibid., 7: 458–59.
40. Ibid., 13: 265–66.

cliques based upon mutual family connections and favoritism, as well as upon more reputable motives. The boards served as massive counterweights to the power of the king. They could obstruct, delay, and falsify reports, but they were incapable of assuming active leadership of the State.

Mediocrity of the Subaltern Personnel

Naturally the whole of the work of the core bureaucracy could not be undertaken solely by the councillors and other executives of the boards or by the ministers and their junior partners, the privy finance councillors of the General Directory. The real work was entrusted to a host of underlings, the so-called "subalterns," as well as the more lowly messengers, guards and nonskilled workers of other types.[41] Traditionally these persons were recruited from two main sources, inso-far as is known. Many if not most of them, were retired noncommissioned officers and ordinary soldiers, while some were unlucky aspirants to councillor posts at the executive level and came from the bourgeoisie. The latter group included individuals who had failed to complete a university education, for example, and yet lacked the familial and social connections to obtain posts as *Auscultator* or unpaid apprentices in one of the boards. They were thus permanently excluded from promotion to executive rank. If the criteria of selection were vague for *Auscultator* and councillor posts, they were even more vague for subaltern posts, and the quality of such persons could not have been high. For minor clerical posts, however, aspirants usually had to demonstrate ability to copy in a clear hand and some rudimentary ability to collate paperwork. In the Foreign Affairs Department a knowledge of French and the ability to write in non-German script was a practical asset in finding employment. The pay of clerks

41. Although good information is lacking concerning the number of subaltern and executive personnel in the local level organisations, the appendix 1 includes some estimates. In the Electoral Mark board in 1754, for example, the subaltern personnel numbered 29 (11 Secretaries, 10 chancellory clerks, 3 *Commissarii*, and 4 supervisors). By 1766 some 16 secretaries, 15 chancellory clerks, and 17 copyists were employed. Potsdam, Rep. II, A, Allgemeine Kammersachen, A 367, 2, 230.

and copyists was very low, perhaps 40 talers a year on the average, which only permitted a living at the subsistence level. The parsimony of eighteenth-century governments, including the Prussian, is indicated by the fact that veterans received preferment for employment; such persons could be fed from the public trough while they were accomplishing needed work.[42]

Neither Frederick nor his officials ever thought it necessary to improve the selection and working conditions of these humble toilers despite frequent evidence that many of them in sensitive positions, such as excise collection, regularly received bribes and performed at a low level. In fact, this easygoing corruption, while frequently exposed by Frederick, was not unusual anywhere during the century. The British customs service in North America prior to 1763, for example, cost £4,460 a year to administer, but brought in receipts totalling only £1,856 a year.[43] Because of lack of interest in the subaltern personnel, Frederick, in his quest for greater efficiency and loyalty from his civil service, always believed that the whole organization could be reformed at the top. But the suspicion remains that those who carried out orders in humble ways constituted a really effective limit to overall efficiency. This lesson becomes clearer when one examines the work of the General Excise Administration (the *Regie*) after 1763. The *Regie* was organized by a consortium of profit-seeking French entrepreneurs to collect certain taxes and proved to be quite efficient because stringent control was exercised over lower ranking tax collectors.

Local Government in the Countryside

In addition to the personnel directly employed by the General

42. Merseburg, R 9, L 8, Fasc. 11, 1–7, Fdsc. 6, 9, 10. All of these documents concern applicants for subaltern posts shortly before the Seven Years' War.

43. Thomas C. Barrow, *Trade and Empire: The British Customs Service in Colonial America, 1660–1775* (Cambridge, Mass., 1967), pp. 74–75. Naturally the *Regie* was not a total success and it was abolished by Frederick William II. The reasons for its demise had little to do with its efficiency in the narrow sense of this word. See chapter 7 below.

Directory and the boards, one must consider three subbureaucratic categories: the *Landräte*, the domain administrators (*Beamte*), and the municipal *Bürgermeister*. Without the work of these three subbureaucracies the work of the core bureaucracy would have been impossible. The *Landräte* acted as intermediaries between the provincial board and the aristocratic landowners of the countryside, while the *Bürgermeister* performed a similar service in regard to the chartered towns and the realm. Both of these quasi-officials were holdovers from the *Ständestaat*; the *Landräte* had always been local aristocrats who represented the interest of a group of landowners in a particular district (*Kreis* or county), and the *Bürgermeister* had formerly been selected by the patrician bourgeoisie to administer municipal affairs in the local *Rathaus*. The *Landräte* resembled the English justices of the peace, while the *Bürgermeister* were similar to municipal aldermen elsewhere. The domain *Beamte*, however, were professional farm overseers who obtained contracts from the king to administer particular blocs of royally owned agricultural tracts.[44] Although a subbureaucratic group, they obviously differed considerably from the other two categories. After 1740, Frederick II came to pay very close attention to the *Landräte*, but not to the *Bürgermeister* or the *Beamte* because he envisioned a particular and important role for these squire–officials in the state at large.

Because Frederick William I and his predecessors had experienced so much difficulty with the nobility in East Prussia and in Cleve-Mark, they had taken away local election rights in those provinces. The *Landräte* in the latter provinces were appointed directly by the king. Elsewhere they were elected by county aristocratic associations (*Kreisstände*), but this mode of selection did not make them really different from their royally appointed colleagues. Everywhere the *Landräte* had to cultivate the support of local aristocrats in order to do their jobs.

Obviously, one of the most difficult administrative positions any official might occupy is one that stands on the very perimeter of the official bureaucratic corps. In fact, the *Landrat* stood between the

44. Stadelmann, *Preussens Könige*, pp. 8 ff., 119 ff.

State, which was represented by the core bureaucracy, and the subjects of the king. He was a spokesman for the *Junker* landlords in his county, yet he also held an official position. As a local landowner he performed his official functions as a part-time auxiliary duty. The records reveal countless instances of recalcitrant *Landräte* who could not or would not enforce policies that were unpopular in their districts.[45] In many instances they found themselves between Scylla and Charybdis, between angry fellow landlords and angry provincial councillors.

The core bureaucracy and the king expected great things of these amateur and easygoing squire–officials. To the boards the *Landrat* was a permanent obstruction on the road of administrative process. The councillor (*Krieg- und Domain Rat*) could seldom make him do what the board desired. The board could seldom resist the temptation to interfere in the local elections in the hope that they could install persons sympathetic to them. Frederick II viewed such attempts to be examples of "chicanery" on the part of the councillors.

In order to make sure that the core bureaucracy did not obtain effective authority over the landed aristocracy, Frederick II attempted to secure control of all *Landrat* appointments in the realm. He protected the local election rights of the nobility in the New Mark, the Electoral Mark, Pomerania, Magdeburg, Halberstadt, and Minden. According to an edict of 1756, the county aristocracy associations were to elect those officials within these provinces and the king would then approve them. The boards and the General Directory had no authority to reject someone selected by a county *Stände*. Only in Cleve-Mark would the General Directory recommend a candidate for Frederick's approval. Frederick in another instance retained the right to make all appointments to *Landrat* posts in East Prussia.[46]

45. F. Gelpe, *Geschichtliche Entwicklung des Landratsamts* (Berlin, 1902), pp. 58 ff. Georg Rohde, *Die Reformen Friedrichs des Grossen in . . . Geldern* (Göttingen, 1913), pp. 5–20. O. Hintze "Der Ursprung des Preussischen Landratsamts in der Mark Brandenburg," *FBPG* 28 (1915): 357–80. See the comments of Rosenberg, *Bureaucracy*, p. 69. The role of the *Landräte* in political consensus will be further clarified in chapters 6, 7, and 8 below.

46. Elsbeth Schwenke, *Friedrich der Grosse und der Adel* (Berlin, 1911), dis-

Such attempts to control placement did not prove very successful. Frederick could not possibly know all the aristocrats within the realm, nor could he prevent the boards from exerting pressure on certain aristocratic associations. Finally, he could not determine whether the nominations of the General Directory or the boards had been validly arrived at. He characteristically resorted to two devices to circumvent these difficulties. On occasion he would veto the candidates submitted by both the county associations and the General Directory. More importantly, he began to tell the county associations and the boards that he preferred former military officers. The reports of provincial boards specified the nature of the candidate's military service after 1744. Even in areas which supposedly possessed the right to select *Landräte*, the king sometimes preferred to make his own appointments from the army retired list. Such was the case when large numbers of officers were discharged at the conclusion of the War of the Austrian Succession or the Seven Years' War. For years these ex-officers were appointed in Magdeburg despite the opposition of the local aristocrats.[47]

In general Frederick paid scant attention to consideration of what background and training a *Landrat* should possess. He assumed that training as a child on the paternal *Rittergut* would acquaint the potential *Landrat* with the realities of rural life such as serfdom, the management of agricultural production, and the nature of the relationships between the nobility and the State. A title was often sufficient since it implied that the holder possessed these vague qualifications. Because of this indulgent and careless attitude Frederick often appointed misfits and failures.

By 1756 Frederick had gradually developed a new policy towards the *Landräte* of the realm, a policy designed to enhance the prestige and power of these quasi-officials. He came to believe that the *Landräte* were excellent prospects for councillor and presidential

cusses Frederick's regard for the Junker most intelligently. *AB*, 10: 571–72; 9: 426–31. See also F. Schill, "Der Landrat in Kleve-Mark," *FBPG* 22 (1909): 327–37.

47. *AB*, 9: 91–92, 280, 426–31, 437–45; 10: 571; 13: 223–24. Rohr, "Landratsamts," pp. 187–89.

posts in his boards. In line with his policy of using them as an auxiliary provincial administrative system, he decreed that each board would henceforth admit all *Landräte* to its sessions during a four to six weeks period once a year. "In the *Collegium* they will rank equally after the Directors and sit between the Directors and the first Councillor."[48] He also apparently believed that the county aristocratic associations (*Kreisstände*), which previously had met only to nominate new *Landräte*, might be encouraged to meet frequently to handle unspecified administrative chores. Finally, he continued, and even increased, his preferences for the appointment of aristocrats to board councillor posts. The effect of all these half-formulated policies would have been to make his aristocratic placemen rank over his own professional bureaucrats in provincial government and to decentralize that government by strengthening the individual county governments.

All such proposals failed. The *Landräte* were not as knowledgeable about bureaucratic business and procedures as their superiors, the councillors, and, more importantly, all of the councillors and their presidents combined to form solid fronts of resistance to such a substantial alteration of provincial government. Prior to this ill-conceived "council-stuffing" plan of the king, the lines of authority were rather firmly drawn: the career officials of the boards told the rural subbureaucracy, composed of the *Landräte*, what to do, and the latter tried, to some extent, to execute these orders. Frederick's problem, as he evidently saw it, was to make the *Landräte*, and even the county associations, important cogs in the bureaucratic machinery, to amalgamate the subbureaucracy into the core bureaucracy and thus make the aristocratic element predominant in provincial government. He liked this idea because he believed that in the realm the aristocracy alone had a real stake in the enhancement of monarchical power. Such a belief was disputed, even in the eighteenth century, but it was obviously a potent concept in the minds of many contemporary monarchs. Faced with a very serious challenge to their

48. *PKPSA*, 11: 2. 263. See also *AB*, 6: 2. 651 ff., 9: 551–52. See also chapters 5 and 9 below.

authority, the councillors refused to cooperate with the king, and the gulf widened between monarch and provincial government. Frederick failed to amalgamate the *Landräte* into provincial government, but he did succeed in keeping them free of complete control by the boards. Nevertheless, because the boards and the king could not supervise the *Landräte* continually and carefully, rural administration remained lax, and the great mass of the people of Prussia continued to look to their landlords for governmental and judicial guidance instead of to the State. Weak and poorly qualified *Landräte* were to prove embarrassments in the great crisis of the Seven Years' War.

Local Urban Government

Until after the Seven Years' War, Frederick II largely followed the municipal governmental policies of his predecessors. Since the issuance of the decrees establishing the war and domains boards in the provinces to complement the new General Directory in Berlin, the key local official had been the *Steuerrat*. When Frederick finally decided to alter his policies substantially, it was largely because of his unhappiness with the efficiency of the *Steuerrat*. But this provincial board councillor was only one of the people entrusted with the governance of municipalities. The magistracy, the garrison commander, the local merchants organized collectively (*Kaufmannschaft*), and the board itself in the provincial headquarters also played roles in city government. Municipal government was still left in the hands of the local town council in most cities, yet the *Steuerrat* was supposed to be able to impose his will on these patricians.[49] The boards spent a large proportion of their energy and time in attempting to regulate the activities of the town councils.

Frederick distrusted the councillors, or *Steuerräte*, because he considered them lazy and incompetent. The *Steuerrat* was in reality a

49. Magnus Friedrich von Bassewitz, *Die Kurmark Brandenburg . . . in 1806* (Leipzig, 1847), pp. 131–33. Hugo Preuss, *Die Entwicklung des deutschen Städtewesens* (Leipzig, 1906), p. 163. P. Schön, "Die Organisation der städtischen Verwaltung in Preussen," *Annalen des deutschen Reiches* (1891), pp. 725 ff. K. W. Rath, *Stadt und Kreis* (Berlin, 1926), pp. 1 ff.

busy official. He was responsible for the supervision of a number of municipalities of various sizes within a county. In practice his duties required that he constantly travel from one area to another between sessions of the provincial board. By 1740 the Potsdam *Steuerrat* no longer possessed "seat and voice" in the Electoral Mark board and was supposed to make his headquarters in the royal "residence" city while periodically inspecting other cities in his county. It is possible that other *Steuerräte* elsewhere had also lost their right to participate in board sessions, but evidence for this is lacking. Frederick did not appoint many of these officials throughout his reign for reasons of economy. There were only 42 *Steuerräte* in the realm outside of Silesia and usually ten in that province. No wonder that the pressure of work made many of them careless and dilatory in performance. The average *Steuerrat*, for example, probably tended to approve the actions taken by the magistracy during his absence.[50] If law and order were maintained, the taxes collected, and if no superior official was currently instituting a special reform or investigation, this dusy councillor probably felt that the magistracy was doing a good job. In Potsdam again, none of the *Steuerräte* between 1720 and 1790 made attempts to visit other cities regularly and probably devoted themselves to military quartering and other problems in Potsdam itself. It is astonishing to note that Frederick William I had thought that one annual inspection trip was sufficient for the *Steuerrat*. The central government could be very petty about the granting of per diem allowances and seemed to place more value on limiting such expenditures than on maintaining a close control of the towns.

By 1748, when Frederick II decided to amend the regulations of the General Directory, he manifested his distrust of the *Steuerräte* in accusations that some were unable or unwilling to harness the *Bürgermeister* of their towns. But the *Steuerrat* was already coming into conflict with these local officials: the magistrates of the cities of Brandenburg and Potsdam resisted attempts to quarter troops. More frequently, perhaps, some *Bürgermeister* became the personal friends,

50. *AB*, 8: 563–64; 9: 559–62, 89–91, 622–26. Ziekursch *Beiträge*, pp. 32–40. Gloger, "Der Potsdamer Steuerrat," p. 117.

or followers, of the *Steuerrat* and gained considerable influence over him.[51]

Frederick attempted to extend his authority over the towns between 1740 and 1756. Perhaps he realized that the *Steuerrat* was not performing adequately because he had too many duties and too many responsibilities. He, in effect, circumvented this official and the boards by resorting to the appointment of officials to handle the "police" side of municipal administration. In 1752 Alberti was appointed *Polizeidirektor*, with nearly coequal rank with *Steuerrat* Voss in Potsdam. In Silesia the local garrison commander always possessed wide authority over municipalities after 1741, and the *Steuerrat* consequently found his authority limited. Finally, in Berlin and Koenigsberg the boards themselves suffered some loss of authority when new municipal administrations under royally appointed and responsible officials were installed. Admittedly these were special cases, but the number and variety of such innovations meant that the *Steuerräte* were being relegated to the smaller and less important urban centers.[52]

All of these "special" changes were concerned with a general attempt on the part of the king to make both tax collection and municipal government in general more efficient. Voss in Potsdam, for example, was supposed to concentrate on tax collection in his city of residence and to continue his regular duties in the smaller cities. Alberti as "police director" was in charge of police, fire protection, street maintenance, and other activities as defined in the eighteenth century by the term *Polizei*, solely in Potsdam. In Berlin a *Polizei Direktorium* was established by Frederick II in 1742. Berlin administration was divided in the same year into four departments, concerned with the administration of justice, economic life, and finance, as well as regular municipal administration. Breslau in Silesia was placed under a similar ordinance, as was Koenigsberg. Everywhere the king seemed dissatisfied with the state of the tax collections.[53]

51. Gloger, "Der Potsdamer Steuerrat," pp. 99 ff.
52. Ibid., p. 116. Ziekursch, *Städteverwaltung*, pp. 84–90. Schrader, "Berlins," pp. 94–97; Gause, *Königsberg*, 2: 142–43.
53. See note 52 for citations. Frederick William I had encountered difficulty as

Frederick also endeavored to separate the administration of justice from the workload of the *Steuerräte* and was obviously influenced by his shrewd and ambitious chancellor of justice Cocceji in developing this policy. Included in municipal councils throughout the realm were several *Bürgermeister*: one in charge of general administration, one of the municipal court, and one of fiscal affairs. Prior to 1740 these *Bürgermeister* had either been selected by the town councils or by the provincial board, except in Magdeburg and the western enclaves where the mercantile class of the cities still possessed election rights. In practice the provincial board became the decisive appointive body due to the meager authority possessed by the town councils (magistracy). In 1749 Frederick decreed that in the future the municipal council would nominate two or three candidates for a vacant judicial *Bürgermeister* post to the Superior Court. The Superior Court the provincial arm of the Department of Justice, then examined each of the candidates and determined the appointment. Similarly, the town council would nominate several candidates to the provincial board for vacant police or fiscal *Bürgermeister* positions. The board would then examine and place individuals in the vacancies. Due to the influence of Cocceji, and in accordance with his plan to reorganize local courts, Frederick began to shift his position still further. In 1751 several royal edicts emphasized that the provincial Superior Court, not the board, could place judicial *Bürgermeister* without soliciting the approval of any other agency. Frederick had supported the Superior Courts in their efforts to obtain control of municipal judicial functions.[54]

---

early as 1713 in raising taxes in Berlin. Grumbkow was placed in charge of an administrative reform commission which reported that the military treasury was mainly dependent upon excise tax revenues. Frederick II may have noticed that the excise total for Berlin in 1745 was 280,000 talers, whereas it had been 247,000 talers in 1733. Receipts had risen roughly 50 percent between 1712 and 1740, but further increases were modest. In 1752 Frederick II laid particular emphasis on the necessity of instituting better tax collections and preventing fraud. He stated that the new police administrations of Koenigsberg and Berlin were to concern themselves with this problem. Potsdam. Pr. Br., Rep. 30, A Tit. 39, No 1, Vol. IV, 98–117. Schrader, "Berlins," p. 71.

54. Schön "Organization," p. 727. *AB*, 8: 385–86; 9: 197–98, 247, 411; 10: 327. Schrader, "Berlins," pp. 150–51, claimed that most members of the Berlin

The garrison commander of the army found that his authority over the inhabitants of cities was likewise decreased. Both the provincial board and the army found, in fact, that the king wished to limit their vague but wide control over municipal affairs. The garrison commander possessed a considerable amount of authority over civilians within the cities primarily because he commanded as much as one third of the inhabitants. He possessed almost absolute authority over the soldiers and their dependents quartered in urban areas. This military official forced the *Bürgermeister* to find quarters for his troops in the houses of townsmen. In turn, the resentful civilians often came into conflict with unruly soldiers. Both officers and men felt that they need pay no attention to ordinary municipal laws. They brawled in the streets and insulted the burghers with impunity. Frederick decreed on one occasion that the *Bürgermeister* possessed full power to arrest such miscreants in the absence of a military officer. He subsequently ordered military personnel to protect the lives and property of civilians. One one occasion several junior lieutenants and soldiers were actually courtmartialed and imprisoned for insulting a *Bürgermeister*. Finally Frederick decreed in 1752 that "no military or regimental commander can usurp authority over the magistracy and townsmen." Mixed military courts, composed of army officers and civilian jurists, became more common as the increasing size of garrisons created more and more unrest in the cities. It is difficult to determine if such sporadic edicts actually increased the authority of the town councils over the garrison commander, but it is significant that the king came to rely more and more on the Department of Justice to help the aldermen protect themselves from the army.[55]

---

city council had started their careers as apprentices in the municipal courts. It is probable that many university graduates in law came into municipal administration in many different cities, but it would be difficult to prove this without a personnel study of great magnitude and difficulty.

55. Ziekursch, *Beiträge*, remains the most discerning of studies on this topic. Horst Krüger, *Zur Geschichte der Manufakturen und der Manufakturarbeiter in Preussen* (Berlin, 1958), pp. 33, 280. *CCM*, 3: 1. 76–86; *AB*, 13: 28, 746–47; Johannes Ziekursch, *Städteverwaltung*, p. 79.

Frederick explained his policy regarding the municipalities in the *Political Testament* of 1752: "I have allowed the cities in the old provinces freedom to elect their magistracies, and will only interfere in these elections if some illegality results and certain families arrogate all power to themselves."[56] In truth only the cities in the western enclaves and in Magdaburg actually could elect their own officials; elsewhere the "election right" consisted of the right of the *Bürgermeister* in the council to appoint an outsider to the vacant post of a colleague (cooptation). The *Corpus Constitutionum Marchicarum*, the public collection of royal decrees published between 1737 and 1800, includes several edicts designed to protect local cooptation and none prohibiting it.[57] Apparently Frederick left the town governments in local hands in the smaller municipalities.

No champion of grass roots democracy, Frederick sought to promote decentralization of the core bureaucracy.[58] He tried to create a balance of power between the *Steuerrat*, the *Bürgermeister*, and the garrison commander. He also assisted the attempts of the Department of Justice to obtain control of municipal courts. At the center of controversy up to 1756 was the hapless *Steuerrat* whose supposed lack of success prompted royal attacks. Previously the *Commissarii Loci* and their successors, the *Steuerräte*, had managed municipal affairs with efficiency, but by 1756 they were faced with new problems of population growth, increased military garrisons, and a relatively inflexible tax revenue base. Frederick determined to narrow their jobs by appointment of other, equally ranked, officials and to increase the size of their staffs. These administrative changes would continue after 1763.

Stalemate

Observers from other countries who visited Berlin between 1740

56. *AB*, 9: 363.

57. *CCM*, 6: 1. 407, 438.

58. Erich Becker, *Gemeindliche Selbstverwaltung* (Berlin, 1941), pp. 144–50, advances the curious thesis that Frederick II encouraged local self-government. *AB*, 9: 278–79, 363; Friedrich Holtze, *Geschichte der Stadt Berlin* (Tübingen, 1906), pp. 72–79; Ziekursch, *Städteverwaltung*, pp. 79–111.

and 1763 were obviously puzzled by the nature of the relationship between Frederick and his officials. Thomas Villiers commented in 1746: "Nothing is certain but what comes from this King himself, and I don't find, that any body is entrusted with the Secrets of his mind." Another Englishman stated: "His Prussian Majesty, whatever he intends, asks no Body's Advice, and makes his ministers speak plain Truth," and the ministers of the crown "may be honest, able, and well-meaning People, but they neither can, nor dare do any Thing without positive Instructions, and are even disavowed sometimes for what they have said or done by Authority." Sir Andrew Mitchell commented, finally, "no reports of the marches or encampments of Prussian troops, or indeed of any other public affairs in that monarchy, deserve much credit, till it is given them by royal edicts or declarations, or by the executions of the things themselves." Naturally, these diplomats had more contact with the minister of foreign affairs, von Podewils, than with the officials of the General Directory, but they apparently formed their nearly universal opinion concerning the "despotic" nature of the entire Prussian administration from these contacts.[59]

Of course, all of these observers noted the existence of a lack of confidence in the ability and loyalty of subordinates on the part of the king, but their conclusion, that the king did everything himself and made his officials errand boys, is fallacious. Frederick was indeed operating at cross-purposes with the General Directory and was

59. Manfred Schlenke, *England und das friderizianischene Preussen 1740–1763* (Munich, 1963), pp. 268–69, quotes these and other passage from the published writings of English travellers. John Douglas commented in 1749: "A prince, however extensive his capacity, can never know the real situation and circumstances of his people, without admitting those, who have drawn knowledge from age and experience, to give him advice, to expose the wants, and represent the distresses of the state, and to suggest the proper remedies." And, because of the large standing army and its constant demand for recruits, the populace is unduly burdened: "There is no more unfortunate land than Prussia" (pp. 270 ff.). These contemporary English views have undoubtedly been the foundation of the more modern, British, attitude that Frederick's Prussia was a despotic, militarily dominated state wherein the king did everything and his ministers were mere puppets. See the biographies by Carlyle and Robertson, their views are so well known that no more documentation is necessary. (Sir Andrew Mitchell was British ambassador to Prussia during and after the Seven Years' War.)

interfering with the delicate mechanism of the provincial governments in an effort to secure more efficient operation and to bypass the obstructive tactics of his ministers.

Frederick discovered that all parts of the structure were interdependent when he attempted to incorporate the *Landräte* into the provincial boards and when he tried to bypass the General Directory to deal directly with board presidents. His sporadic efforts to work directly with municipal governments were likewise frustrated because of the resistance of all officials to any change in the line of command and the chain of hierarchical responsibility. Fortunately, Frederick was an extremely intelligent, if inexperienced, administrator, and he did not push these destructive policies to the point where administrative coherency was utterly lost. He had to acknowledge that the ministers of the General Directory were in charge of the core bureaucracy if he hoped to maintain minimal efficiency in the organization. But the net result was a growing awareness on the part of officials of all levels that the king could not be depended upon to support them. No improvement in the core bureaucracy could be expected until the king and his officials had altered their attitudes.

The differences which separated the king from his officials were also due to the social milieu in which they lived. The Prussian civil service was dominated by a group of old-line and parvenu aristocrats, those of old families and those ennobled recently by Frederick William I or by his predecessors. Rosenberg believes that the "bureaucratic nobility" emerged primarily after 1740,[60] but it may be true that it amalgamated as early as the administrative reforms of Frederick William I. The core bureaucracy had been built into a tax collecting elite by 1740, but its members still viewed their functions and offices partly as perquisites and artificial social benefits. Embezzlement was relatively easy because of the deficient understanding of the difference between public and private funds, because of overlapping administration of treasuries, and because officials did not receive salaries according to some rational criterion but depended, individually, upon the largess of the king when he made appointments.

60. Rosenberg, *Bureaucracy*, pp. 137 ff.

Frederick disliked the cosy, clublike, atmosphere of the core bureaucracy with its obvious aristocratic and patronal *modus operandi*. He
particularly distrusted the patronage system, whereby senior officials
gathered around themselves coteries of juniors aspiring for placement
or promotion. These senior officials tended to view themselves in
somewhat the same light as the great *robe* aristocrats of France.[61]
They had, after all, built the administration since 1722 and considered
it the vehicle of their ambitions.

The stalemate that emerged between the king and his officials
during the period 1740 to 1763 was due to mutual misunderstanding
and to the efforts of the bureaucrats to protect their elitist position
in Prussian society. Frederick would have to work outside of the
core bureaucracy in order to bring about his desired innovations.

61. See the piquant commentary by Rosenberg, ibid., p. 86. Naturally, the
formation of this bureaucratic elite within the core bureaucracy was similar to
the regrouping of officials of various kinds within the French bureaucracy as
suggested by Franklin L. Ford, *Robe and Sword* (Cambridge, Mass., 1953).

III

THE ECONOMICS OF

BUREAUCRATIC ANARCHY

Frederick knew that an increase in the revenue of the State, reflected in a greater yield from direct and indirect taxes, could come about only if the commerce within the realm was in a consistently prosperous state. Mercantilistic and cameralistic writings of this time concentrate on the search for means to obtain a favorable balance of trade through the exchange of goods. What better way existed to insure this desirable state of affairs, Frederick thought, than to create a superagency responsible for all commercial, industrial, and settlement programs? He considered the settlement of foreign artisans a keynote to economic development. Such a bureau could collect statistics on these subjects, dispatch inspectors to supervise them, and coordinate the work of the boards in such a manner that trade would flourish. Scarcely a month after he came to the throne Frederick established a new agency, the fifth department of the General Directory, to fulfil this function.[1]

On June 27, 1740, Frederick dictated to his cabinet secretary, Eichel, a general decree providing for the foundation of this additional department within the General Directory to take charge of "commercial and manufacturing affairs."[2] It was to be headed by Samuel von Marschall, a minister who had previously served in the third department under von Boden. Marschall had been a minister since 1733 and had served for twenty years as a cabinet secretary to Frederick William I. He had been ennobled by that monarch and had

1. *AB*, 6: 2. 30–32.
2. Ibid.

married into the aristocracy. Frederick, lacking experience, may well have thought that this veteran official, so closely associated with the affairs of the previous monarch, would be able to secure the cooperation of the other ministers of the General Directory. Unfortunately, the post of cabinet secretary was one that conferred authority on a person, but only the reflected authority of the king, and the ministers in the General Directory may well have felt that Marschall was an outsider. Also, the hostile attitude of old-line aristocratic officials towards the newly ennobled still persisted, although evidence of it was to be seen mostly in the judiciary. Marschall had never worked in harness with other officials and his social background, that of a parvenu, did not help. Frederick also appointed two privy finance councillors, Beyer and Hille, to assist Marschall.[3]

Hille had initiated Frederick into the operations of the core bureaucracy while the latter was recovering from the wrath of his father in 1731. He had thus established a friendly relationship with "our illustrious *Auscultator*," and had taught him some of the cameralistic lore of the day. Hille was interested in expanding trade abroad and in making Prussia imitate England: commerce, not industry was king in his thinking. As Hinrichs remarked: "He revealed himself as a mercantilist in the west European sense" by stressing the balance of trade as a key to general economic prosperity. In fact, Hille thought that Prussian trade with Silesia, Poland, Bohemia, and with Hamburg and Holland could be funnelled through Frankfurt on the Oder so that the cheap raw materials of eastern Europe would be exchanged for the manufactured products of western Europe to the advantage of Prussia. Even though the crown prince had not seemed very interested in these and other economic theories in 1731, his subsequent correspondence with his guardian, Grumbkow, revealed that the lessons were remembered.[4] Hille had suffered because of great op-

3. Hintze, ibid., 1. 171–72.
4. Carl Hinrichs, "Hille und Reinhardt, zwei Wirtschafts- und Sozialpolitiker des preussischen Absolutismus," *Preussen als Historisches Problem* (Berlin, 1964), pp. 164–69. Reinhold Koser, ed,. *Briefwechsel Friedrichs des Grossen mit Grumbkow und Maupertuis, PKPA* 72(1898). Koser, *Geschichte Friedrichs des Grossen* (Berlin, 1912), 1· 62–63, 79.

position within the core bureaucracy to his "radical" theories, and his appointment signified a new direction of state policy. The chief opponent of this courageous official was Privy Finance Councillor Reinhardt, who tended to look at economic problems from a conservative angle. He was not very interested in sponsoring great overseas trading corporations or businessmen who became "poor patriots" because they put profit over everything else. Instead, Reinhardt hoped that the tax-collecting system would be modified so that it rested lightly on the urban artisans. The State would not help entrepreneurs, but would keep them from making "beggars" of the laborers they exploited. Hille wanted to expand the mercantile economy through aggressive sponsorship of entrepreneurs in trade abroad; Reinhardt wanted to preserve the existing economy and society and to protect the urban lower classes from exploitation. Although our sympathies should go to Reinhardt, Hille had a greater real understanding of the times. Reinhardt, in fact, expressed the narrow, provincial attitude of his colleagues in the core bureaucracy while Hille looked westward.[5]

Thus, the fifth department began its work under difficult conditions. Its executives had not served as part of the old-line core bureaucracy: they were outsiders and "radicals."

Jurisdictional Problem of the New Fifth Department

Once the fifth department was established by royal edict, the ministers of the General Directory had to establish some kind of *modus vivendi* with it. Conversely, the new department had to establish a meaningful place for itself in the existing administrative structure. Frederick did not prove of much assistance to either the ministers of the old departments or to Marschall in the subsequent ticklish negotiations. In the June decree he had given Marschall extraordinary authority over existing and new industries as well as the colonization of artisans. As an afterthought, however, he instructed Eichel to note on the margin: "By the way, it is His Majesty's inten-

5. Hinrichs, "Hille und Reinhardt," pp. 164–69.

tion that Marschall and his two officials will confer with the General Directory concerning important matters in every instance."[6] If no consensus could be developed, the final decision was to be left to the king. The jurisdictional limits of the fifth department were not clearly defined even in the edict establishing that agency.

After June, 1740, a curious bureaucratic conflict developed between the fifth department and the other four departments of the General Directory. The contending parties subtly maneuvered for advantage in this essentially doubtful and fluid situation. At the basis of it was the unresolved question of control over the vitally important manufacturing and commercial activities of the realm.[7] Frederick did not realize how intimately these matters were connected to the very structure of the core bureaucracy. The yearly tax balances depended in large part upon the efficiency of those entrusted with the management of commercial affairs. In the final analysis the whole core bureaucracy was judged by its imperious master on its balance sheets. Needless to say, the shrewd ministers of the four old departments had no intention of abdicating control over these economic matters. Equally certain was the attitude of Marschall and of his subordinates. They possessed a unique opportunity to assume extraordinary influence and prestige within the core bureaucracy if they were victorious in the jurisdictional struggle.

The jurisdictional question was first pinpointed by a subordinate official within the General Directory, Manitius, who was slated to work in the fifth department. In August of 1740 Manitius prepared a detailed memorandum outlining the difficulties which the new department would have to face. First of all, he indicated, the fifth department would have to be assigned definite prerogatives or functions. Manitius did not suggest that his superiors consult with Frederick. Instead, he recommended that the fifth department prepare a circular at once for distribution to all the boards. He realized that the real

6. *AB*, 6:2. 26–29.
7. August Skalweit, "Die Getreidehandelspolitik und Kreigsmagazine Verwaltung Preussens, 1756–1806," *AB Getreidehandelpolitik*, 4: 36–42. Paul Goehls, "Berlin als Binnenschiffahrtsplatz," *Schmollers Jahrbuch*, 147, p. 13. *AB Akzise und Zollpolitik*, 3:1. 496–98, 502 3.

victory lay in securing the domination of his agency over the boards in all economic questions. He asked rhetorically whether the boards would be allowed to introduce new industries and artisans within their provinces without submitting a "report for each occasion to the Minister von Marschall?" Manitius's shrewd memorandum may have been the first sign of gathering opposition to the General Directory within the fifth department.[8] Scarcely two weeks before, the ministers of the first four departments had audaciously decided to allow the fifth department to handle only "improvements" of existing manufactures or the introduction of new ones. Viereck and Happe stipulated that if no such improvement was involved, but merely the administration of existing economic institutions, the boards would have complete charge. The General Directory also claimed complete responsibility for all "treasury" matters.[9] Manitius's memorandum implied that the fifth department would undertake supervision of "new" manufactures and of "improvements" in the old ones through manipulation of tariff schedules, the collection of trade statistics and other matters. On the surface he merely kept within the limits the General Directory had set but he correctly suggested that these functions could not be exercised without granting to the new department far-ranging authority over tax and toll collections. This little war of August, 1740, did not settle any major issues but merely cleared the ground for subsequent fighting.

Despite long and hard-contested bargaining sessions during July, 1740 Marschall and his opponents in the General Directory could not agree on jurisdictional limits.[10] Additionally, although Frederick encouraged these officials to agree with one another, he did nothing substantial to increase the authority of his new minister. In fact, the hapless head of the fifth department was appointed to the onerous duty of supervising the *Chargenkasse,* or repository of fees collected from newly appointed officials at the same time that the king graciously relieved him of other obligations. While Frederick compliment-

8. *AB*, 6:2. 112–15.
9. Ibid., p. 115.
10. Ibid., pp. 35–36.

ed Marschall for being a man of "trust, diligence, and dexterity,"[11] he did seem able or willing to ease his task. In reality the king hoped, perhaps, that the bureaucratic struggle would result in a suitable jurisdictional settlement and preferred to keep hands off in the interim.

In the time of Frederick William, Marschall had infrequently attended the sessions of the General Directory and his relations with the other ministers had been cool and even hostile.[12] After his appointment as head of the fifth department he found that these colleagues refused to give up any of their prerogatives. "Everything in the land" including established manufactures and existing trade between provinces was to be "solely" under the members of the four original departments, according to a statement issued by the *Collegium* in January, 1741. In fact, "the Fifth Department has only to do with the colonization and establishment of all sorts of artisans, manufacturers, who are not presently in the realm and must be brought in from elsewhere." Granting strictly limited authority to Marschall over the mints, the *Lagerhaus*,[13] and the state-owned alum factory, the ministers claimed that all other actions, except the introduction of new settlers, would have to be countersigned by themselves. Marschall realized that he and his department had suffered an important defeat because his ministerial colleagues determined to make him work in harness with them.

Again, Frederick's position was equivocal; he finally settled the jurisdictional squabble by promising everything to all parties. Such a "solution" really hamstrung the work of the infant fifth department. On the one hand, for example, he gave Marschall responsibility for "all commercial matters" insofar as the prospective establishment of new trading concerns and the improvement of old ones was concerned. But, even though the king went on to grant him authority over the supervision of old and new manufacturing activities, Marschall

11. Ibid., pp. 30, 77–78.
12. Hintze, ibid., 1. 169–72.
13. The royal textile warehouse and factory. See subsequent remarks in this chapter.

found that his role was to remain as one within the chorus of the General Directory. Frederick imparted this blow by stating that "all such matters must be concerted with the other members of the General Directory whenever a particular province is affected."[14] So ended the formal struggle of power between the General Directory and the upstart fifth department. Marschall had to content himself with independent authority in the collection of reports on settlements, but nothing else. It is impossible to say whether Frederick realized the import of his decision of February, 1741. The old-line bureaucrats had won.

The Economic Development Scheme of the Fifth Department

Unfortunately, neither Frederick nor Marschall realized as early as 1742 that the real and effective basis of authority of the infant fifth department had been destroyed. Its main theoretical functions still remained very broad: to raise the economy to parallel that of an advanced western European State. As the cameralists had often emphasized, the productivity of industry was dependent upon a favorable balance of trade and a stable agricultural condition. Since peasants were often part-time artisans, a very close connection existed between two apparently different branches of the whole economy, manufacturing and agriculture. Similarly, commerce tied both the other sectors together and served as the main measuring rod of economic development. Marschall and his subordinates thus believed that all three sectors must be simultaneously developed, but the teeth of the department had been pulled, and it could do nothing without first undergoing extensive and onerous negotiations with the General Directory and the various provincial boards. Additionally, none of these officials really understood how to administer an agency that was to play a revolutionary role in economic development, that was to sponsor change and improvements in society at large rather than concentrate on the tried and proven techniques of tax collection. This lack of administrative expertise hampered all governments of the

14. *AB*, 6: 2. 191–92.

Old Regime. The most successful of them was Colbert's administration, but it fostered so many squabbles among officials and merchants that it received, perhaps, less recognition than it deserved in France and Europe later.

The problems that confronted eighteenth-century governments when they presumed to institute economic development programs were different from those faced by modern, highly industrialized states. In order to promote the textile manufacturing in a pre–industrial revolution context one had to seek weavers and spinners from those parts of Europe, particularly France and the Netherlands, that seemed to have a surplus work force in these trades. In truth, during the eighteenth century the textile artisans in Lyons and elsewhere in western Europe were generally poorly paid and not averse to moving eastward.[15] But why should the Prussian government desire to promote this particular branch of manufacturing? The tariff schedules reveal the answer: one of the most costly import items was fancy cloth such as silk and velvet. In common with other greatly valued imports such as French brandy, these commodities were considered luxuries permanently beyond the reach of the vast majority of the king's subjects, but they were necessary ingredients in the aristocratic and wealthy bourgeois style of life everywhere. Under the putting-out system both weaving and spinning were accomplished in rural and urban settings; peasant–artisans did some of the work and urban artisans the rest.[16] Therefore, Marschall, if he desired to promote the textile industry generally, had to consider the inhabitants of the domains, of *Rittergüter*, of villages, and of chartered municipalities. He could not, if he wished to sponsor an ambitious program, restrict himself to just one or two of these potential arenas.

Marschall's difficulties can be readily appreciated if one examines the nature of Prussian agricultural administration, for example. He discovered that the domains, while theoretically under the boards, actually were administered by entrepreneurs who were, according to

15. Krüger, *Zur Geschichte der Manufakturen* . . . (Berlin, 1958), pp. 134 ff. Many artisans came from Bohemia and western Germany in addition.

16. Krüger, *Zur Geschichte der Manufakturen*, pp. 167–260, discusses the dual nature of manufacturing in Prussia.

Otto Hintze, "trustworthy and *kapitalkräftig.*"[17] These entrepreneur–officials obtained almost unlimited authority over their contracted portions of the crown lands. Their cooperation was necessary before new settlements could be established, but the boards possessed little influence over them between contract-signing times. It was almost impossible to make the entrepreneurs institute agricultural improvements unless these were stipulated in their agreements with the State. But if the domain entrepreneurs were almost autonomous agents, the owners of private lands were so protected by traditions and law, as well as by royal edict, from bureaucratic regulation that any attempt to force them to settle peasant–artisans, for example, were bound to be frustrated because they were not willing to change their ways. Agricultural land owned by chartered towns was subject to the same kinds of legal and semifeudal encumbrances.[18] Since the fifth department could not deal directly with such local units, and since the boards did not intend to cooperate, Marschall's attempts to sponsor settlement programs always failed.

Of course, settlement programs were in fact undertaken between 1740 and 1756, but they were always promoted by the king in the first instance and the boards in the second instance. In 1742, for example, Frederick ordered the boards to remove any domain entrepreneurs found guilty of oppression of the serfs. While thus stressing a familiar theme, the conservation of the peasantry, he also warned the board councillors not to engage in "chicanery" with the domain administrators. If he did not work directly with the boards, he used the offices of the Chancellor of Justice Cocceji and even military commissions to supervise agrarian projects.[19] The fifth department was bypassed by the king himself.

17. *AB*, 6: 1. 24–25.
18. M. Beheim-Schwarzbach, *Hohenzollern Kolonisation* (Berlin, 1888), p. 361. Robert Stein, *Geschichte der Ostpreussischen Agrarverfassung* (Jena, 1918), pp. 108–11, 127–30. Walter Mertineit, *Die Friedericianische Verwaltung in Ostpreussen* (Heidelberg, 1958), p. 138.
19. *PKPA*, 11: 253–54. The domain entrepreneur–administrator became extremely important in the provincial administration of East Prussia after 1756. Domhardt, president of the boards in that province after 1763, began his career in that capacity. After the onset of the "enterprise" system, contracted land

Although Marschall tried to lead the campaign in Western Europe which was designed to lure artisans with promises of exemption from military service, monetary subsidies, and relaxed manorial service,[20] even such propaganda activities had to be shared with others. Each board proceeded with its plans with varying amounts of energy and interest, and the fifth department discovered that neither the General Directory nor Frederick had any concerted settlement plan in mind. This lack of central direction and planning was symptomatic of the general failure of the new department: a failure which Frederick finally understood in 1749 when he decreed that the fifth department would no longer have any jurisdiction over rural settlement programs of any type.[21]

The promotion of industrial development in the cities involved problems of management nearly as great as those in rural areas, as Marschall discovered. Industry within the cities of the realm was concentrated mostly in Berlin, Magdeburg, and Cleves, although countless smaller municipalities harbored craftsmen. Silesia possessed an extensive rural industry and the city of Breslau served as a financial center unifying this industry. Magdeburg, however, was an economic dependency of Hamburg, Cleves of Amsterdam, and Breslau of Vienna and Leipzig. These industrial and commercial centers belonged to economic spheres outside the Prussian realm. Frederick gradually came to believe that all of these cities had to be subordinated to Berlin, which was the administrative center of the realm, and his realization had much to do with the subsequent development of the capital into a *Grossstadt* in central Europe.[22]

---

passed from father to son for many generations and the dynasties thus formed differed little from those of the landed nobility in wealth and influence. See the comments of Walter Mertineit, *Die Fridericianische Verwaltung in Ostpreussen* (Heidelberg, 1958), pp. 112–16. Frederick stipulated in domain contracts after 1763 that the entrepreneur had to settle a certain number of colonists during his contract period. If he was successful, the board was required to renew his contract automatically. This constituted the "enterprise" system.

20. H. Troger, *Die kurmärkischen Spinnerdörfer* (Leipzig, 1936), p. 19.

21. Beheim-Schwarzbach, *Kolonisation*, pp. 361, 272 ff. *AB*, 7: 262, 578; 8: 433 ff.

22. August Skalweit, "Getreidehandelpolitik," *AB Getreidenhandelpolitik*, 4: 36–42.

Before 1747, however, he had not developed this centrist doctrine very far. Marschall had a golden opportunity, if he had been able to see it. But his attempts to secure control over the highly important construction of canals linking Berlin with the Oder and Elbe came to nothing because the Electoral Mark board was already heavily engaged in this work.[23] Aside from an abortive attempt to introduce silk making in the Electoral Mark,[24] the fifth department experienced frustration in any part of municipal industrial promotion. In Berlin itself the department had no real authority.

Growth of the Entrepreneurial Elite

The failure of the fifth department to obtain supervisory authority and control over the diverse types of economic endeavors of the realm was only part of a more general failure of the Prussian government. Despite the confident claims of the cameralists, the administrative manipulation of business and economically important groups was poorly understood and imperfectly instituted by the king and all of his advisers. A truly remarkable story begins to unfold in Berlin during the eighteenth century; the evolution of a new class of entrepreneurs, large and small, with fiscal, commercial, and manufacturing interests. This apparently heterogeneous group rose parallel with the growth of the administrative apparatus of the State. Was it the creation, intelligently planned, of Frederick William I? Did it, after 1740, prosper because of the benevolent activities of the fifth department? The answers to both questions are negative.

State-subsidized industrial programs had originated early in the reign of Frederick William I. Two enterprising Pomeranian small businessmen, David Splitgerber and Gottfried Daum, were saved from destitution by the king in 1710 after they had failed to obtain entrance into the tightly organized guild system of Berlin. These entrepreneurs attracted the attention of the "Soldier King" primarily because they

23. Detto, *FBPG*, 14: 165–86. *AB*, 9: 346–47.
24. *AB Seidenindustrie*, 1: 100–1. W. Bassewitz, *Die Kurmark vor 1806* (Berlin, 1854), p. 454.

attempted to establish weapons and munitions factories and could secure gunpowder and other necessities of war from Amsterdam in quantity and at reasonable cost.[25] From the beginning, the central warehouse (*Lagerhaus*) which the king erected served the business interests of the two entrepreneurs. These interests soon broadened to include the importation of western European nonmilitary goods including textiles. Finally, the *Lagerhaus* became a textile factory under state control. Frederick William I, knowing little about such matters, entrusted authority to a merchant–official named Krautt, and that canny businessman soon confused his private profit-making motives with state business. In short, the alliance that soon arose between Krautt and the entrepreneurs, who now numbered more than just the favored Splitgerber and Daum, resulted in a mutual greasing of palms and the general multiplication of corrupt practices. When Krautt died, in possession of extensive landed property, his Pietistic royal master confiscated it.[26] From 1730 to 1740 the entrepreneurs cautiously expanded their business, which now included export–import trading, and weapons and cloth manufacturing, under the eyes of their choleric overseer. By 1740 the tiny world of Berlin entrepreneurs numbered about a dozen, and one should not imagine that they presided over an industrial revolution. The volume of goods traded, the numders of entrepreneurs involved, and the limited amount of capital available were small.[27]

When Frederick II came to the throne in 1740 he discovered that the *Lagerhaus* had been effectively seized by Splitgerber and Daum and their friends; it no longer served as an official regulatory agency, but was now a kind of mutual protective association designed by its business executives to keep new entrepreneurs out of the tiny world of Berlin business. Frederick also found that this monopoly had aroused

25. F. Lenz and O. Unholz, *Die Geschichte des Bankhauses Gebrüder Schickler* (Berlin, 1912), pp. 1–42. Wilhelm Treue, "David Splitgerber, ein Unternehmer in Preussischen Merkantilstaat," *Vierteljahrschrift für Sozial- und Wirtschaftsgeschichte* 41 (1954): 253–67.

26. Stephen Skalweit, *Die Berliner Wirtschaftskrise von 1763 und ihre Hintergründe* (Stuttgart, 1937), pp. 2–3.

27. H. Rachel und P. Wallich, *Berliner Grosskaufleute und Kapitalisten* 2 (Berlin, 1938): 251 ff.

great enmity and jealousy among outside businessmen such as Johann Wegely, the porcelain manufacturer. In 1739 the new and underprivileged entrepreneurs petitioned the Electoral Mark board for redress of their grievances and the destruction of the *Lagerhaus* monopoly.[28] The dispute, still alive after 1740, came under the purview of Marschall, who was now head of the *Lagerhaus*. Unfortunately the new chief of the fifth department was not able to cope with the problem and thus to take a dominant role in Berlin entrepreneurial life. Frederick liked Splitgerber and had used him as an agent for the purchase of French books while crown prince. Splitgerber thus continued to enjoy a kind of immunity, and the rebels under Wegely failed to undermine his position.

To the new king, perhaps, these entrepreneurs were nothing more than "tradesmen" who had served him well, if also profitably, in the past. After the nearly impecunious days of Rheinsberg, Frederick felt somewhat obligated to Splitgerber, to whom he owed 1,518 talers. Another astute merchant had taken care to befriend the crown prince and was to be suitably rewarded after 1740, Johann Ernst Gotzkowsky. The scion of an impoverished Polish noble family, Gotzkowsky had established a textile factory in Berlin after 1730. Because he took the trouble to journey to Rheinsberg later to offer commercial services and advice he had become, by 1740, the chief provisioner of fancy imported cloth to Frederick and his sisters. Gotzkowsky enjoyed good relations with the *Lagerhaus* monopolists and supported Splitgerber and his colleagues when Wegely began his campaign. Frederick, advised by such interested parties, refused to do anything about the *Lagerhaus* problem. Marschall, as head of the *Lagerhaus* and chief of the fifth department, also, and understandably, did nothing.[29] In Marschall's defense one could say that the situation was fraught with uncertainties and dangers. Gotzkowsky, not Marschall, was the expert Frederick consulted about the problems of the silk industry in the decade after 1740. Splitgerber enjoyed immunity.

28. Horst Krüger, *Zur Geschichte der Manufakturen* (Berlin, 1958), pp. 476–79. *AB Akzise und Zollpolitik*, 2: 1. 754 ff.

29. Otto Hintze, "Johann Ernst Gotzkowsky," *Historische und Politische Aufsätze* (Berlin, 1908), 2:109–10.

Therefore Marschall and his fifth department colleagues came to gravitate towards the Gotzkowsky–Splitgerber clique out of expediency and necessity.

Instead of relying upon the fifth department Frederick resorted to the creation of a multitude of commissions and semi-independent agencies to supervise the Berlin entrepreneurial community. Significantly, he did not feel that such supervision was necessary until 1743, when he appointed a commission composed of two Berlin magistrates, two deputies of the Electoral Mark merchants, a member of the Electoral Mark board, and two from the Berlin entrepreneurs to arbitrate disputes between the *Lagerhaus* monopolists and their business opponents. Since neither the General Directory nor the fifth department was involved in this commission, and since no provision was made for really moderating the influence of Splitgerber and Gotzkowsky, the plan failed. By 1748 it had been abolished upon the recommendation of the merchants involved.[30] When the Berlin Police Directory was established in 1742 it was ordered by Frederick to spy on the workshops of the industrial entrepreneurs and to arbitrate disputes between masters and workmen.[31] Kircheisen, a councillor of the Electoral Mark board, became its president and expanded his responsibilities to include the arrest of vagabonds and their placement in workhouses.[32] Similarly, the fifth department was not able to dominate or even influence the Potsdam Orphange Commission, which supervised silk production by its wards, nor any of the two other silk regulatory bodies established after 1742.[33]

But all of these commissions included substantial representation from the Electoral Mark board and the Berlin municipal government. The degree of cooperation between these two agencies can be understood when one discovers that Kircheisen remained a councillor of the board when he was appointed city president in Berlin in 1742.[34]

---

30. Krüger, *Manufakturen*, pp. 78, 475 ff. *AB Akzise und Zollpolitik*, 3: 1. 381.
31. *AB Seidenindustrie*, 1: 207–8, 199–200, 358–59.
32. Krüger, *Manufakturen*, p. 600.
33. *AB Seidenindustrie*, 1: 85–87, 103–5, 260–62.
34. Potsdam Pr. Br. Rep. 30 A Tit. 39, Pol. Dir. zu Berlin organ. #1, Vol. IV, 1742–1786, pp. 98–117 Schrader, *Verwaltungs Berlins*, pp. 91 ff.

The ministers of the General Directory took this opportunity to bypass Marschall and place Kircheisen directly under their orders. When the municipal regulations of 1742 and 1747 were drawn up by the General Directory, the fifth department was not consulted. Karl Stephen Jordan, an intimate of Frederick's since the Rheinsberg days, was elevated to the post of director of the Potsdam orphanage in 1742. His duties included the establishment of a training program to transform the children into productive silk workers, and Frederick rewarded him for his services, as well as for past friendship, by membership in the Academy of Science. He enjoyed the confidence of the king and was not really subordinate to anyone else.[35] As a consequence, the direction of important manufacturing activities in Berlin not only was kept from the hands of the fifth department, it was not placed under any one supervisory body. Such a development proved highly dangerous because Splitgerber and his friends could easily play commission against commission and official against official and thus increase their own profit-making opportunities without suffering too much from bureaucratic direction. They tended to act in concert with one another while the officials tended to rival one another. Outside of Berlin, and particularly in newly conquered Silesia, Marschall discovered that his hands were similarly tied. The ambitious and intelligent minister of the new province, von Münchow, seized most of the private mines in the province and made lucrative contracts with Splitgerber and Daum before Frederick took the reins. The supervision of the Silesian industry thus became a responsibility of the provincial government and not of the General Directory or the fifth department.[36]

This complex and poorly developed structure of bureaucratic control over enterpreneurial activity reflected the uncertainties and

35. Koser, *Friedrichs*, 1: 107 ff. *Oeuvres de Frédéric le Grand*, ed. J. Preuss (Berlin, 1846–57), 7: 7. Krüger, *Manufakturen*, pp. 595–96.

36. H. Fechner, "Die Königlichen Eisenhüttenwerke Malapane und Kreuz zu ihrer Übernahme durch das Schlesische Oberbergamt, 1753–1780," *Zeitschrift für Berg-Hütten- und Salinenwesen*, 42: 81–82. Hans Buchsel, *Rechts und Sozialgeschichte des Oberschlesischen Berg- und Hüttenwesens 1740–86* (Breslau, 1941), pp. 18–27.

ambiguities of royal and ministerial policy alike. Before 1747 Frederick only dimly understood the teachings of councillor Hille, and particularly the argument that economic development had to be centrally coordinated and planned. Because he distrusted the General Directory, Frederick had instituted the fifth department. Because the fifth department had not been able to establish itself independently of the old-line ministers, he had bypassed it. Because he wished to encourage manufacturing in Berlin and Potsdam, he appointed ad hoc commissions to work on specific projects and enlarged the authority of the Berlin municipal government. But afterwards locally instituted controls proved ineffectual because the entrepreneurs worked on a national and, even, an international basis. The results were governmental weakness combined with a liberal subsidy policy and the growth of a group of profit-seeking entrepreneurs.

Fäsch and the New Direction of the Fifth Department

Despite the hopes of certain officials within the General Directory that the fifth department would be abolished when Marschall died in 1749, Frederick declared that he would shortly announce the appointment of a successor. In truth, the department had been reduced to supervising the settlement of artisans in Pomerania and the Electoral Mark, a gift of the ministers of the General Directory and not of Frederick, who wished to take even these duties away and return them to the other four departments. Marschall claimed near the end of his career that he still held authority over *Generalia* in *Lagerhaus* matters, but this statement was nothing more than sound and fury. Always aware that he was a parvenu, ennobled by Frederick William I, and with a marriageable daughter for whom he wished to find a secure position in the highest social stratum, Marschall had never been able to make his department important, nor his career outstanding.[37]

For a short period Frederick undertook direct supervision of the fifth department, but he then appointed the former Prussian com-

37. *AB*, 8: 433–37, 605–7, 621–33. Hintze, *AB*, 6: 1. 169–72.

mercial agent in Amsterdam, Johann Fäsch, to replace Marschall. The preliminary negotiations between Fäsch and the king began a month before the ailing Marschall died and resulted in the appointment of this knowledgeable friend of Amsterdam businessmen to the subministerial rank of privy finance councillor, but with a ministerial salary. Beginning his career under ambiguous circumstances because he had not served in the core bureaucracy in subordinate positions, Fäsch nevertheless possessed excellent qualifications and experience. Most valuable were his personal contacts in the chief money market of Europe, Amsterdam, which he continued to maintain through his brother, a merchant in that city. To the directing ministers he was a "new man" and therefore a puzzle. They did not know whether he would find a place for himself in the complex and interlocking bureaucratic power structure.[38]

Frederick, on his part, began to see that the fifth department could do its job more effectively if he sponsored its efforts. He supported Fäsch against the Electoral Mark board in a matter concerning the Leipzig fair of 1750, stating that no action affecting manufacturing could be instituted without prior consultation with the fifth department.[39] Fäsch also found his position strengthened when the king warned the rest of the core bureaucracy that "not even the most minor commercial and manufacturing matters"[40] could be decided without the approval of the chief of the fifth department. The ministers hastened to assure Frederick that they had no such intention. When Fäsch left Berlin on an inspection trip the ministers were similarly warned not to interfere in the work of the fifth department in his absence. Culminating this story of the gradual increase in the powers of the fifth department was a jurisdictional agreement concluded in January, 1752. Fäsch outlined his concept of the duties of his department and the ministers agreed completely.[41] Frederick had apparently backed him strongly at every point and the ministers had no choice but to acknowledge the changed situation.

38. *AB*, 8: 637, 672–73, 790–91.
39. *AB Seidenindustrie*, 1: 207–8.
40. *AB*, 9: 84, 218, 267–71.
41. Ibid., pp. 289–92.

Wars are seldom won by paper agreements between protagonists, however, and the bitter, if bloodless, feud between the fifth department and the old-line core bureaucracy continued to be fought sub rosa. At least Frederick had decided to cooperate with his own ministers instead of remaining a disgusted spectator at the bureaucratic circus. But the king still hesitated to interfere in a way which would insure that neither the General Directory nor the fifth department would predominate in economic matters. Undoubtedly he saw by 1752 that if he made the General Directory wholly responsible for such matters the fifth department would become superfluous. But he could not make the new department supreme over all the facets of commercial, industrial, and financial policy because such responsibilities were deeply involved in the total workload of the core bureaucracy.

Facing this difficulty well, if not squarely, Frederick decided to change the whole nature of the fifth department from a policy- and decision-making organ into a statistical and technical information center. When two officials were retired in 1751, the king replaced them with one; Privy Finance Councillor Ursinus. This left the fifth department the most understaffed of all departments in terms of executive personnel.[42] Fäsch committed an error when he recommended that no further state funds be expended on new manufacturing projects. The king denounced this conclusion as "superficial" and ordered the department to undertake a complete survey of each province to see what new projects could be launched in order to reverse the unfavorable balance of trade. From this time on Frederick became more and more concerned with study of trade statistics and began to make Fäsch and Ursinus develop more informative reports as a consequence. The final transition in his thinking occurred in June, 1753 when he ordered Fäsch to send all trade reports from the provinces of East Prussia and Magdeburg to Ursinus, who would draw up import and export statistics or "balances" for all the provinces for Frederick's perusal.[43] At the point where Fäsch seemed to

42. Ibid., pp. 278–80.
43. *PKPA* 11: 306. *AR*, 10: 41, 305.

be ready to make his department a directorate of economic development, the king refused to cooperate and changed the entire nature of that department.

The truth of the matter was that Fäsch was never really in a position to make his grandiose dream come true. He never had the complete support of the king, he was never able to bypass the General Directory, and the boards steadfastly refused to cooperate with him. But his most important failure was none of these; it was that he could not harness the business community of the realm. In common with Marschall, Fäsch experienced great frustration and ultimate defeat in any attempt to force the bankers and merchants to take orders from his office. The coterie headed by Splitgerber and Gotzkowsky was much stronger than it had been in 1740. The story is complex, but must be narrated in order to show that despite the efforts of Fäsch and others, the businessmen of Berlin succeeded in evading administrative controls and became a powerful, wealthy, and influential entrepreneurial elite.

Fäsch Attempts to Harness the Entrepreneurial Bureaucracy

Curiously enough, Fäsch actually encouraged the profit-seeking entrepreneurs of Berlin to work together and to consolidate themselves into an elite that seemed to be virtually independent of the government. When he assumed office in 1749 he discovered that the business community had prospered through liberal subsidies and privileges dispensed by the various commissions and by the fifth department. By 1756 some 687 entrepreneurs had established firms in the Electoral Mark.[44] These smaller firms were humble dependents of the entrepreneurial elite and shared crumbs from the royal table. Splitgerber, Gotzkowsky, and a handful of others had succeeded in

44. Lenz und Unholz, *Schickler*, pp. 5–87. Krüger, *Manufakturen*, pp. 153–54. W. Hassenstein, "Zur Geschichte der Könige Gewehrfabrik in Spandau," *Technik Geschichte* 4 (1912): 27–40. Rachel and Wallich, *Grosskaufleute*, 2: 258–59. E. Winter, "Die Wegelysche Porzellanfabrik in Berlin," *Schriften des Vereins für Geschichte Stadt Berlin* 35 (1898): 14–15. Hintze, *Gotskowsky*, pp. 111–120. *AB Akzise und Handelspolitik*, 3: 2. 576–78.

dominating the business community and could not be dislodged by anyone apparently.

The partnership of Splitgerber and Gotzkowsky managed to keep the support of the king. In truth, both men were more than leaders of the business community; they were also chief officials of what one can call an entrepreneurial bureaucracy. An "elite" becomes a "bureaucracy" when that elite is incorporated into the administrative system of the realm as a semiautonomous organization. At first, between 1740 and 1749, the energies of the Berlin entrepreneurs were occupied with the tasks of carving out places for themselves in the economy of the realm, but later they succeeded also in tying themselves to the state so that most of their activities, besides being profit making in nature, were quasi-official. No firm line separated governments from business communities in this mercantilistic century, as Adam Smith recognized and criticized. Splitgerber, for example, began his relationship with Frederick in the role of private banker and after 1740 simply cultivated the king in order to become an important financial advisor and, ultimately, the leader of a vast number of commercial, mining, and industrial firms. By 1750 this entrepreneur made considerable money through involvement in state subsidized shipping firms, sugar refining, and syrup production. Frederick amiably altered the tariff schedules to protect Splitgerber's interest. But banking and currency exchange speculation became the cornerstone of the business of this astute investor. Frederick really considered Splitgerber to be a kind of state minister; he issued orders to him in the same fashion he employed with board presidents and allowed him to sit on the boards of directors of the Bengal shipping monopoly and other state supported organizations. Thus, the entire banking community of Berlin and much of the lucrative import–export business were really under the supervision of Splitgerber. Gotzkowsky dominated the silk industry, the favorite industrial project of Frederick, by 1750, and became a kind of official in charge of an activity that was almost totally supported by state funds.[45] Other businessmen such as the Jewish bankers and mint purveyors

45. Merseburg. Rep. 96. 421 B, 17, 23.

had to cultivate one or the other of these leading businessmen–officials.

But the Berlin business community was in the process of reorganization between 1750 and 1756; small entrepreneurs such as the procelain maker Wegely were falling under the control of the great business leaders. In 1752, for example, Splitgerber and Gotzkowsky led the entrepreneurial elite which persuaded the king to keep new entrepreneurs out of their sphere and to prohibit Jews from engaging in silk making. Step by step this elite developed into a bureaucratic organization. First, all members of the business community were extremely dependent upon the king for monetary support and for help in importing and exporting. Secondly, within the business community the less wealthy and influential entrepreneurs became the clients of the great such as Splitgerber. Third, Frederick dealt directly with the leaders in many industrial and commercial projects in a way that suggests that he believed that they were informal hirelings of the State. In short, the entrepreneurs were organized hierarchically and collegially, their organization was primarily dependent upon financial support from the State, and it was given administrative direction by the king himself. The element of business competition was notably absent since the leaders had succeeded in allocating markets and productive specialties among themselves and their clients and had effectively eliminated outsiders. Of course, a formal organization in the bureaucratic sense did not exist, but its absence was unimportant since in all other ways these entrepreneurs were so tied to the king that they became informal members of a bureaucratic organization.

Fäsch discovered that he could do little to control these informal wielders of influence and power. In fact, he had to cooperate with the entrepreneurial elite in order to foster his desired economic reforms. Concerning himself first with the international trade position of Prussia, Fäsch hoped to use Splitgerber's services to advantage. Hamburg had previously supplied the Prussian realm with sugar; Fäsch talked to the chief Berlin banker and succeeded in interesting him in sugar production within the realm. This conversation of January 16, 1751[46]

46. Merseburg. Rep. 96, 421 B, 17, 23. This firm hoped to obtain a sugar sale

was followed by the collaboration of Splitgerber and the head of the Fifth Department in other spheres as well. Specifically, the two wished to make Emden in East Frisia a world shipping center. But such grandiose plans failed to be executed because the various trading schemes that Fäsch contemplated, and the king approved, always seemed to lack capital. Fäsch also collaborated with Splitgerber in the establishment of mines and smelters in Neustadt-Eberswalde during the ensuing decade. He endeavored to recruit about 300 miners and metal workers from the Ruhr to aid the new scheme in 1751.[47]

Splitgerber and his colleagues continued to work behind the scenes with Frederick, various ministers of the General Directory, and the Silesian minister. In addition they possessed influence with the directors of the Berlin police, the Potsdam orphanage, and the managers of the *Lagerhaus*. The entrepreneurial bureaucracy managed to prosper under the pluralistic management system established by Frederick because it could establish its autonomy in the face of a disorganized and weak opposition. Since it had, in fact, obtained organizational integrity, it resorted to various devices to limit recruitment into its own ranks, for example. So many officials and businessmen had their hands in business regulation that it was difficult to discern which of them was the most influential and should be courted by the merchant–novice who hoped to enter the charmed circle of Berlin business. The subordinates of the fifth department tried to assert their authority by devising rules and procedures which the neophyte merchant or manufacturer had to meet. These rules proliferated to such an extent that the newcomer would often despair of obtaining any satisfactory

---

monopoly in Cleves and East Frisia for twenty years, exemption from taxes, military service, and also hoped for stiff tariffs to keep out other sugar importers. In addition it wished exemption from "all bourgeois burdens" or, more clearly, exemption from municipal employment, marketing, and excise taxes and, perhaps, exemption from the rule that householders in cities would quarter soldiers. Such privileged status was often granted to officials, clergy, lawyers and members of other more prestigious professions, and to important merchants (the relief from "Bourgeois burdens"). This concession, typical of many Old Regime proposals, would have tied up the sugar business for twenty years. Splitgerber succeeded in convincing his new friend, Fäsch, that he, and not Albrecht, should handle the sugar business.

47. On the collaboration of Fäsch with Splitgerber in the Neustadt-Eberswalde project see Merseburg. Rep. 96. 421 B, 9.

action because of delay, red tape, and bureaucratic squabbles. One merchant complained, "anyone who desires to establish a manufactory must have a strong constitution, English patience, and much money to lose, or the work can not be undertaken."[48] Thus, by 1756 the most important elements of the Berlin business world had consolidated themselves into, first, an elite, and secondly, a bureaucracy; business associated itself with the State.

Graumann, Fäsch, and the Central Bank Schemes

If the entrepreneurial bureaucracy had been able to achieve remarkable results in profit making as well as in the state service, this success had not occurred without opposition. Curiously enough the opposition to Splitgerber, Gotzkowsky, *et al* did not come from the core bureaucracy; no official in the four main departments of the General Directory or in the Electoral Mark board seemed to be upset. Only two men became aware of growing business power: Fäsch and Johann Graumann, after 1749 the director of the royal mints. Both were well experienced in public and business finance and both had previously worked in more complex economic spheres in western Europe. From 1749 on each tried to develop administrative controls that would force the semiautonomous entrepreneurial bureaucracy to become subordinate to either the fifth department (Fäsch), or to the mint directory (Graumann). Although Fäsch and Graumann each had certain self-seeking goals in mind and could not cooperate very effectively with each other, both agreed that the key to control of the business bureaucracy lay in the acquisition of currency control. The role of Frederick in the controversy was one of disinterest, at least until the business panic of 1763. He supervised the entrepreneurs himself and saw no real need for the recommendations of Fäsch and Graumann.

Before 1750 the royal mints were small-scale establishments that never provided enough coinage to serve the needs of trade within the realm. Not a little of the prosperity of such private bankers as Split-

48. Krüger, *Manufakturen*, pp. 128.

gerber and Schütze was due to their monopoly of the exchange of currency. These shrewd financiers obtained a virtual monopoly of the exchange of the favored Dutch coinage and bills of exchange with the frequently debased and distrusted coinage of central and eastern Europe. Fäsch drew up a plan in 1751 which he claimed would put an end to this domination over monetary exchange. In effect, he proposed the establishment of a state owned and operated bank. Frederick, however, did not intend to damage his friend Splitgerber in any way and refused the suggestion with the excuse that the time was not yet ripe for it and it was too "vague."[49]

Nevertheless the king believed that the State could regulate commercial and financial activities through manipulation of specie issue. Prussian coinage, he hoped, would replace that of Amsterdam, Hamburg, and Leipzig in the market place. The private money changers such as Splitgerber would lose a source of profit and power, but Frederick apparently did not immediately discern this truth. In common with most of his contemporaries he believed that money was a commodity rather than merely a medium of exchange. The minting of coinage thus possessed an inflated importance to him since he believed that the objective of trade was to secure for the realm as much specie as possible and to export as little as possible. At first Frederick hoped to limit the export of specie by means of prohibitory edicts such as the one issued in 1747, which prohibited shipment of specie of value of over 300 talers by any individual. After the General Directory recommended a decrease in mint production in order to improve control over counterfeiting, Frederick began to view the problem in a different light. He decided to remove the entire mint system from the hands of the directing ministers and to administer it himself.[50] In late 1749 he hired the mint director of Brunswick, Johann Graumann, as Mint director with the title of privy finance councillor.

Graumann was given "Seat and voice" in the General Directory and complete responsibility for the mints. He was placed directly

---

49. *AB Akzise Handelspolitik*, 3: 1. 396.
50. Heinrich Schnee, *Die Hoffinanz und der moderne Staat* (Berlin, 1953), 1: 13–14, 117.

under the king rather than under the ministers. This change, which may appear minor, actually caused great consternation among the directing ministers, who could see no reason for what they considered an act of royal displeasure. Several times Minister von Viereck of the fourth department sent obsequious letters to Frederick in which he protested his innocence of wrongdoing, and each time Frederick denied any such intention to punish. Graumann was made absolute administrator of the new mint system. Frederick had hired a foreign expert to head his expanded mint system instead of promoting a junior from the General Directory.[51]

At first the entrepreneurial bureaucracy must have been elated; the new mint director did not immediately try to assume control over the currency exchange business but concentrated on the purchase of specie. His reorganization of the mints posed no apparent threat to Splitgerber and his colleagues since the latter hoped to be recipients of lucrative specie contracts. Although they stood to lose part of their customary business, they still hoped to continue as the faithful bankers of the king. The resultant contracts with Splitgerber, Moses Isaak, Ephraim and Sons, and others provided for the delivery of specie worth millions of talers, as for example in 1752. These entrepreneurs had to deposit bonds amounting to hundreds of thousands of talers. Such business transactions dwarfed ordinary commercial dealings.[52]

Graumann, however, was no mere master minting craftsman, he was also a cameralist of considerable acumen. He had studied the western European banking and credit system in some depth, and in 1762 he published a treatise in which he summarized his ideas concerning the importance of the mints in the total economy of the State. Briefly he maintained that the State could effectively prevent inflation and deflation through increase or decrease in the amount minted at appropriate times. Unlike Frederick, who thought the Prussian economy was in good condition if "more gold comes in" than goes out, Graumann had shed many of the naive assumptions of the lesser

51. *AB*, 8: 645–47, 658–59, 665–67.
52. Ibid., p. 602. *AB Münzwesen*, 2: 352–55, 329–30, 319–20. Schnee, *Hoffinanz*, 1: 122–23.

cameralists. Grauman stated: "The value of our coinage rises and falls in relation to other coinage, primarily if our land sends out more or less products and receives payment for them."[53] The mints of a State, he suggested, should coin a large issue to be put into circulation promptly if a great quantity of specie is received through trade and little is exported. If a country exports a great deal more specie than it receives, little new coinage should be placed in circulation by the mints. Graumann thus considered the mints as an essential part of the economy. The question of how the mints should be managed assumed major proportions to him. The mints would, he implied, assume a commanding role in economic planning by the State. The mint director would have to have access to official trade statistics, intimate contact with the important entrepreneurs, and absolute authority to regulate issue as he deemed necessary. Although he did not outline in detail the nature of his centrally directed economic system, he nevertheless suggested that the State would have to assume absolute control over banking and finance. No longer could the State allow powerful private bankers to control the dispersement of official funds or to regulate the exchange of money.[54]

Even though these ideas appeared in print during the Seven Years War it is obvious that Graumann had already developed them as early as 1753. On January 31 of that year he sent a memorandum to the king in which he advocated the establishment of a State owned and operated *Giro-Leih und Zettel Bank*. Its purpose would be to exchange foreign money for Prussian *Friedrichs d'or* in order to keep the exchange ratio in Berlin on a par with that of the Hamburg banks. Immediately Splitgerber, the mint contractors, the Berlin and Breslau merchants, and others involved in financial transactions, rose up in anger to fight this proposal. In a petition to Frederick the following March they stated:

The basis of the project for the projected bank remains inap-

53. Johann Graumann, *Gesammelte Briefe von dem Gelde, von dem Wechsel und dessen Curs, von der Proportion zwischen Gold und Silber* . . . (Berlin, 1762), pp. 170–73.
54. Ibid.

plicable to our country, and we must protest humbly that the establishment of such a bank will not incease the commerce but will hinder intercourse until the present minted pieces are made equal in value. Otherwise, it will be of no use to Your Majesty himself, nor to your loyal subjects who await such a secure basis in the future.[55]

In fact, the protests of the merchants took another form: they decided to propose a central banking scheme of their own.

In the same year, 1753, an important consortium of these disgruntled businessmen submitted a detailed proposal under the signature of one Thresler. Some seven or eight bankers operated in Berlin, and the resources of all of the private banks amounted to no more than 20,000 talers. This small number of bankers could not by themselves regulate the mercantile economy of the realm. Agreeing with Graumann and other officials, the consortium recommended the establishment of a central bank, a bank to be administered, however, under the auspices of a board of directors composed of Splitgerber, other bankers, and selected manufacturers such as Wegely. If the king were prepared to agree, each of the directors would contribute 100,000 talers a year to the central bank of issue, and it alone would exchange foreign money. In fact, the bankers promised to accomplish the same objectives as stated by Graumann and Fäsch; they simply wanted to control the new bank themselves without any interference from government officials. If the Thresler bank project had been approved by Frederick, the entrepreneurial bureaucracy would have consolidated itself as an organization responsible to the king alone, and the core bureaucracy would have lost very substantial authority over the economy. Ultimately, perhaps, the highly important public responsibility of a central bank of issue would be undertaken by entrepreneurs for profit. Frederick may not have understood all of the ramifications of the currency question but he was not naive. The project was vetoed.[56]

55. Lenz and Unholz, *Schickler,* pp. 62–63.
56. Merseburg. Rep. 96, 410g, 1–33 includes material on the Thresler Bank Project.

Since 1751 Graumann and Fäsch had worked with the chancellor of justice, Cocceji, on the establishment of the central bank. They and Privy Finance Councillor Magusch were concerned over the long-run effect of the haphazard subsidization of Splitgerber and other entrepreneurs by the State. In fact, in February, 1753 Magusch warned that these businessmen were becoming dangerous because they controlled a very large share of credit and financial power in the realm at large, tending to equate the public welfare with their own private profit seeking.[57]

Frederick expressed interest in Graumann's scheme, despite the possibility that it might damage his old provisioner Splitgerber. In January he had forced the merchants to consult with Graumann in an effort to work out a satisfactory compromise. At that time they had already declared the plan "unacceptable."[58] Frederick nevertheless established the bank the following October and gave it authority to exchange money in such a way that it mirrored the current exchange in Hamburg. In November he again ordered the merchants to confer with Graumann, but again they refused to cooperate. Finally he ordered Councillor Kircheisen to start the bank without further consultation with the entrepreneurs. He soothed the latter with assurances that their property would be safeguarded and that Graumann would have no voice in the management of the bank.[59] Frederick had once again decided to establish a new agency.

The ministers of the General Directory had not played major roles in this drama; in fact they might have supported Graumann and Fäsch and given counsel to the king. But they were silent, perhaps because they either did not understand the problems involved or because they were simply not interested in supporting their own fiscal experts, Graumann and Fäsch. Of course, some might have had elephantine memories. The two officials were both outsiders with no contacts in the civil service and had been appointed by the king without consultation with the General Directory. Frederick probably knew the state

57. Merseburg. Rep. 96, 410e, includes the proposal of Magusch.
58. Lenz and Unholz, *Schickler*, pp. 62–63.
59. *AB Akzise und Handelspolitik* 3: 1. 396–98.

of their collective mind and did not try to secure their cooperation. He thus hoped that the new bank, under the joint aegis of the head of the fifth department and of the mint director, would obtain necessary authority to control the Berlin business elite, but he made a miscalculation. The bank soon ceased to exercise much authority over the entrepreneurs. Splitgerber and other private bankers continued their financial operations with little difficulty. As a result they were in an advantageous position by the time of the Seven Years' War. Frederick was forced to lean upon them for support in the darkest days of that conflict, when the combined weight of his adversaries threatened to overcome him. In 1763, as a consequence, the private bankers had once again recovered all their old influence. Later in that decade, after a severe financial crisis had brought Frederick's attention to them once more, two other officials reestablished the State Bank.[60]

Frederick's Intentions: Centralized Economy and Diversified Control

It would be a mistake to assume that the failure of the fifth department to assert itself, the indifference of the General Directory, and the perplexing policies of Frederick combined to insure that no effective developmental programs were instituted in the Prussian realm between 1740 and 1756. Curiously, great progress was manifested in the commercial arena; the entrepreneurial bureaucracy could never have prospered unless concomitant development in trade occurred throughout the realm. Frederick also presided over the birth of Berlin as a great commercial and industrial center of central Europe.

Integration of Berlin within a cohesive commercial system directed by the State became a policy of Frederick by 1752, but the idea had been considered by Frederick William I and Councillor Hille long before. If Berlin were to become a commercial center, it had to obtain good transportation connections with the old and important traffic lanes of the Oder and Elbe rivers. Prussia had always been at a disadvantage in international trade because the Elbe commercial traffic was dominated by Hamburg and the Oder traffic by Breslau in Silesia

60. Ibid.

and by Electoral Saxony. Frederick had concentrated since 1743 on the construction of a network of canals designated to shift the courses of these old commercial routes. The Plaue Canal in 1745 joined the Havel to the Elbe; the Finow Canal later joined the Spree to the Oder. Both of these canals resulted from the suggestions given by Minister von Görne. Frederick entrusted the construction to Görne at first, but was disgusted with the delays and official procrastination which he thought characterized both projects. The third canal scheme, and the most important, called for the changing of the course of the Oder River to provide a better shipping channel and to provide some 44,200 acres of reclaimed bottom land for future colonization and cultivation. Despite preliminary planning initiated under Frederick William I, nothing concrete had been accomplished by 1745.[61] Frederick was faced with two main problems in the middle of this decade: the completion of three important transportation connections to the main streams of international trade, and, secondly, the selection of appropriate agencies to supervise the massive construction program. Only when this program was completed would Berlin, Breslau, and Stettin be integrated economically.

Characteristically, Frederick was loath simply to confer appropriate authority over this gigantic task to a single agency, especially to the General Directory. In 1746, for example, Marschall was told to supervise the surveying and general planning of the Oder Canal and drainage project after Frederick became dissatisfied with the record of the Electoral Mark board and of the General Directory in the first phase of construction of the other two canal projects. Frederick, however, was dissatisfied with the progress of work in late 1749 when Marschall died; he ordered the General Directory to refrain from "obstruction" and "chicanery" and to allow the fifth department to complete the work quickly. Even after Councillor Haarlem of the Electoral Mark board, a man of engineering skill, had taken over the direction, the Oder Canal project was still slow in completion and beset by technical difficulties as well as squabbling between various bureaucratic agencies. In the final stages of work Frederick appointed

61. Detto, *FBPG*, 16: 165–85.

a committee of investigation, which revealed a complex substratum of paper warfare between the General Directory, the Electoral Mark board and the fifth department. Nevertheless this important program was finally completed[62] and must be recognized to be a massive feat of civil engineering and a tangible sign of what determined governmental action could accomplish. The lesson of the canal construction programs was simply this: all had been finished because enough funds had been made available, expert engineers had been hired, and the king, acting as "straw boss" had devoted attention to encouraging and browbeating the various administrative agents into working diligently. Nothing had resulted from the work of one office because no one office had in itself the requisite technical expertise, financial resources, or planning staff. Unfortunately, Frederick then tended to downgrade the importance of both the General Directory and the fifth department: Fäsch never achieved any true authority over commercial regulation or the new Oder–Elbe waterways system.

The ministers of the General Directory might have rejoiced over this disgrace of the fifth department, but that would have been foolish. They too were bypassed to a considerable extent by Frederick, who preferred to establish several independent commissions to regulate trade on the Oder and Elbe rivers. These commissions were ultimately dominated by two able men: the Silesian minister, von Münchow, and the Pomeranian board director, von Schlabrendorff. From their two headquarters, Breslau and Stettin, these collaborators really formed the new Oder trade system by abolishing internal tariffs and tolls, by forcing merchants in both cities to act in concert, and by

62. Ibid., pp. 165–86; *AB*, 9: 346–47. *AB Akzise und Zollpolitik*, 3: 1. 409, 410. *PKPA*, 11: 265–66, 283. *AB*, 8: 638. In 1746 the preliminary work on the Plaue Canal came to a halt when a serious disagreement between Councillor von Haarlem, and the contracting engineer, a certain Mahistre, arose. Mahistre contended that the proposed route was wrong, insufficient attention had been paid to the problems of dike construction and to clearance for vessels. This dispute eventually reached the king. Unfortunately, no official seemed to have the engineering competence to determine the justice of the matter. This example of *Vielschreiberei* is included in Merseburg. Gen. Dir. Magdeburg, Tit. CLVII, I, Vol. II, pp. 6–65. The canal projects outlined the need for engineering expertise in the civil service: a need that was not met until after the Seven Years' War. See chapter 9 below.

trying to establish joint trading regulations. Frederick encouraged these initiatives because he now wished to make Silesia an economic as well as a political part of the realm. Throughout, all of these plans were instituted by the king in conjunction with the Silesian minister, certain board presidents, the General Directory, and the fifth department. The important task of reorientation of trade on the waterways had to be solved the same way that the initial construction of the means of trade, the canals, had been solved.[63]

The entrepreneurial bureaucracy was a real beneficiary of these programs. Splitgerber secured a seat on one of the commissions entrusted with the regulation of the Oder trade. He also consummated an alliance with the Silesian minister and became one of the most important businessmen in that province. The prominent Breslau firm of Eichborn and Company, which occupied a leading position in Silesian trade and finance, worked with Splitgerber in devising mutually agreeable commercial arrangements.[64] Where business was concerned, the leading entrepreneurs of Berlin, Stettin, and Breslau could work together. As a consequence of a number of factors such as the improvement of river routes, the abolition of some tolls and restrictive trading privileges, the pluralistic managerial system, and more promising business opportunities, these merchants consolidated themselves into a new power elite within the realm. Because they worked in harness with the king and with official agencies of one kind or another, they now constituted an interprovincial entrepreneurial bureaucracy.

Frederick had obtained excellent results by utilizing ad hoc expedients of administration. Unfortunately, he now believed that all innovations could be introduced without any cohesive central direction, or, at least, without the central direction provided by the General Directory. His officials had sometimes warned him that the businessmen of Berlin had almost obtained dominance of the economy of the

63. *AB Akzise und Zollpolitik*, 3: 2. 80–130. *AB*, 8: 169–171, 54, 638; 9: 346–52, 676–77, 681–82; 10: 140–47. Krüger, *Manufakturen*, pp. 56–57. H. Freymark, *Zur preussischen Handels- und Zollpolitik von 1648–1848* (Halle, 1897), p. 13.

64. Lenz and Unholz, *Schickler*, pp. 73–87. K. F. von Eichborn, *Das Soll und Haben von Eichborn und Co.* (Munich, 1928), pp. 14–15.

realm. They were poorly regulated and controlled by the government.

What a difference existed between the recommendations of the cameralists and the reality of governmental action in the economic sphere! To contemporary "experts" such as Justi, the supervision of commercial, industrial, and agricultural sectors of the economy posed difficult problems. First, one established a unified bureaucratic organization staffed with persons who possessed high qualifications as administrators, as well as agronomists, fiscal experts, and engineers. Secondly, this organization would automatically prepare comprehensive and long-range developmental plans and should have the capital available to carry them out. Finally, those who actually farmed or traded or manufactured commodities would do what they were told by the government.[65] No government could staff an organization solely with disinterested persons who possessed both administrative skill and expertise because such persons were, and still are, remarkably few in number. Lacking capital and cognizant of the need to maintain many programs, such as the army, with funds which could not be diverted, Frederick could not indulge in massive long-range planning which might not reveal tangible results in a lifetime. The subjects of the king of Prussia had their own selfish interests and did not sacrifice them to the demands of officials. Economic development may well have resulted from lax direction by a multitude of offices, commissions, and ambitious individuals who could only act if they worked in harness with businessmen who had additional capital and expertise. Who could wonder that these businessmen tried to make the government their servant by trying to subordinate the entire economy to their control?

Frederick doubtless realized by 1749, when Marschall died, that few if any of his officials possessed adequate knowledge about the international trade sphere or about the details of industrial work. In order to promote his objective, which was to make it possible for Prussia to obtain a permanently favorable balance of trade, he used the technical services of Graumann and Fäsch, he "westernized" his economic policy. But the multitudinous programs which the king

65. Johnson, "Concept of Bureaucracy," pp. 379 ff.

sponsored with the help of these officials had to be launched with the aid of the Berlin entrepreneurs because they possessed capital and because Frederick had no intention of establishing "state capitalism" or socialistic enterprises. Important leadership for great industrial and waterways schemes thus came from without the core bureaucracy since the old-line officials were unable to work with such problems. The creation of the entrepreneurial elite, which became, in fact, a new bureaucratic organization, was a by-product of the economic programs of the period 1740 to 1756. This new organization was led by a consortium of the most influential bankers and merchants and tried to become completely autonomous, as the Thresler project implied. By 1756 both Graumann and Fäsch were anxious to subordinate the entrepreneurs to their own direction; the Frankenstein's monster was proving itself to be powerful and, perhaps, unmanageable.

IV

RISE OF THE

JUDICIAL BUREAUCRACY

Frederick William I had created the war and domains boards within the provinces and had effectively subordinated local associations, in the forms of the estates and the municipal corporations, to the will of those directorates. During the course of this centralization of authority within the provinces the aristocratically controlled court system was also reduced to near impotence. These courts (*Regierungen*) served as the judicial and administrative arm of the old feudal state and were thus considered by Frederick William I to be both unnecessary and dangerous. His successor was not happy, however, with the boards and would have liked to make them more efficient. He did not, however, find administrators of sufficient ability to accomplish this task before 1763. Fortunately for the judiciary, Frederick II recognized early the need for wholesale reconstruction of the courts and listened to the advice of the few jurists who seemed to be working for a better and more just legal structure. He supported Cocceji and saw the courts remolded and strengthened to the point where they could serve as organizational examples to the boards and could rival them in influence in the realm at large. The judicial reforms resulted in the creation of a new public bureaucracy within the provinces which was to serve as an effective rival to that of the boards and of the core bureaucracy.

The reconstituted courts were the work of an exceptionally astute jurist, Samuel von Cocceji, and of his protégés.[1] Cocceji's reforms

1. Standard accounts of Cocceji and of his reforms can be found in: Adolf Stolzel, *Brandenburg-Preussens Rechtsverwaltung und Rechtsverfassung* (Berlin,

were possible only after he had secured the support of the king, large numbers of the jurists, and, finally, of the estates. Judicial reformation did not come simply because Frederick II approved certain edicts prepared by Cocceji. The creation of an effective public bureaucracy necessitated securing the acquiescence, if not the support, of those to be subjected to the authority of the new agency. Most of Cocceji's really important accomplishments occurred after he had negotiated with the jurists in the various provincial courts as well as with the representatives of the estates. Needless to say, he depended ultimately upon the approval of Frederick. The king placed the cloak of legitimacy over his actions. The study of the judicial reforms initiated by Cocceji found the courts mere auxiliaries of the landed nobility and left them powerful challengers of the power of the core bureaucracy.

Frederick II became convinced, perhaps because of the persuasive arguments of Cocceji, that the entire judicial structure would have to be overhauled and gave his chancellor of justice considerable authority between 1746 and 1755 to undertake this enormous labor. Cocceji believed that the existing courts were vestigial remnants of an age when the elector had been comparatively weak and the aristocrats strong; they had served as helpmates of the *Ständestaat* and had cooperated with the provincial estates and with the municipal oligarchies. His main ambition was to construct a judiciary which would be independent of the aristocrats and of the town councils even at the lowest levels and would acknowledge no master except the king. In a sense, then, he hoped to reform the judiciary along the lines of the administrative reforms of the Great Elector and of King Frederick William I. Instead of competitive courts there would be one Superior Court in each province which would handle appeals from the local rural and municipal courts. The Department of Justice in Berlin

1888), 2: 141–235; Conrad Bornhak, *Geschichte des Preussischen Verwaltungsrechts*, 3 vols. (Berlin, 1884–86), 2: 199–221; Otto Hintze, "Einleitende Darstellung der Behördenorganisation und allgemeinen Verwaltung in Preussen beim Regierungsantritt Friedrichs II," *AB*, 6:1. 111–14, passim. Friedrich Holtze, *Geschichte des Kammergerichts in Brandenburg-Preussen* (Berlin, 1890–1904), 3:186–94, passim. An adequate summary of the foregoing is Herman Weill, *Frederick the Great and Samuel von Cocceji*, (Madison, 1961).

would then serve as a kind of equivalent of the General Directory except that the chancellor of justice would be the director of everything and the focus of final appeals within the whole system. Cocceji as chancellor of justice would then report directly to the king with thorny cases which neither he nor his subordinates could decide. Such an integrated judiciary would need, he thought, a common code of laws, a professional system of recruitment and promotion of jurists, and, finally, it would draw its financial support directly from the treasuries of the State and would no longer have to depend on court fees. Cocceji also wished to establish a lasting basis for the authority of the courts within Prussian society by claiming as their responsibilities all problems involving the ownership of property and the determination of the social status of individuals.

Since many of the reforms of Cocceji have been adequately described it will not be necessary to give another exposition of them. Instead, since Cocceji was the founder of a new bureaucratic organization as well as a codifier of laws and a legal theorist, the discussion will concentrate on his political and administrative accomplishments. He had to struggle with many enemies within and without the courts and was not uniformly successful in putting his ambitious program into practice. This struggle was concentrated in several key stages in his career as chancellor of justice. Briefly, these stages included crises arising in his relationships with Frederick II, with opponents in the courts, with the landed nobility, and with the core bureaucracy. Cocceji was able to institute his judicial reforms only after he had successfully emerged from these power struggles. In fact, the limits of the authority of the new court system were to be determined by the partial nature of his victories.[2]

Reform of the Judicial Organization

Cocceji began his extraordinary career in the early years of the reign of Frederick William I. He earned the confidence of this ruler by suc-

2. The following discussion will consider the problems associated with the allocations of political power between Cocceji, Frederick, and other individuals, as well as groups. It will not describe the formal history of the judicial reforms, which is well known and explained above.

cessfully reorganizing the courts of East Prussia in 1721. Subsequently he rose to become minister of justice and head of the newly established Department of Justice in 1738. Cocceji owed his rise to power to the relatively liberal social policy of Frederick William, whose distrust of the nobility was so great that he frequently promoted enterprising burghers and newly ennobled officials to high office. Due to his dubious social origins as well as his reforming proclivities, Cocceji came to be regarded by the aristocratic judges of the higher courts as an overly ambitious and ruthless upstart. He had adequate personal reasons for engaging in battle with the conservatives in the court system. Due to a resurgence of the influence of his enemies he found himself temporarily excluded from the exercise of power after 1738. This forced exile extended until 1743.[3]

Frederick II, occupied with his Silesian campaigns during the first years of his reign, did not pay much attention to problems arising out of the administration of justice. Cocceji, intent upon obtaining the patronage of Frederick, which he realized would be essential before he could resume his reforms, composed a pleasing *pièce justificative* which attempted to legitimatize the Prussian seizure of Silesia. But some years were to pass before Cocceji was to secure Frederick's complete support. Between 1743 and 1746 the chancellor was given charge of the Prussian organization of the newly acquired province of East Frisia. Despite this work and the previous recommendation of Frederick William I, the new king did not place complete trust in him until 1746. The judiciary tended to accept the leadership of von Arnim of the *Kammergericht*, a superior court in Berlin, rather than to obey the chancellor. Arnim despised Cocceji and had been chiefly responsible for his eclipse from power. At first, in 1743, Frederick refused to consider a judicial reform plan prepared by Cocceji, but changed his mind three years later; the chancellor then possessed his complete confidence.[4] Cocceji proposed to select one province to serve as the

3. Hintze, *AB*, 6:1. 106–125. Holtze, *Kammergerichts*, 3:187–94.
4. Weill, *Cocceji*, p. 32, states the usual interpretation that Frederick's support of Cocceji was "based upon the conviction that the judicial process must be fast, inexpensive, and impartial if it is to be called just." Cocceji prepared a long "plan" for consideration by Frederick in 1746 in which he did stress the benefits that would accompany the elimination of the old, competetive courts and their

stage for a pilot reform experiment. He suggested, shrewdly enough, that Arnim, his arch-rival and fellow minister, de given a free hand in the renovation of the courts in a different province. Frederick rejected this second proposal despite Cocceji's boasts that Arnim would fail and his own plans would be proven. The king then forwarded to the chancellor an anonymous complaint, evidently from a noble, which accused the Pomeranian courts of inefficiency and corruption. Cocceji selected these courts for his "experiment" and appointed an extra-ordinary commission composed of his lieutenants who were entrusted with the reform project.[5] In a revealing letter to the powerful royal secretary, Eichel, the chancellor stated: "With your Excellency's sentiments conforming to mine, I hope, with your assistance, to show the world and the king that nothing will interfere with the shortening of trials and the elimination of chicanery. My whole work is based upon the desire to aid the fatherland." In a further effort to flatter Eichel, he mentioned that he "will request the help of my esteemed friend, von Jariges,"[6] who was a close friend of the secretary. At the request of Cocceji, the king ordered the Pomeranian estates to pro-vide deputies to aid in the proposed reform work and, at the same time, he admonished the superior courts not to accept new trials un-less absolutely necessary in the interim. Provincial justice in Pomera-nia was studied by Cocceji and his team for several months. Finally, he combined the two superior courts and the provincial ecclesiastical

---

replacement by a new, unified, system. "This Labyrinth" which caused "con-fusion, venality, and jealousy" in previous court systems in European history, had, he felt, resulted in the formulation of the great unified codes in the past: The Roman and canonical codes in particular. But, since the Reformation, German jurisprudence had been divided between Catholic and Reform groups, each tak-ing bits and pieces from the old, foreign codes. The system had to be reworked from the ground up: old and incompetent jurists had to be dismissed, surplus tribunals eliminated, and a new university-trained corps of legal experts had to be employed. All of these measures would accomplish the aims Weill outlines above. Cocceji did not preach along these lines, but he was completely logical and hardheaded. He opposed any tribunal which operated outside his own system and came into conflict with the civil bureaucracy headed by the General Directory as a result. See Merseburg, Rep. 92, Cocceji, No. 8, vol. 3 pp. 1–22 for Cocceji's own formulation of the legal reform problem.

5. Holtze, *Kammergerichts*, 3: 190–94. *AB*, 6: 2. 616–18; 7: 6–10.
6. *AB*, 7: 139.

tribunal into one body. One presiding judge was pensioned and several other jurists were dismissed or transferred. He had established a "Perquisite Treasury" as a repository for all court fees, from which officials were to be paid set amounts as determined by royal edict. The enormous backlog of pending trials was quickly eliminated.[7] In short, the Pomeranian judicial reforms completely disrupted the existing procedures and bureaucratic lines of authority within the court system of that province. Due to the support of Frederick and the *eminence grise* Eichel, Cocceji had achieved outstanding success in one province.

A shudder of alarm passed throughout the judiciary in the wake of such a revolutionary accomplishment. As soon as the commission's work began in Pomerania, Cocceji had sent copies of his proposed reform plan to all of the provincial superior courts. Their replies were masterpieces of evasion marked by thinly veiled hostility. Some courts, for example, protested that their trial backlogs were not too large and that they needed no assistance from an extraordinary commission in catching up in their work. The entrenched aristocrats in the unreformed courts also began to attack Cocceji through a series of complaints and petitions addressed to the king. The *Kammergericht*, for example, expressed puzzlement over the inclusion of so many "unknown" officials in Cocceji's entourage. Fortunately for Cocceji he stood in such high esteem in the eyes of Frederick II at the conclusion of the Pomeranian reforms that he could challenge his enemies within the judiciary at all levels with some hope of success. He chose to carry the battle to the *Kammergericht*, which was controlled by, and served as the focal point of, his rival, Arnim's, opposition.[8] He realized that systematic reconstruction of the rest of the court system could only come about when such major opposition was crushed. The dispatch of the Pomeranian reform plan to all other superior courts constituted a challenge to Arnim and the other distributors of patronage.

7. Ibid., pp. 153–55, 335–37. Local municipal and rural courts were not yet reformed.
8. Ibid., pp. 220–27, 433–34.

As soon as Arnim and his supporters saw that Frederick was determined to back Cocceji in the reconstruction of the judiciary, they attempted to find means to preserve their own power while seeking to cooperate in the reforms. President von Görne of the *Kammergericht*, one of the central appellate courts, prepared two plans for the "reform" of his court. The first was approved by his fellow jurists. Under this plan, two judges, whose conduct had made them vulnerable to charges of corruption, would be allowed to resign quietly. Cocceji rejected this scheme with the significant remark that Görne must take his deserved "odium." No change in the *Kammergericht*, he stated, would be allowed until the completion of the Pomeranian reforms. The imperious chancellor remarked that he intended to deal with the *Kammergericht* himself in order to make sure that "venality" ceased and to insure that the king would have no cause to complain. Cocceji also claimed to have evidence of corruption which he had uncovered in a trial handled by the *Kammergericht*. Some months later Arnim was told that a commission would be sent to reorganize the *Kammergericht*. To the charge that this tribunal had been dilatory in clearing its trial load, Arnim tactlessly replied that "precipitate justice" would do more harm than good. The long standing rivalry between Cocceji and Arnim thus came to a head in early 1748. When Cocceji complained of Arnim's lack of cooperation, the latter was ordered by Frederick II to set aside his "private jealousy" or face dismissal.[9]

The defeat of Arnim and Görne and their protégés marked the end of the most decisive struggle for power engaged in by Cocceji in his attempt to secure absolute control of the judiciary. Frederick II, while initially distrustful of Cocceji, gradually came to support him throughout the Pomeranian reforms and the reorganization of the *Kammergericht*. This process, which ended in the discrediting of Arnim, taught a lesson to all of the judges. They realized that their careers rested in the hands of Cocceji. Cocceji, mindful of the internal opposition to him and his policies, proceeded cautiously to win the support of the old-line jurists. He did not intend, in fact, to make a clean sweep, but merely to obtain absolute control over the courts. Cocceji, of course,

9. Ibid., pp. 220–21, 433–34, 449–50.

had not received the backing of most judges at the time of the Pomeranian reforms. The other provincial courts had resisted his proposed
reforms until Frederick had disgraced Arnim. In the aftermath of the
Pomeranian reforms, Cocceji had placated the jurists. He obtained
their support first by throwing fear into them. By dismissing and
disgracing a handful of judges he intimidated the rest. But in his extended conversations with the provincial jurists he undoubtedly took
great pains to make clear to them that they need not fear dismissal
if they accepted the bureaucratic reforms and acknowledged the supremacy of the Department of Justice headed by himself. He was able
to extend the reform plans to all the provinces in the ensuing years
precisely because he had made an informal "bargain" with the jurists.
The courts did, in fact, henceforth acknowledge his supremacy.

The reformation of the judiciary proceeded with little effective
internal opposition after 1748. Cocceji introduced a variety of innovations designed to speed the course of justice: procedure was simplified, official duties more carefully defined, and the appellate structure
was streamlined.[10] As a result of this radical transformation some
eleven judges were transferred or dismissed. Subsequently all of the
provincial court systems were centralized and reformed as a result of
"visitations" by Cocceji and his proteges from 1748 to 1755.

Development of Professional Standards

Cocceji, bureaucrat par excellence that he was, next attempted to
institute a professional recruitment, training, and promotion system.
He gathered around himself a highly competent group of lieutenants
in the course of his reforms. Later these individuals were dispersed
throughout the provincial courts as well as in the central appellate
tribunal. Most of these individuals were intelligent and highly ambitious bourgeois who possessed a clear understanding of the operations of the power elites encountered in local areas and in head-

10. Ibid., pp. 359–61, 378, 400–5, 444–46, 474–80, 497 ff. Stölzel, *Rechtsverwaltung*, 2: 193–94. These matters again have been well explored. Bornhak,
Verwaltungsrechts, 2: 220 ff.

quarters. Social status made little impression upon Cocceji; he warned that "young noblemen will be held responsible for a solid knowledge of the law."[11] Due to his efforts all of the judges of the superior and appellate courts ultimately were appointed only after they had successfully undergone a rigorous examination administered by a Central Examination Commission in Berlin.[12] As a consequence, these officials, who corresponded in rank to the provincial councillors of the boards (some also corresponded in rank to administrative bureaucrats of higher rank), soon became a highly trained, hand-picked, bureaucratic elite. As the old guard jurists retired, these experts took their places. Cocceji did not neglect the institution of a regular system of recruitment of trainees for these positions. Known as *Referendäre*, these apprentices constituted a revolutionary bureaucratic innovation. Young men, after serving one year as *Ausculta-toren*, or junior apprentices, were admitted to internship as *Referendäre* after completing academic training in law and fulfilling the quaint requirement of being able to "write in a fully legible hand."[13] The *Referendar* was shifted from one senate to another within the provincial or appellate court every three months in order to familiarize him with all phases of judicial work. Most interesting was the requirement that all such apprentices who had served five years or more were to be sent to Berlin for examination when a judgeship in a provincial court fell vacant.[14] Again the task of rationalization of the judicial system was advanced when judicial appointments came under increasing central control.

By 1763 the level of competence of judicial officers was undoubtedly superior to that of their rivals in the General Directory and the boards. The latter did not institute an examination system until 1771. Even then it was not as elaborate, nor as suggestive of the techniques of modern civil service, as the judicial Central Examination Commission. Unlike his rivals in the General Directory, Cocceji could rely

11. *AB*, 7: 45.
12. Ibid., 10: 352–54.
13. Ibid.
14. Ibid., pp. 317–22.

upon the universities for academic preparation of trainees.[15] The General Directory and the boards were staffed with people who owed more to experience gained while working in subordinate posts than to perfunctory, or in most cases nonexistent, university training. By control of higher education the jurists long impeded the development of a system of training for prospective core bureaucrats.

The General Directory and the boards responded to this challenge, but to little avail. The *Auscultator* system was enlarged, but Frederick continued to prefer to appoint his regimental quartermasters and *Auditeure*. The "conduct list" system was instituted in response to the judicial "visitation" of the regular inspection of the provincial boards by experts dispatched from Berlin, but it soon became a perfunctory whitewash of all councillors except the personal enemies of the board president. Recruiting of officials remained as haphazard as ever, and technical competence as rare. Unfortunately, neither the General Directory nor the boards could produce a rival to Cocceji. Cocceji was brilliant, unscrupulous, disdainful of the niceties practiced by his rivals, as well as opportunistic. He was an organizer who combined rare ability with a hard grasp of the requirements of power politics.

In one sector of the proposed scheme for strengthening the judicial bureaucracy, Cocceji experienced great difficulty and bitter frustration. Expert officials could only be retained by paying them salaries commensurate with their functions and training. Because of this need for more financial support, Cocceji was to call upon the landed nobility to contribute loans and grants to the superior courts. The near-impotent provincial estates thus obtained an opportunity to assume new power within the provinces. Because of the neglect of the court system by Frederick William I, judges' salaries had been curtailed. By 1740 the jurists had constructed a system designed to augment their diminished income, a system which, in effect, fostered corruption, delay in trials, and judicial favoritism towards wealthy litigants. In

15. Ibid., 15:113–22. The core bureaucracy could not persuade the universities of Halle and Frankfurt on the Oder to institute courses in "cameralistic science" because all educational institutions were controlled by the Spiritual Department which had strong connections with the judiciary.

brief, every stage of judicial proceedings was subjected to a heavy payment of special fees, collected individually from litigants by the judges and their subordinates. The longer the trial, the greater was the opportunity for the enrichment of jurists. Cocceji determined to eliminate this source of graft, since he realized that the reformation of the judicial administration depended upon the establishment of a stable source of income for judges.[16] This financial source had of necessity to be independent of the repository of court fees. At first he suggested to Frederick that judges' salaries be paid from the treasury in the same manner as those of the fiscal bureaucrats. Frederick refused, with the excuse that the treasury could not support such an additional burden. Cocceji then decided that fees should be collected according to a fixed schedule and deposited in a rigorously controlled treasury in each Superior Court. Judges would then be paid set amounts from this repository according to a schedule compiled by the Department of Justice. This plan constituted merely a stopgap until a better source of revenue might be available.

Cocceji, frustrated in his attempts to obtain increased allowances from the royal funds, decided to approach the estates in each province. Such collections would serve as a substitute for support from the State. As he arrived in a particular province to begin reorganization of the courts, he asked the estates to name deputies to confer with him. Cocceji managed to obtain monetary grants in this manner for periods extending over several years. In return he offered vague promises to the landed nobility who dominated the estates. He promised, for example, to agree to appoint only those born within the province to judicial posts within that province. But he then stipulated that if the Central Examination Commission could not find a qualified person from within the province, an outsider could be substituted. More important than this concession were the soothing assurances of Cocceji that the courts would continue to serve the interests of the landed nobility. The aristocratic landowner continued to exercise his "patrimonial" justice over his serfs, and he would be tried before the provincial Superior Court in the first instance if accused of a crime or

16. *AB*, 6: 2. 616–18; 7: 6–10.

involved in a civil suit. The provincial courts continued to safeguard landed property by recording deeds and by acting as legal guardians for the orphans of deceased aristocrats. Henceforth the landed nobility and the reformed judiciary were uneasy allies. Cocceji and his successors did not, in fact, give the nobility much voice in the management of the superior courts. Both Cocceji and Jariges, his successor, believed that the future of the judiciary depended upon the training of able jurists. Burghers, rather than aristocrats, proved willing to undergo the academic preparation deemed necessary for advancement.[17]

In Conflict with the General Directory

The judiciary had been strengthened internally as a result of bureaucratic innovations, reorganization, and the hierarchical arrangement of the courts. But such reforms had only affected the highest courts in the provinces and the central court in Berlin. The lowest local courts remained under the hands of the aristocrats in the countryside and the boards of aldermen in the cities. Cocceji was forced to continue patrimonial justice under the control of the landowners in the countryside, but determined to obtain control over the municipal courts. He was concerned about the administration of criminal justice and civil suits involving private individuals. The supervision of local courts that handled these matters came under the justice *Bürgermeister* who served on the Board of Aldermen. As explained earlier, Frederick II cooperated in Cocceji's efforts to make the justice *Bürgermeister* subject to control by the provincial courts rather than by the board. But Cocceji also wanted to make the justice *Bürgermeister*, or some other jurist, responsible to the Superior Court in the province responsible for the trials of persons accused of tax evasion, smuggling, violation of the military quartering laws, and similar cases where the State, rather than some private individual, was involved in litigation with the king's subjects.[18] In many states a

17. Ibid., 7: 6–10, 253–56. See chapter 9 for the social ramifications of the judicial reforms.
18. Ibid., pp. 649–52.

difficult problem has existed: what tribunal should try persons who are accused of violating statutes concerned with taxation, customs and excises, embezzlement of official funds and such matters that directly involve the State as litigant? What tribunal should try government officials accused of such crimes? By 1740 the General Directory and the boards had established almost complete jurisdiction over cases involving such administrative legal statutes (*Kammerjustiz*), especially in the cities. Cocceji did not intend to allow the core bureaucracy to continue to wield this power unchallenged. From 1745 to 1755 he launched a concerted campaign against the boards and the General Directory.

Cocceji tried to alter the situation to his advantage in several ways. First, he hoped to persuade Frederick II to specify, by royal edict, much greater authority over local justice to the superior courts in the provinces. He also attempted to strengthen the position of the general fiscal officer and of his subordinates within each of the boards. These *Fiscals* were bureaucratic spies placed within the official ranks by Frederick William I originally to halt corruption and intrigues. Independent of the board presidents and of the General Directory, these unpopular watchdogs gradually came under the control of the Department of Justice. Frederick II invariably held the chancellor responsible for the conduct of the *Fiscals*.[19] The final line of attack proposed by Cocceji was to be directed against a large corps of officials in the boards which had gradually taken control of "cameral justice." These councillors were experts in the apprehension and trial of criminals involved in fraud, tax evasion, smuggling, and the like. They, as well as their subordinates, who were termed *Justitaire*, provided the judicial arm of the boards.[20] Cocceji thus hoped to limit the authority of some of the board officials by use of the *Fiscals* and by circumscribing the effectiveness of the *Justitaire* and the *Kammerjustizräte*.

19. Dorn, "Prussian Bureaucracy," 47: 91–92, mistakenly places the *Fiscal* independent of both the General Directory and the judiciary. Schmidt, *Fiskalat*, pp. 149 ff.

20. *AB*, 8: 144.

Within the General Directory, the so-called "cameral justice" functions were assigned to four privy judicial councillors, who corresponded at this higher level to the *Kammerjustizräte* of the boards. They were ordinarily distributed among the four departments, but met together periodically as a Review Commission by 1740. First established in 1724 under a separate minister, these officials had played little part in the operation of the General Directory over the years, until they were replaced by the perfunctory Review Commission.[21] As a consequence the entire judiciary was not centrally directed but left to the indifferent supervision of the board presidents. By 1750 Cocceji took advantage of this neglect to suggest to Frederick II that two councillors be given charge of the entire cameral justice system. The new councillors, he remarked, could not be recruited from the ranks of the core bureaucracy because they required special training unobtainable in this structure. Such trained personnel could be found only outside the realm, where academic preparation of administrative lawyers had been developed. Cocceji was, of course, interfering in the affairs of a rival agency in a purely illegal and impudent manner. Evidently, when the king notified the General Directory of this impending change, the protesting ministers at least hoped to appoint the councillors from within the ranks of its own bureaucracy. Cocceji then obtained the opportunity[22] to select these officials according to this stipulation. In effect, this so-called "reform" of 1750 did not result in better central administration of cameral justice, since the General Directory insured that the new councillors would receive little or no cooperation from other officials. In 1772 still another attempt was made by the king, the General Directory, and the Justice Department, to establish a central judicial authority: the Supreme Review Board.[23] Cocceji had not succeeded in thwarting the core bureaucrats in their control of their own judicial functions, but he had forced them, ultimately, to review these functions.

21. Hintze, *AB*, 6: 1. 179–81.
22. *AB*, 8: 713–15.
23. Hintze, *AB*, 6: 1. 179–81.

Not content with this destructive activity in the anterooms of the General Directory, Cocceji next attacked the humble *Justitiar*, the judicial agent of the boards who conducted the majority of trials for excise and tariff fraud in the cities. In 1750 some board councillors complained of Cocceji's proposed division of judicial functions between the boards and the superior courts. Cocceji replied to the king that these complaints indicated "a clear proof that one can expect the conduct of justice by the boards to be biased." Going further, he remarked "that everything depended upon the *Justitiar's* ability in such cases, and, if he does not understand the case, or is negatively inclined, the parties must lose all hope. In contrast, the Superior Court, which is filled with able men, can deal with such cases in expert fashion." At the root of this attack was Cocceji's radical, if sophistical, interpretation of what constituted "cameral justice" as opposed to that appropriate to the superior courts. He acknowledged that excise, tariff, hunting, and other cases involving fraud came under the jurisdiction of the boards, but "if the question is whether anyone has a claim to exemption from a tariff, hunting or other such regulation, or a complaint against supposedly incorrect collection of taxes and thus comes in contact with the *Fiscal*, and, equally, if anyone has a complaint involving the nature of a hunting right, . . . or such, these belong to the jurisdiction, not of the board, but of the Superior Court, which alone can prevent great injustice."[24] The *Justitiar* was to find himself the center of a hotly disputed jurisdictional conflict.

Cocceji attempted to wrestle control of primary courts away from the hands of the municipal patrician oligarchies as well as from the boards. In 1748 Frederick opened the path for such an endeavor by asking Cocceji to place the financial affairs of the magistrates' courts in order. The chancellor immediately suggested that the judges of the municipal courts were "inferior" in legal training and should be examined by judicial experts from the superior courts to determine their competence. The General Directory protested, stating that these courts had been subject to the jurisdiction of the boards since 1713.

24. *AB*, 8: 144–47.

Nevertheless Frederick supported Cocceji. Stalemate between the superior courts and the boards appeared subsequently, however when the king decided to base appointments of municipal judges upon the recommendation of the magistrates and the boards rather than of the superior courts.[25] Adding to the confusion was a particularly vague and conflict-producing section of the Jurisdictional Regulation of 1749, which decreed that local judges must de examined by the Superior Court, and that they must confer with the latter in matters of a "private" nature.[26] In 1755 Jariges, one of Cocceji's protégés, attempted to place all of the judicial magistrates into a *Landgericht* which would be directly under the Superior Court in Cleves. The Cleves board protested energetically. Jariges supported his stand with charges of incompetence in the proceedings of the city courts. As an example of malpractice he cited the case of the physician who supplemented his income with part-time magisterial duties in one town.[27] Thus the municipal courts remained a bone of contention between the superior courts and the boards.

The *Fiscals* within the boards, as well as their chief the general fiscal officer, Uhden, found that Cocceji began to espouse their cause concurrently with his attempts to strip the core bureaucracy of its judicial powers. Frederick II (always fascinated by the espionage functions of these officials), ordered Cocceji in March 1748 to make sure that they obeyed orders and that the *Fiscals* assigned to each superior court received such edicts. "Edicts, orders, and such promulgations sent to the courts by me will be communicated to the *Fiscals* of these courts so that contravening activity against such orders and edicts might be uncovered by adequate vigilance and reported."[28] Although attached to the superior courts, the *Fiscals* actually performed most of their work within the boards. They were ordered in 1750, for example, to watch the war and domains councillors to make sure that these officials were not allowing nobles to

25. Ibid., pp. 230–36.
26. Ibid., pp. 230–34.
27. Ibid., 10: 149–53.
28. Ibid., 7: 461–62.

leave the country for foreign military service. In 1764 Jariges, then chancellor of justice, possessed the authority to appoint *adjunctis Fisci* within the Boards.[29] These pariahs long served as a hidden source of information and control within the ranks of the fiscal bureaucrats. The judiciary knew something of what was transpiring in the chambers of its arch rival.

The conflict between the judicial and the core bureaucracies reached its hottest stage in the period from 1748 to 1751. During these years Frederick II attempted to carve out separate spheres of influence for each organization. In the course of the year 1748 he studied the original General Directory *Instructions* of 1722, which had first established that body and specified its functions, and finally, he issued *Revised Instructions* in 1748. Article 37 of this document attempted to preserve a delicate balance between the boards and the superior Courts by giving the latter complete authority over cases involving serfdom, the conflict of nobles and serfs over debts and property lines, as well as over domain units (*Ämter*) or cities involved in such litigation. In general the Superior Court was to be responsible for cases involving personal, or "private" litigation.[30] But, due to Cocceji, Frederick decided to issue a separate jurisdictional regulation in 1749. Cocceji outlined his objections before and after the 1749 decree. He claimed that the present, or the 1748, regulation decreed that "the boards have cognition of all judicial and other matters which are not specifically given to the superior courts." Cocceji intended to revise the regulation to read: "all trials and suits should belong to the cognition of the Department of Justice except those specifically relinquished." But Frederick vetoed this change with the comment that "it is too vague." Frederick intended that "the nobility will be subject in all cases involving the boards and the cities to the superior courts, while the cities and the domains come before the board in economic matters."[31] But he did approve Cocceji's suggestion that the Superior Court should have jurisdiction over conflicts

29. Ibid., 8: 791–92; 13: 383.
30. Ibid., 7: 649–52.
31. Ibid., 8: 388–90.

involving disputed serfdom and building contracts. The *Jurisdictional Regulation* of 1749 attempted, then, to establish an even finer distinction between functions than the General Directory instructions of 1748. Basically, the superior courts were to have jurisdiction over all private litigation such as peasant hereditary tenure rights and property indebtedness. The boards would have jurisdiction over peasants on domain lands involving suits aimed at increasing or decreasing the size of plots, changing methods of cultivation, and other *ad statum oeconomicum*. The personal indebtedness of board officials fell under the cognizance of the Superior Court. Complaints of private property holders that involved eminent domain rights necessary to the construction of dams, bridges, and roads, also came under the superior courts. But tariff and license cases went to the board.[32] This last point, of course, had elicited strong opposition from Cocceji. He realized that jurisdiction over tax frauds gave the board almost absolute control over commerce and industry and the persons involved in these activities.

The battle for bureaucratic precedence cloaked in this bitter, if bloodless, strife over jurisdictional spheres spread throughout the entire administrative and judicial hierarchies in the ensuing years. In East Prussia, for example, the Königsberg board under the leadership of von Blumenthal and, later, of Domhardt, continually refused to pay for the support of new churches and schools because of its rivalry with the Superior Court in that province. The same bitter struggle affected corresponding programs in the Lithuanian province. In 1769 Frederick allowed the astute, if unscrupulous, Domhardt, then president of the East Prussian boards, to lead an investigation into the affairs of the East Prussian consistory director, Minister von Braxein. Braxein complained that the investigation provided the core bureaucrats an opportunity to get revenge on their judicial rivals.[33] Cocceji had earlier experienced great difficulty in Cleves

32. Ibid., 8: 235–36,391.
33. Hartwig Notbohm, *Das Evangelische Kirchen- und Schulwesen in Ostpreussen* (Heidelberg, 1959), pp. 62–72. The administration of churches and schools ultimately came under the Department of Justice.

because of the sullen resistance of the board there at the time he attempted to establish a "land court" upon request of the estates.[34] Within the provinces, by 1755 Cocceji had failed to obtain absolute control over all judicial processes. He had succeeded in extending the jurisdictional areas of the Superior Court to include most of the legal matters of a "private" nature. But Frederick II prevented him from interfering in tax trials. The boards continued to wield absolute control over the collection of excise taxes as well as the trial of tax evaders until 1766.[35] Nevertheless the boards did experience a definite loss of authority as a result of the jurisdictional fight. More important, they now had to face the opposition of the superior courts day in and day out, because the judiciary continued to fight for additional authority.

Reconstruction of the Religious and Educational Consistories

It is extremely doubtful that the Spiritual Department would ever have acquired administrative authority of importance without the prior reorganization of the judiciary. Cocceji had tried, since 1730, to reform this complex agency which was charged with the supervision of all ecclesiastical and higher educational institutions. Only in 1746 was he able to obtain the support of Frederick; prior to that year his enemies within the agency had thwarted attempts to revive this moribund institution.[36]

Of all the vaguely defined functions of the Spiritual Department, none was more important than control over the universities. These institutions were the scenes of violent conflict between the orthodox Lutheran, rationalist, and Pietist professors by the middle years of the eighteenth century. This internal squabbling encouraged Frederick William I to interfere in their affairs to an increasing extent. Despite the support of Cocceji, for example, Christian Wolff was discharged from Halle when the orthodox theologians persuaded

34. *AB*, 9: 500–9, 525–39, 568–76.
35. Until the establishment of the *Regie*. See Chapter 7.
36. Hintze, *AB*, 6: 1. 134–50.

Frederick William that their rival was preaching heretical and subversive doctrines. Such conflicts within the theological faculties affected the entire development of universities because the majority of students matriculated in theology. Frederick II and Cocceji could thus embark after 1740 on a thorough housecleaning of the universities with the excuse that the long internal conflict between professorial cliques was detrimental to the educational functions.[37]

Probably due to the influence of Cocceji Frederick established a University Commission in 1742. Initially this board included Cocceji, Marschall and Brand, but the last was replaced by Jordan in 1745, in conformance with the wishes of the king. Freed from control by the Spiritual Department, this commission probably was dominated by Cocceji. Marschall was also head of the fifth department and occupied primarily with its thorny management and Jordan, chief of the Potsdam orphanage, probably lacked knowledge of Prussian educational problems. Jordan died in 1747, and Frederick appointed another Rheinsberg companion, the baron von Bielfeld, in his place. In this edict he specified that the commission was responsible for obtaining "learned and famous subjects"[38] for vacant professorships, as well as looking after the welfare of the universities in general. Bielfeld, a widely traveled cosmopolite and a prolific writer on cameralism and jurisprudence[39] seemed to agree with Cocceji, and there is every reason to suppose that the two cooperated well with each other. Frederick chose to state in this edict appointing Bielfeld that the University Commission and not the Spiritual Department was responsible for the placement of professors.[40] By 1748, Cocceji had succeeded in achieving a dominant voice in the administration of the universities.

37. Konrad Bornhak, *Geschichte der preussischen Universitätsverwaltung bis 1810* (Berlin, 1900), pp. 159–61. Karl Aner, *Die Theologie der Lessingzeit* (Halle, 1929), discussed Wolff's place in German theology at great length. See also Henri Brunschwig, *La Crise de l'État prussien a la Fin du XVIIIe Siècle* (Paris, 1947), pp. 10 ff. Koppel S. Pinson, *Pietism as a Factor in the Rise of German Nationalism* (New York, 1934), pp. 70–71.
38. *AB*, 7: 388–89.
39. Jacob von Bielfeld, *Institutions Politiques*, 3 vols. (Leiden, 1767).
40. *AB*, 7: 338–39.

Cocceji began to think seriously about the possibility of reorganizing the consistories as well as the Spiritual Department at this time. In 1748 he asked Johann Süssmilch,[41] a member of the Electoral Mark consistory as well as pastor of St. Peter's Church in Berlin, to make recommendations concerning the regulation of educational and spiritual problems. Süssmilch was most concerned about the possibility of establishing some official agency to supervise the training of prospective pastors. Many unworthy persons were certified by local *Bürgermeister* and other officials who did not possess competence in such matters, he claimed. He thus suggested the establishment of a Superior Consistory (*Oberconsistorium*), to rectify this evil condition. Süssmilch suggested that the Superior Consistory could dispatch trained inspectors throughout the realm to supervise the training, placement, and performance of pastors. We should remember at this point that Cocceji, Süssmilch, and their subordinates always considered the question of regulation of all branches of education to be inseparably connected to that of religious bodies. Frederick, however, chose for reasons of his own to regard the two questions separately. He remained cool towards various projects, calling for the establishment of a superagency or *Oberconsistorium* to assume control over these important functions. Cocceji did not allow Süssmilch's plan to be forgotten, however; he began to correspond with other prominent leaders of Prussian Protestantism, and in 1749 both Süssmilch and Pastor Baumgarten sent detailed recommendations to him. Süssmilch recommended that the prospective *Oberconsistorium* consist of five or six members of which two would be the chief Lutheran pastors in Berlin. This board would assume wide supervisory powers over schools and universities, as well as religious bodies.[42] Baumgarten approached the problem from the Evangelical side and suggested that the proposed superagency take charge of the placement of clergy as well as its training. The board,

41. A demographer, statistician, and cameralist in addition. See his *Göttliche Ordnung in den Veränderungen des menschlichen Geschlechts*, 3 vols. (Berlin, 1775–76).
42. *AB*, 8: 394–403.

he stated, could insure that theological students in the universities received "the necessary discipline and preparation."[43] Cocceji had secured the support of two prominent Protestant pastors for his proposed *Oberconsistorium*. Aiding Cocceji at this juncture was the death of Minister Brand, the ineffectual chief of the Spiritual Department. Cocceji knew that Frederick had long believed that the Spiritual Department was inefficient and impotent, and took this opportunity to suggest that Minister von Dankelmann be placed in charge of the department in order to clean it up. In case Frederick approved of this recommendation, Cocceji was willing to work on an overall reorganization plan with Dankelmann to eliminate future "mistakes." Frederick chose to interpret this suggestion as a means of eliminating the "jealousy" that existed between Evangelical and Lutheran bodies in his realm. He did not mention in his reply any other points of cocern, such as the universities, but he later gave Dankelmann considerable authority over religious bodies by granting him supervision of certain ecclesiastical revenues upon the death of Marschall.[44] Cocceji also secured the approval of Frederick for the establishment of a Lutheran Superior Consistory in 1750 which he intended to use to supervise that denomination. His first recommendation to Frederick in May of that year skirted the question of university administration, but the final edict of August, 1750 gave the new Superior Consistory power to examine theological students as well as to recommend persons to professorships of theology, but the actual supervision of the universities remained under the separate University Commission.[45] Thus, by August of 1750 the basic reorganization of the central administration of the religious and educational functions of the realm had occurred.

Cocceji had successfully obtained general authority over all educational and religious functions within the realm with the exception of those in Silesia, and after 1750 he proceeded to reform the provincial consistories and to attach them to the superior courts. In the

43. Ibid., p. 408.
44. Ibid., pp. 316–17.
45. Ibid., 9: 50–59.

course of periodic inspection trips to the various superior courts, he and his subordinates regularly studied the operations of these consistories.[46] The reorganization of these agencies resulted in giving the Department of Justice greater police authority over the subjects of the king of Prussia. The authority of the Prussian State over religious and educational bodies was increased. The authority of the core bureaucracy and of local pressure groups of all kinds, including the aristocratic associations, was decreased. Frederick approved this substantial reapportionment of administrative power.

Unlike his dogmatically Calvinistic father, Frederick II was an admirer of Christian Wolff. Cocceji and Frederick supported Wolff's protégés in the law and theology faculties of the universities, and after 1750 theological training came to reflect Wolff's attempted synthesis of "reason" and "revelation," or the combining of certain elements of the philosophy of the Enlightenment with some of those of traditional Lutheranism. This alteration in the curriculum gave a pronounced secular bent to theological training and resulted after some time in many students taking degrees in theology while actually pursuing studies in mathematics, mechanics, optics, classics, and philosophy.[47] The law faculties came to have close relationships with the theologians because of the leadership of Wolff, who was both jurist and theologian. The whole curriculum of the university changed rapidly from semimedieval to something approaching a training course for ecclesiastical jurists and administrative lawyers. Cocceji intended to fill the ranks of the judicial and consistorial system with carefully trained and worldly minded bureaucrats.

Cocceji tightened supervision over the curriculum, the standards for the granting of degrees, and the conduct of students and professors. By 1756 the Consistory for Higher Education conducted regular inspections of the universities and prepared efficiency reports on professors, recommending those it considered worthy of continued employment.[48] Periodically the consistory prepared elaborate decrees

46. Ibid., pp. 238, 139, 518, 451 ff., 512, 513.
47. Hartwig Notbohm, *Das Evangelische Kirchen- und Schulwesen in Ostpreussen* (Heidelberg, 1959), pp. 86–7. See note 10 above.
48. Ibid., pp. 111–12.

for the signature of Frederick, listing the courses to be given by all the faculties as well as the requirements for matriculation and for graduation.[49] The judiciary now possessed almost absolute control of the operations of higher educational institutions.

Frederick believed that the reorganized universities would continue to prepare lawyers and clergymen for positions in the court system and the religious bodies. He did not believe that prospective officials in the core bureaucracy needed such an educational background; training in economics and rural management could best be acquired by working with merchants and domain administrators rather than in the universities.[50] The ministers of the General Directory disagreed with this pragmatic approach to the education of recruits in their service. Cameralists such as Justi also disagreed with Frederick. The King's penchant for the appointment of former regimental quartermasters to important board councillor or *Steuerrat* positions was likewise subject to criticism by leading members of the core bureaucracy. The General Directory hoped to obtain its recruits from the universities and tried to introduce faculties of "cameralistic science." Due to the opposition of the king and of the judiciary under Cocceji, however, these attempts failed. When the two existing chairs of cameral science fell vacant in Halle and Frankfurt, the General Directory sent officials to hold periodic lectures in an attempt to lure students away from the faculties of theology and jurisprudence. But these lectures were poorly attended and subsequently were cancelled.[51] In 1770 the General Directory again tried to introduce cameral science into the curriculum. Theological students, it was suggested, should study such matters because country pastors could help solve rural problems by recommending the introduction of new methods of cultivation and agricultural management to the conservative peasant and to his lord. Such a request fell upon deaf ears in the *Oberconsistorium* and was never put into force.[52] In subsequent years the

49. Bornhak, *Universitätsverwaltung*, pp. 159–61.
50. Ibid.,
51. Johannes Ziekursch, *Beiträge zur Charakteristik . . .* (Breslau, 1907), p. 4.
52. Bornhak, *Universitätsverwaltung*, pp. 159–61. Ziekursch, *Beiträge zur Charakteristik,* p 4

universities proved to be a fertile ground for dissemination of the doctrines of Adam Smith, and for the spokesmen of other movements in opposition to the quasi mercantilism of the General Directory.[53]

Through its control of the consistories the judicial bureaucracy was also able to wield some influence on the preparation and placement of professional people in society at large. Since the consistories maintained supervision over the recruitment of schoolmasters and pastors, the occupations favored by a large majority of university graduates, it became easy for these agencies to reduce such professional persons to the status of minor bureaucrats. This process was naturally aided by the fact that the consistories also controlled the salaries paid to such persons. In some areas, however, such as the countryside of Silesia, the aristocracy continued to wield considerable authority over the selection of pastors and teachers, but, even in such cases, the provincial superior courts held ultimate veto power.[54] Since the consistories also controlled entrance to such professions as law and medicine, it is obvious that practically all university students found themselves regulated by the judicial bureaucracy, especially since Frederick prohibited study in foreign universities. Caught in the web of the judiciary, the student embarked upon a course of study determined by the State, obtained a position with the sponsorship of the State, and could never escape the conclusion that he was a quasi bureaucrat.

Cocceji, with the help of Frederick, had scored a great victory for the cause of absolutism by finally subordinating the educational and religious bodies to the State. As long as he lived he possessed control over both the *Oberconsistorium* and the University Commission since he was the chairman of both. Frederick tried to keep the two separate afterwards, but the chancellor succeeded ultimately in subordinating the universities to the *Oberconsistorium*.[55] The Spiritual Department, although nominally independent, remained part of the Department of

53. Brunschwig, *Crise*, pp. 124–25.
54. Bornhak, *Universitätsverwaltung*, pp. 71–78, 156–59. Notbohm, *Evangelische kirchen*, pp. 110 passim. Johannes Ziekursch, *Hundert Jahre Schlesische Agrargeschichte* (Breslau, 1927), pp. 120 ff.
55. By 1754. See *AB*, 10: 162–64.

Justice. The General Directory, the boards, and the municipal magistrates undoubtedly lost a substantial amount of authority which they had previously exercised over the schools and churches. A substantial redistribution of administrative power had, in fact, occurred.

The Judiciary by 1756

Frederick pursued a consistent policy in regard to the judicial reform plans of Cocceji. He encouraged the chancellor to challenge the entrenched authority of the boards and of the General Directory. He permitted him to reform the courts, to remove incompetent personnel, and to regularize the appellate system. But he effectively hamstrung Cocceji when he thought the new judicial bureaucracy was powerful enough in its own right to claim independent status within the State. Frederick did not intend to allow the judiciary to become a substitute center of power for the core bureaucracy. Instead, he never really allowed Cocceji to establish the finances of the courts on a stable basis, nor did he allow him to obtain absolute jurisdiction over all legal questions in the realm. Behind Cocceji's schemes Frederick discerned that his chancellor desired to limit the effectiveness of the boards and to augment the authority possessed by himself and by his proteges. By astutely playing off the judiciary against the core bureaucracy, Frederick effectively stymied any such radical change.

The provinces thus formed a battleground on which several competitive administrative agencies vied for supremacy. Provincial administration can be understood only if it is studied as a composite whole that was the result of three different types of functions interwoven with one another. The functions of some officials were designed to reflect the interest of local groups. The boards of aldermen reflected the desires of the urban patricians while the estates and the *Landräte* reflected those of the landed nobility. Some officials represented, within the province, the top level agencies and the king: the *Fiscals*, supposedly, as well as outside investigators and commissions. Most of the functions of the board and of the Superior Court were "intermediary" in nature. Each of these agencies had to reconcile top level policy with local conditions. The *Steuerrat* functioned both as a central agent and as an intermediary, as did the councillors on the domains. The *Justitiar* functioned as a central agent, supervising the magistrates in the interests of the board. Naturally no official exercised only one of these three basic functions, but some reflected an emphasis on one of them to the partial exclusion of others. These basic bureaucratic functions, embodied in the duties of different officials, existed in provincial administration by necessity. Hohenzollern absolutism continued to exist by allowing local interests to assume "seat and voice" in provincial affairs, and by providing intermediary mechanisms in administration. One fact, often ignored by administrative historians, is that official edicts in themselves do not necessarily result in action. Edicts must be enforced, and can be enforced only with due regard for the existing social, political, and economic conditions. Frederick II and Cocceji both desired to rationalize and perfect the central control of Prussian society. Both realized, but Frederick sometimes forgot, that *ex cathedra* decrees do not govern social relations. Behind the scenes the political leader must make alliances with powerful groups; he must compromise, cajole, reward, dissimilate, and, finally, endeavor to preserve his own position by setting one group against another. The functions of the political leader differ, however, according to his initial mastery of the situation. Cocceji was a political innovator. He was interested in augmenting the power of the judicial branch in the State. His approach, therefore, required constant conflict with the General Directory and the provincial boards. In order to win this battle, he had to elicit support from other elements in society such as the king and local groups in city and countryside. Compared with this "parvenu" leadership, that of Frederick II was essentially different. His was the leadership of arbitration. The king did not desire the predominance of one group over all others: he wanted all groups to engage in "free competition." In such a fluid situation, he could hope to preserve supreme power because he remained the only master of the situation. He could also hope that the best solution would emerge.

The history of judicial reform from 1740 to 1763 reveals the interplay of three main power-seeking drives. Cocceji tried to make the superior courts the final repositories of judicial functions. The boards tried to retain their favored position. Frederick tried to set limits to the development of the superior courts and to preserve some of the power residing in the boards. As a result, a state of equilibrium emerged: the superior courts became counterweights of the boards. This equilibrium came about, more precisely, because of the struggle for control over the lower courts, because of the alliance between the superior courts and the estates, because of the strengthening of the superior courts internally, and, finally, because of the policies of Frederick II.

V

THE VICEROYS

OF SILESIA

Cocceji succeeded in reorganizing the judiciary in the Prussian State, but encountered more difficulty in the new province of Silesia than elsewhere. Frederick ordered the invasion of this large and economically productive territory soon after he came to the throne. He grimly defended his conquest in two major wars thereafter. Reserving major policy decisions to himself, Frederick relied on officials such as Cocceji to determine the actual framework of government of Silesia. Great administrative problems had to be faced once the glamor of military victory was forgotten. In the long run Cocceji and his rivals in the core bureaucracy discovered that they could not simply transplant the Prussian government to Silesia in unchanged form. Officials resorted to unusual expedients and succeeded in developing administrative techniques which would be applied to the rest of the realm later.

Following the orders of the king, Cocceji prepared a brief which justified the conquest on the grounds of natural law.[1] He accomplished two small victories by this effort: first he ingratiated himself with Frederick soon after that monarch gained the throne, and second, he involved himself, tenuously, in the future administration of Silesia. But a lawyer's brief could not eliminate the possibility that

1. Friedrich Meinecke, *Machiavellism* (New Haven, 1958), pp. 297–300, tries to reconcile the Frederick who wrote the *Antimachiav·l* and the Frederick who was carried away by a "demonic" spirit when he embarked on the conquest of Silesia. Stölzel, *Rechtsverwaltung*, 2: 141–233, gives an excellent account of Cocceji's career without stressing his diplomatic services. Preuss, ed. *Oeuvres* 2: 50–57, includes Frederick's discussion of his own dilemma.

Silesia might once more pass into Austrian hands. The coup had been spectacular,[2] but few could claim that it would result in the permanent possession by Prussia of the stolen property. Between 1744 and 1764 a cloud of uncertainty remained over the heads of those officials who travelled from Berlin to Breslau to establish the new administrative system. An air of imperious necessity marked their endeavors: they had to consolidate control over the inhabitants of the new province as quickly as possible. This atmosphere of apprehension, haste, and determination had a great, if undefinable, influence upon the actual administrative system.

The cameralists were of no more help than the jurists in providing guides for the Prussian administration of Silesia. Invariably these writers considered the State to be complete before economic policies were initiated and did not address themselves to the means to be used to secure an ill-gotten conquest.[3] Practical officials, who had little time or patience for the cameralists, knew instinctively that they faced perplexing economic and social problems in their task of incorporating Silesia into the Prussian realm. At first they may well have believed that the Prussian State could eventually absorb the new territory without difficulty. The actual administration of the province was to be a radical experiment in decentralized control, however, and it was to be established and maintained outside of the regular bureaucratic structure.

Frederick II was the chief formulator of the Prussian administrative system in Silesia. He was inexperienced in matters of administration when he determined to undertake the conquest of Silesia in 1740.

2. Schlenke, *England*, pp. 167 ff., discusses the controversy that raged in England following the Silesian invasion: some English commentators called Frederick a "robber" but others were fascinated by an apparent major upset of the European balance of power. Stephen Skalweit, *Frankreich und Friedrich der Grosse* (Bonn, 1952), pp. 21 ff., reveals a similar French reaction.

3. The cameralists did not devote much attention to prospects of enhancing the wealth of a country through direct military conquest; they were interested in Colbert's economic conquest of international trade. Justi, for example, said that the wealth of a state could be increased in three ways: by an increase in the population, by promoting foreign commerce and by mining. J. G. Justi, *Staatswirtschaft* (Leipzig, 1758), 1: 157–59.

In addition, he was forced time after time to abandon administrative duties between 1740 and 1748 because of the requirements of military leadership in the War of the Austrian Succession. Because of the fitful nature of the king's supervision over the province, his distrust for the General Directory, his rather low opinion of the competence of his ministers, and because of the remoteness of the officials dispatched to Breslau from Berlin and their relative independence of judgment, the new administrative structure in Silesia was to become independent of the General Directory by 1746.

Establishment of the Silesian Ministry

Upon the invasion of the province, Frederick established a temporary commission (*Feldkriegscommissariat*) to rule the populace as well as to provide supplies for the Prussian army. For this purpose he detached two privy finance councillors, von Reinhardt and von Münchow, as well as an expert in grain storage and its distribution, Councillor Deutsch, and a financial expert, Councillor Köppen, from the General Directory to form the new governing board.[4] Subsequently Frederick divided the province into four districts to be governed by the four councillors, eliminated municipal election rights, and eliminated the right of the Silesian estates to collect taxes.[5] These first steps taken by the Prussian conqueror indicated very clearly that the old *Ständesstaat* would be eliminated and the whole province brought under the administration of outside (Prussian) administrators.[6]

Once Frederick was no longer preoccupied with military problems, he replaced the *Feldkriegscommissariat* with two war and domains

4. The standard account of the Prussian conquest and subsequent occupation remains the somewhat antiquated Colmar Grünhagen, *Schlesien unter Friedrich dem Grossen* (Breslau, 1890), vol. 1, particularly pp. 311–543. See also the pedestrian Conrad Bornhak, *Preussische Staats- und Rechtsgeschichte* (Berlin, 1903), 2: 194–99.

5. *AB*, 6: 2. 188–89, 205–35, 278–85.

6. Colmar Grünhagen, "Die Entstehung eines schlesischen Sonderministeriums," *Forschungen zur Brandenburgischen und Preussischen Geschichte* 20 (1907); 107–9.

boards, one at Glogau and one at Breslau. Councillors Münchow and Reinhardt, after being appointed to head the respective boards, were told by the king to ignore the General Directory in appointing their own subordinates and in drawing up their own administrative regulations.[7] This epoch-marking decree of October 11, 1741 revealed that Frederick intended to grant his officials in Silesia extraordinary authority.

From October 1741 to March 1742 a struggle raged between the General Directory, the king, Münchow, and Reinhardt over the allocation of authority within Silesia. Again, Frederick took the initiative by firmly eliminating the General Directory and intimating his future plans to appoint "a Directing Minister of the Silesian Department." The erstwhile colleagues Münchow and Reinhardt, who had fought the claims of the General Directory, now suddenly turned on each other in rivalry; each hoped to obtain the ministerial post. Münchow secured the confidence of the king first because he had greater success in obtaining a staff made up of officials drawn from throughout the core bureaucracy and because he seemed to be more efficient than Reinhardt. Münchow, not having to negotiate with the powerful Silesian aristocracy and other interest groups because he directed the less important Glogau board, could sit back while poor Reinhardt struggled in Breslau. By February, 1742, Reinhardt was forced to return to Berlin after Frederick castigated his entire effort: "Everything has been treated with nonchalance."[8] Münchow, on the other hand, was appointed minister of Silesia in March and was placed directly under the king and remained independent of the General Directory.

From the beginning, the history of the establishment of the Silesian ministry and the eventual triumph of Münchow presents a picture of improvisation. First, Frederick was concerned with the quick exploitation of whatever goods and services might be available

7. *AB*, 6: pt. 2, 233–38. See *AB*, 7: 659–839 for a series of general regulations for different boards drawn up by the General Directory and approved by Frederick during 1748.

8. Ibid., 7: 2. 247–48; 6: 2. 278, 308–09, 316, 323, 347–48, 359–60, 377–78.

in Silesia for his army; hence the formation of the *Feldkriegscommissariat*. This was obviously a haphazardly contrived agency with an immediate military purpose behind it, rather than a permanent system of administration. The subsequent establishment of two boards at Breslau and Glogau, and the eventual establishment of a Silesian minister to head these boards may also be a result of Frederick's growing view that Silesia possessed unusual military advantages. It was strategically located between Brandenburg and Austria and Bohemia where the focus of military operations centered, and it possessed vast supplies of horses, forage, and grain which the Prussian army could quickly utilize. It must have seemed an obvious necessity to keep the Silesian administration directly under his control because of the pressing military requirements. The General Directory was geographically removed from the province and not organized to absorb quickly into itself the management of such a large territory. In addition, Frederick wanted efficient and loyal administration in Silesia and did not believe he could obtain it from the General Directory. Until 1748 the pressing and urgent requirements of war must have influenced Frederick when he came to decide what form the Silesian administration would take.

Münchow Secures Control of the New Administration

Münchow was a remarkable administrator; he was, in fact, a kind of bureaucratic buccaneer. Knowing that his appointment as minister of Silesia would not be sufficient to enable him to establish his personal authority in the province, he first determined to secure the loyalty and enthusiastic support of his own subordinates. He had, in short, to convince these officials that they were to look to him and to him alone for the protection and enhancement of their careers. Several decrees which he issued immediately resulted in the transfer of several officials, including some identified with his discredited rival Reinhardt, and in the tightening of administrative controls over the Breslau and Glogau boards.[9] He took great care to defend his

9. Ibid., 6: 2. 423–25, 438–42, 551–61.

lieutenants from all outside attack, even that coming from the king. "I have made a reply by post today to His Majesty in order to secure justice for the boards,"[10] he announced on one occasion. Soon Münchow had, in truth, brought about a harmonious working relationship of all officials in the Silesian administration. Troublemakers had been eliminated and the remainder worked in his interest, if not always in the public interest: bureaucratic camaraderie did not prevent, for example, officials from leaking secret information to merchants and others in Breslau.[11]

One major factor behind Münchow's success in his dealings with his subordinates was his unending search for ways to increase their authority in local districts. He stripped locally elected municipal *Bürgermeister* of their authority and correspondingly enlarged the authority of the councillors. By softpedalling one of the most divisive issues within the bureaucracy, the tension between noble and commoner officials, he stressed loyalty and performance rather than social origins. Münchow, of course, never violated an unwritten rule of bureaucratic conduct: if mistakes were discovered, they were always blamed on the board collectively, rather than upon a particular official.[12]

Another ruthless and highly intelligent official, Cocceji, once ruefully praised "Count von Münchow, who is accustomed to hazard all risks," when he encountered extraordinary difficulty in trying to obtain a jurisdictional agreement in the province. Münchow determined to be master of his own house and maintained that this house was a unique structure. From the beginning he waged a psychological campaign to convince the king and everyone else of the validity of Silesian administrative autonomy. But all such claims would have come to nought if Frederick had not agreed. The king gave Münchow authority over the provincial postal system as well as over the highly important administration of the grain warehouses in the province.

10. Siegfried Isaacsohn, *Geschichte des preussischen Beamtenthums* (Berlin, 1847–1884), 3: 206–30. *AB*, 6: 2. 429; 7: 13–14.
11. *AB*, 6: 2. 442–44; 7: 386; 8: 173–74.
12. Ibid., 9: 98–104, 412–13, 449.

Münchow eagerly assumed that he need not consult with the General Directory about anything and that he could make the majority of the policy decisions in the province, leaving only a few relatively easy problems to be referred to the king. This astute estimate of the intentions of Frederick proved rewarding, for Münchow established in the mind of the king a feeling of trust. Frederick, in turn, exacted certain payments: he did not allow his minister to marry because the Silesian administration required his "fullest application."[13] By giving the impression that he was performing the duties of a custodian of the *bagatelles,* Münchow obtained vast powers by seizing the decision-making authority, as for example, over ticklish negotiations with the provincial aristocracy and clergy. To satisfy Frederick, he regularly sent in optimistic reports and queries regarding the appointment of *Landräte*—the latter especially because of the king's particular interest in this local office.

Nevertheless, the suspicious Frederick made occasional attempts to place controls over his ingenious underling. After ordering him in September 1742 to send in detailed reports every eight days on conditions in Silesia, he then decided that his minister should travel to Berlin once a year to coordinate his commercial policies with the General Directory. More serious was the king's decision to establish a separate administration over the Silesian county of Glatz, a decision that worried Münchow greatly despite the fact that the ubiquitous cabinet secretary Eichel told him not to "take it to heart." Finally, Frederick threatened to dock his salary and even to cashier him from the service if his reports were not improved and if he tried to institute new taxes without permission.[14] Despite such difficulties, Frederick allowed his Silesian minister to run the province with a minimum of interference.

If the first phase of the Prussian administrative history of Silesia, that which ended with the elevation of Münchow to the post of minister, was due to pressing military requirements as interpreted by Frederick, the second phase, the consolidation of Münchow in power

13. Ibid., 8: 134–35, 664–65; 6: 2. 453–54. Hintze, *AB*, 6: 1. 287–88.
14. *AB*, 6: 2. 498–502, 647–48; 7: 277–79; 8: 52–54.

was to be due primarily to the enterprising and astute planning of this remarkable official. Besides establishing his independence from the General Directory, he had also begun to establish a loyal group of subordinates, the councillors and directors of the two boards, who would increasingly consider themselves the privileged and unfettered members of the Prussian bureaucracy. Some of these subordinates were quite able and they as well as others who joined the boards at Breslau and Glogau later looked to one man, Münchow, as the dispenser of rewards and punishments rather than to the General Directory or even the king. The ramifications of this empire-building activity of Münchow will appear later.

Münchow Secures Clerical and Aristocratic Support

Although Münchow had secured the support of Frederick as well as the loyalty of his subordinates, he could not yet claim success in achieving his goal of near absolute political authority within Silesia. He had to contend with the Silesian landed nobility, the Catholic hierarchy and with the Prussian Department of Justice headed by Cocceji. Both the landed nobility and the Catholic hierarchy profited from a prolonged conflict between Münchow and Cocceji.

Frederick, while professing his approval of the church's spiritual mission, had no intention of granting it political power. Both Cocceji and Münchow hoped to subordinate the clergy, but differed on whether they should come under the judiciary or under the provincial government. Knowing that the cardinal bishop, von Sinzendorff, was in ill health and could not be expected to live long, Münchow began to look for a suitable successor for the diocese of Breslau. Before Cocceji realized what was happening, the Silesian minister found a pliant cleric, the Count von Schaffgotsch, and began to carry on an intrigue with him and with the cardinal bishop, promising to forward their respective careers. Both clerics were ambitious and worldly minded; Schaffgotsch was made coadjutor bishop of Breslau with the connivance of Sinzendorff and Münchow despite papal and internal ecclesiastical opposition. Sinzendorff was rewarded by the bestowal of the Order of the Black Eagle by Frederick and vague promises that he would be made vicar general of all Catholics in the realm. This interesting development came about only after the clergy of the cathedral chapter were browbeaten by the Silesian minister and when the pope finally, and reluctantly, agreed.[15] The foundations were thus laid for effective and long-standing cooperation between the ecclesiastical and administrative chapters of Silesia; Münchow, not Cocceji, won.

Until the Prussian State had secured an effective working arrangement with the nobility, Silesia would remain a mere appendage to the realm. Frederick understood the nature of this problem as fully as Münchow, but differed with him in believing that a policy of repression consisting of the abolition of the *Ständesstaat* associations and the introduction of an officially directed *Landrat* system would in the long run effectively reduce the nobility to obedience. Although Frederick prohibited the election of land elders by the nobility and gave Münchow authority to appoint all *Landräte* in their places,[16] the Silesian minister discovered that the aristocracy soon found ways to preserve its privileges in spite of repressive policies.

Eventually Münchow found that he could enhance his own prestige and authority within the province most effectively by cooperating with the Silesian landed nobility rather than by chastising them. He discovered that in order to secure this alliance he had to battle continuously against the provincial courts, and, ultimately, against Cocceji, who wished to control the courts and possibly the nobility also. Thus the Silesian aristocracy found itself in the flattering position of being courted by two importunate suitors.

When Cocceji and Arnim arrived in the province in 1742 to estab-

15. *PKPSA*, 10: 104, 225, 276–77, 279, 286, 296–98, 303–4, 316–19, 336, 394. Francis Hanus, *Church and State in Silesia, 1740–1786* (Washington, D.C., 1944), pp. 126–60. Hanus is vague about the Schaffgotsch Affair. See note 14 above. Frederick stated: "The Holy Ghost and I have resolved together that the prelate Schaffgotsch will be elected coadjutor of Breslau" (*PKPA*, 10: 398–99). Cocceji, with ideas similar to those of Münchow, was excluded from participation in this affair.

16. *AB*, 6: 2. 223–33, 259–63. Frederick William I had followed a similar policy in East Prussia earlier. See E. Spiro, *Gravamina*, pp. 1–67.

lish superior courts, Münchow defended the judicial privileges of the aristocracy and accused the outside jurists of trying to impede the administration of justice by engaging in a bitter jurisdictional conflict with the Silesian boards. Frederick, adopting Münchow's view, castigated Cocceji for allowing "inefficient strife and paper exchanges"[17] and ordered him to prepare a jurisdictional agreement with Münchow and with Reinhardt. Cocceji did obtain the cooperation of the Silesian minister, however, and the resultant judicial edict was described by Münchow: "This will completely upset the nobility of the country."[18] In fact, Cocceji was forced to allow the Silesian boards to have considerable representation on courts involving the nobility: the Silesian bureaucracy had achieved a triumph it would never achieve thereafter when the total reformation of the judiciary was undertaken. Münchow obtained royal recognition and new respect from many quarters because of the astute role he played in negotiation with the wily chancellor of justice.[19]

The intrepid nature of Münchow's personality continued to be evident in later conflicts with Cocceji; always seizing the initiative, risking his favor with the king, the Silesian minister continued to build his career. In order to obtain the permanent support of the nobility he determined to discredit the superior courts established by Cocceji and to establish courts subservient to himself and independent of the Prussian Department of Justice. In the process of pushing these two endeavors he took pains to assure the aristocracy that he was their one true friend and protector. He first convinced Frederick that the new courts were incompetent by showing that the Glogau tribunal was rent with internal jealousies. Cocceji, sent to investigate by the king, found himself engaged in a perpetual debating match with the Silesian minister, in which he had to defend the prerogatives of an independent judiciary. But Frederick eventually supported Münchow when he permitted the establishment of a new superior court at Oppeln, which would be staffed by Silesian aristocrats and supervised

17. *AB*, 6: 2. 250–56, 271–76, 287–90, 290–96, 306–7, 382–384.
18. Ibid., pp. 397–98.
19. Ibid., pp. 402, 397 ff.

by the provincial government. The most significant aspect of this affair was Münchow's report to Frederick that the estates would "cooperate" in the establishment of the court; the cornerstone of the Silesian power structure planned by Münchow had been laid. Münchow convinced the nobility that he would be a more indulgent master than Cocceji, and as a result of his success was able to increase their taxes and thus to increase the annual revenues from the province.[20]

Frederick called a halt to this fascinating story of power aggrandizement in 1748 and Münchow had to rest content with his previously hard-won laurels until his death in 1753. The redoubtable Cocceji entered the lists again in 1748, but this time he succeeded in reversing the judicial balance of power. The chancellor of justice, now at the height of his power and influence with the king, told Münchow that he intended to suggest changes in the legal codes that affected the Silesian bureaucracy and advised his old enemy to cooperate. Seeing the writing on the wall, Münchow signed a jurisdictional agreement and stood by while Cocceji set out to destroy the Oppeln court. Despite the intervention of the Silesian minister the president of the court was cashiered for corruption on evidence discovered by the *Fiscal* Gloxin. Satisfied with finding evidence of "abominable disorder" in the Oppeln court, Cocceji proceeded to clean out the entire Silesian judiciary and to bring it under rigid central control independent of the provincial government.[21]

Partial Subordination of Local Government

Frederick hoped to destroy the old, semifeudal, local governments

20. Ibid., pp. 515–17. *PKPA*, 2: 197. *AB*, 6: 2. 430–34, 542, 921–23. Frederick's *Political Testament* of 1752 states that the fixed revenues in that year amounted to 3,400,000 talers from Silesia and 8,750,000 talers from all of the other provinces combined. *AB*, 9: 342.

21. Ibid., 6: 2. 859–60; 7: 24–26, 188–192, 501; 8: 35, 38–39, 134–35, 327, 807–34. Wolfgang Leesch, "Die Einführung der Commissarii perpetue (Justizräte) in Schlesien im Zuge der Coccejischen Justizreform," *Forschungen zur brandenburgischen und preussischen Geschichte* 54 (1943): 382–90. *AB*, 8: 759–60; 9: 1–30, 38–39.

in Silesia and to replace them with subagencies of the Prussian type. As a first step he decreed that the locally selected *Bürgermeister* and land elders would be replaced by his own appointees. But the new *Steuerräte* and *Landräte* had to work with subordinate officials and had to elicit the cooperation of aristocratic landlords and the leading merchants and guildsmen of the towns. Therefore, Münchow found himself acting in the role of arbitrator between his master, who was determined to "Prussianize" Silesia, and the large group of powerful aristocratic landlords and municipal families which was equally determined to preserve its prerogatives and benefits.

The new province differed considerably from the rest of the Prussian realm. Legally, Silesia was divided into two feudal holdings, part belonging to the sovereign and part belonging to the Roman Catholic Church. Every inhabitant occupied some feudal position beneath the secular or ecclesiastical overlord. Some cities were still under the feudal control of the lay and ecclesiastical vassals (*Mediat* cities) while others remained directly under the Austrian (later the Prussian) bureaucracy ("excise" cities). The great vassals of the province were either important abbots, bishops, or landed aristocrats. These *Grundherren* were intermediaries between the sovereign and the feudal structure. In Silesia "The lord has vassals, the vassals a lord, and, obviously, the relationship between the two was that of negotiation between members of the feudal property (*Grundbesitz*)."[22]

Moreover, the "vassals" often possessed long-standing privileges, charters, and benefices which encouraged them to act semiautonomously. In Breslau, a *Mediat* city, the leading members of the wool merchants' guild and other guilds dominated municipal administration and local trade commissions. Over the course of centuries the merchants had established strong trading relationships with Saxony, apparently without serious interference from the Austrian authorities. A considerable number of aristocrats, possessing large *latifundii* (market type farms worked by gangs of serfs as entities), naturally

22. Günther Dessmann, *Geschichte der schlesischen Agrarverfassung* (Strassburg, 1904), pp. 2–20. Johannes Ziekursch, *Städteverwaltung*, pp. 79–90. *AB*, 6:2. 233–47, 263–69

wished to retain their important local privileges. Finally, peasants in many areas were fairly well organized and quite determined to protect and to enhance their rights.[23]

Münchow was not confident about the desirability of working with the original municipal officials; he condemned them for "their incapacity and brutal deportment." The seven new *Steuerräte* of the Breslau board, all Prussians, found it difficult to work with the locally selected *Bürgermeister*. In an effort to improve the poor record of his *Steuerräte*, Münchow required them to spend three or more days a year in each town in order to check the accounts. But these officials were only able to establish authority in the 130 "excise" cities since the *Mediat* cities remained under a vassal or *Grundherr*. Münchow strengthened his subordinates' hands by giving them authority to appoint local officials in the "excise" cities, but allowed the *Grundherren* to select their own *Bürgermeister*. Ziekursch was probably right when he indicated in his study of municipal government in Silesia that the actual authority of the *Steuerrat* was vague; his true function was to serve as a middle man between the *Bürgermeister* and the provincial boards. Not until 1751 were the *Mediat* cities threatened with loss of their rights. Cocceji established his own Prussian judicial *Bürgermeister* in these towns. Münchow, somewhat tardily, then eliminated their autonomy with the appointment of Prussian "police" *Bürgermeister*. Thus, in both "excise" and *Mediat* cities the semifeudal administrative system was gradually abolished in favor of a new, Prussian, one.[24] Münchow had not acted quickly enough to destroy local autonomy in the cities; this delay reflects his conservative view of the province as well as his desire to work with the existing local interest groups.

Although Frederick appointed Prussian *Landräte* to replace the local land elders, he and Münchow found that little was actually changed. The heart of the government in the countryside was to be found in the aristocratic properties: "The landlord as administrator

---

23. Dessmann, *Agrarverfassung*, pp. 2 ff. Schrötter, *FBPG* 10 (1898): 142–62.
24. *AB*, 9: 118–24; 10: 363, 83 ff. Ziekursch, *Städteverwaltung*, pp. 79–81, 84, 89.

of the police and courts was a little king, absolute lord in home and castle, in church and school, and in the whole village,"[25] according to Ziekursch. Since *Grundherren* and their aristocratic vassals had long appointed pastors, priests, and schoolmasters and administered local courts, the land elders had held weak positions of authority over them. The Prussian *Landräte*, in common with the *Steuerräte*, were grossly overworked and assigned to supervise large numbers of villages on rural landed property. Ziekursch claimed that the *Landräte* remained weak until 1806 because they had little authority over the landowners.

Münchow did not really push the official policy of subordination very effectively. He, perhaps, wished to continue to work with the established centers of influence and power in the province rather than to embark on a hard-fisted repression of local autonomy. Quite revealing of his attitude was a curious incident: when the first director of the Breslau board, d'Alencon, fell into heavy personal debt the aristocratically dominated estates promptly offered 2,000 talers to him. Münchow was willing to allow this "gift," but Frederick vetoed the arrangement, grumbling that he "paid my own officials." Münchow tried to secure the support of the aristocracy in other ways. He recommended that the candidate for *Landrat* nominated by the local aristocrats be approved. This time Frederick agreed, despite the fact that he had earlier stated that he alone would appoint Silesian *Landräte*. In fact, by 1749 Münchow had persuaded the king to approve locally selected *Landräte* in certain counties, as long as they were not "Austrians."[26] The Silesian minister manifested a similar regard for the rights of the powerful guilds in the cities. Throughout the rest of the reign of Frederick II successive Silesian ministers even tried to defend the peasantry from oppressive military conscription and servile burdens. The king was not interested in these pleas. Recognizing, perhaps, that the social structure of Silesia was too strong to be changed by its conquerors, Münchow very early determined to

25. Ziekursch, *Agrargeschichte*, pp. 129–30.
26. *AB*, 9: 258–59, 318–20. Münchow had earlier obtained royal permission to allow a county meeting for the Brieg election. Ibid., pp. 671 72, 683–84.

become more than just a henchman of the king entrusted with a fruitless job of repression. But one wonders about the net result of both royal "Prussianization" and ministerial accommodation; a disillusioned Prussian official commented in 1806: "Silesia is the same as it was under the Austrians."[27]

Partial Economic Integration

Frederick wished to incorporate Silesian commerce into the general Prussian economy and to funnel trade down the Oder to Stettin. The Breslau and Glogau merchants, on the other hand, had long engaged in a lucrative international trade with Poland, Saxony, and, of course, with the Austrian realm. Münchow, again caught between opposing forces, tried to discover a compromise. His efforts to obtain a guarantee from the king and from the General Directory that Silesian wool would receive preferential consideration in the realm ran into opposition from Prussian merchants who preferred the superior Spanish wool. Frederick nevertheless imposed a high tariff on foreign wool and ordered the Berlin *Lagerhaus* to "buy Silesian." Münchow was not able to stop Frederick from imposing high tariffs on the transit trade between Poland and Saxony. Also, the Austro-Prussian tariff war which developed after 1749 contributed to a general decline of Silesian wool production and its import–export trade. Surplus Silesian wool was no longer imported in great quantity into Saxony, and the Poles searched for alternate ways to transfer their livestock to central Europe. Throughout his term of office, Münchow found that the vested interests of the older Prussian provinces, the king's position of economic integration, and the established trade links of the Breslau merchants prevented him from developing a unified and cohesive commercial policy.[28]

The Prussian conquest thus had long term and unfavorable results

27. Ziekursch, *Agrargeschichte*, pp. 1–7, 119–30.
28. *AB, Handels- und Zoll*, 3: 1, 92, 96, 97, 103, 107, 111–18. Schrötter, *FBPG* 10 (1898): 142–62, 170–80, 259–60. Frederick's views are embodied in *AB*, 9: 677 ff., in the *General Instructions* to Massow.

for Silesia. Trade and urban population declined between 1740 and 1806. Ziekursch indicated that the loss of population of Breslau (from 54,774 in 1756 to 50,524 in 1780) was paralleled by a decrease in the numbers of inhabitants with "bourgeois freedoms" (*Bürgerrecht*). The annual export value of the linen trade averaged between 3 and 4 million talers between 1740 and 1769, a static position. In 1752 and 1753 a temporary price rise in the international market was reflected in an increase to 6 million. Also, it is possible that a recovery began after 1770.[29] In any event, the Prussian occupation did not result in real economic dividends for the province before 1806.

Münchow may well have been the last Silesian minister who really tried to improve the commercial and industrial sectors of the economy. Heinitz accomplished more after 1770, but he had to operate independently of the lethargic minister Hoym. Between 1742 and his death in 1753 Münchow worked diligently to develop mineral resources and earned the admiration of Frederick for his determined efforts to safeguard Silesian commerce and its textile industry. Frederick was aware of the Austrian program of economic containment of Silesia, a tariff policy which aimed to destroy the export trade of its lost province. He also suspected that the Austrian government was trying to establish new livestock and textile marketing centers which would draw trade away from Silesian cities. Finally, Münchow worked to protect the aristocratic and merchant classes by obtaining the permission of the king to establish funds from which mortgage debts of landowners and trade losses of businessmen might be partially repaid by the State.[30]

Münchow's Successors: Massow and Schlabrendorff

The premature death of Münchow in 1753 created a difficult problem. He had built up through the years a kind of psychological aura

29. Ziekursch, *Städteverwaltung*, pp. 1–20, 55–63. *AB Handels- und Zoll*, 3: 1. 571–73.

30. These accomplishments of Münchow were identified by Frederick in his *General Instructions* for Massow (Münchow's successor) in 1753 *AB, 9*: 667–79.

that sanctified his authority in the eyes of those dependent upon him, or subject to his command. His successor could not automatically inherit this charisma; he had to establish some kind of cooperative relationship with the local interest groups before his authority could be acknowledged. Unfortunately, this successor, von Massow, lacked the qualities of intelligence and diplomatic skill so necessary in this position.

Massow, a veteran bureaucrat with an undistinguished career, arrived in Silesia and suddenly acquired unaccustomed ambition and energy. By ignoring long-standing rules of bureaucratic conduct, he failed to retain the cooperation of his subordinates. He antagonized the influential clique of officials headed by Councillor von Pfuel in Breslau, for example, by telling the king that the Silesian bureaucracy was corrupt, inefficient, and rent by petty jealousies. But, more seriously, he suffered great loss of prestige and support from the king when he fired the postmaster, Hänel, for corrupt practices without ascertaining first if a successor could be found. Frederick was loath to allow Hänel to leave the province because of his intimate knowledge of the postal system. The dismissed official remained behind in Breslau to intrigue with his former colleagues.[31]

As if this unfortunate and obstinate minister had not brought enough troubles on himself, he next managed to convince Frederick that he was a rebellious and arrogant administrator. Massow protested the recruitment of peasants into the army and complained that these serfs were undergoing great hardships due to oppression by their landlords. Frederick became even more exasperated when his new minister continued to insist that the army was "draining the land" of manpower. Massow, by attacking the sacred military cow, overtly opposed the policy of his superior; his predecessor had once protested military conscription, but had sense enough to forget this problem when Frederick slapped his fingers.[32] Through this lack of tact Massow gave the impression that he was "telling" the king what

31. Ibid., pp. 664–67, 667–79. *AB*, 10, Preface by Schmoller, Hintze, and Koser, 8–9: 1–2, 32–33, 41–42, 62 ff.
32. Ibid., 10: 88–94; 7: 344.

should be done, but Frederick could not be moved by such gestures. Only Cocceji, Münchow, and a few others knew how to present proposals to the king in such a way that he felt he really made the ultimate decisions.

Massow failed to listen to the protests of the bishop of Breslau when Cocceji returned to the province to subject church property to secular judicial control. In fact, and in contrast to Münchow, he supported Cocceji. Frederick received a very poor impression of Massow when both Cocceji and the bishop, Schaffgotsch, ignored the minister in the course of their bitter conflict.[33] At the same time the disloyal lieutenant, Pfuel, began to spy on Massow; this completed the destruction of his prestige and authority. Pfuel had actually persuaded the king to allow him to engage in this activity by pleading that Massow was confused and incompetent. "My enemies have finally triumphed over me,"[34] the hapless minister reported when he sought resignation on the ground of ill health.

Fortunately for the Silesian Ministry the next appointee, in 1755, was von Schlabrendorff. At 35 he was one of the younger, university-trained bureaucrats who retained a flexibility of mind and courage. Schlabrendorff was determined to rectify the mistakes of Massow. He ordered the reinstatement of the indispensable postmaster, Hänel, but quickly obtained the transfer of the troublemaker, Pfuel, out of the province. By protesting Frederick's decision to transfer a councillor he earned the thanks of his own subordinates who believed that the bishop of Breslau had been responsible for the king's decision. The Breslau board councillors were constantly in conflict with the ecclesiastical establishment. Similarly, Schlabrendorff curried favor with his own subordinates by recommending one of them to the king for ennoblement—a flattering even though useless gesture since the king did not ennoble bourgeois bureaucrats.[35] Schlabrendorff refused to cashier an inefficient official, preferring instead to find him a job as custodian of ecclesiastical property with the bishop of Breslau. He

33. *PKPA*, 13: 395 ff.
34. Ibid., pp. 430–35. *AB*, 10: 108–10, 225–26, 309–12.
35. Ibid., pp. 336–41, 386–87, 399–402, 391–96.

did not intend to create another disgruntled Hänel. Petty as these personnel changes appear to be, they were nevertheless only miniature equivalents of the displacement of rival and high ranking courtiers around a throne when a new monarch, or other chief executive, seeks to establish his authority.

Schlabrendorff, like his predecessors, continued the difficult and frustrating conflict with the Catholic hierarchy in the province as well as with the judiciary and the landed nobility. He enjoyed the confidence of Frederick and the loyalty of his subordinates.[36] He also rescued the Silesian ministry from possible subordination to the General Directory after the disastrous career of Massow. Henceforth the General Directory was not to have an opportunity to interfere.

Novelty of the New Silesian Ministry

By 1756 the Silesian Ministry was an established organization. It had been built by the king, by successive ministers, and by the corps of officials that composed it. In origin it was Prussian, but as it developed it acquired certain unique characteristics. Its distinct personality was formed of three specific factors: integration of the Prussian civil service into the local political life, a new experiment in decentralization of monarchical authority, and a new bureaucratic professionalism.

One great achievement of Münchow was to mold his civil service to fit the political realities of Silesia. A study of his administration serves to clarify certain important questions concerning the nature of the eighteenth-century "absolute" State. This narrative of apparently petty bureaucratic, aristocratic, and ecclesiastical intrigues, replete with repulsive personal rivalries, constituted the warp and woof of politics in this authoritarian regime. In a modern parliamentary State politics is relatively open: political parties exist, politicians jockey for the support of interest groups and electoral blocs, and much of the haphazard conduct of public business is carried forth under the light of publicity. In the authoritarian State of Old Regime

36. Ibid., pp. 392–93, 396–97, 403, 451–53, 569–71. *PKPA*, 13: 700, passim.

Europe, political functions were carried on in a covert and clandestine manner. We must not assume that interest groups did not exist. Effective political authority, or power, had to be solicited by the autocrat. His authority rested on the cooperation of his nominal subordinates as well as on that of the elites that dominated social and economic life. By astute negotiation with powerful aristocratic landlords, ecclesiastical leaders, prominent businessmen, and his own lieutenants, Münchow was able to make his office important.

Frederick wondered how he could establish an administrative system in the new province that would be free of the bureaucratic evils of the Prussian government, and yet would be an effective instrument of absolutism. He eventually decided to separate it completely from the General Directory and to place it directly under his own supervision. But he had many other duties and preoccupations. Perhaps unwittingly he surrendered a degree of authority when he created the Silesian ministry. Münchow could have adopted the following courses when he took command: he could have assumed that he was nothing more than the mouthpiece of the king and proceed to act only after obtaining permission for each decision. Or, he could have assumed that he was in charge, *de facto,* and make all the decisions, being careful to keep the king informed. Both courses of action represent theoretical extremes and both would have led to disaster. Frederick did not wish to be bothered with what he called the "bagatelles," but he also wished to believe that he made the important decisions. Münchow was able to make the ministerial post the most important in the whole civil service because he defined his own limits of action realistically and courageously. His technique consisted of first seizing the initiative in recognizing a political problem; second, formulating a provisional solution for that problem; third, approaching the king for approval of his course of action. For example, he did not wait until the cardinal bishop of Breslau became so restless that he wrote directly to the king. He was in the antechambers of the episcopal palace waiting to negotiate. Münchow also made real attempts to solve the economic dilemmas of the province by supporting the wool producers and exporters and by arranging for capital investment for mining with the Berlin bankers.[37] As a result of his extremely fruitful years of service, Münchow left behind a powerful ministerial office. Monarchical authority had been decentralized.

Moreover, the creation of the new Silesian ministry constitutes the first true break with the collegial system and with the pattern of administration that had been established since the founding of the General Directory. Administration became hierarchical and more professional in concept and in execution. Unlike the board presidents of the old provinces, the Silesian minister was able, from the beginning, to select the officials he wanted from the entire civil service. He did not have to wait weeks or months for the collegial machinery of the General Directory to provide guidance on difficult economic problems, for example, but could approach the king directly with plans, estimates, and budgets. Unlike a minister of the General Directory, he could ascertain the problems of the province at first hand. Münchow used these opportunities to build a first-rate civil service. Naturally he did not have enough *Steuerräte* to effectively manage the cities; this explains his relative failure in municipal government. But his officials were encouraged to use their initiative in developing mining and other economic programs. Only in the Electoral Mark were board councillors able to exercise a similar authority. In both Silesia and the Electoral Mark the boards were constantly involved in ambitious canal and mining schemes, working hand in glove with local authorities and with Berlin entrepreneurs. For years board presidents elsewhere in the realm would complain that Silesia took the best officials, leaving mediocrities for the rest of the civil service. Heinitz, after 1770, was also able to obtain the talent he needed for his economic programs in Silesia continuing a long tradition. In short, the Silesian civil service was an elite of the Prussian bureaucracy.[38] In Silesia officials received a good training in the difficult art of negotiations with military commanders and with local

37. Lenz and Unholz, *Schickler*, pp. 73–87. Eichborn, *Soll und Haben*, pp. 14–15.

38. *AB*, 13: 660, 686–89. Lenz, *Schickler*, pp. 73–87. Eichborn, *Soll und Haben*. pp. 14–15.

interest groups. Some would use this experience elsewhere in the realm during the Seven Years' War and afterward. Münchow and Schlabrendorff also tried to reward promising officials and to encourage the development of competence.

No doubt should exist at this point regarding the importance of the Silesian ministers and of their nearly independent positions of authority. Frederick himself admitted as much when he wrote a long set of instructions to guide Massow after the death of Münchow in 1753: "Vous recevez le département de la Silésie, la plus belle place que j'aie a donner dans le civil." Naturally the king expected the holder of this "most attractive position" in the whole bureaucracy to "render an accounting of your conduct," but the details of the position would be determined by the Silesian minister himself, not the king: "I have prepared this instruction to serve as a regulation of your conduct." In tone, in language, and in organization, Frederick's *Silesian Instructions* of 1753 bore a remarkable resemblance to the *Political Testament* of 1752 which he prepared for the guidance of his own successor. Throughout the document reveals its writer's attention to the general lines of policy to be employed in economic, political, and diplomatic affairs. Frederick constantly referred to the policies instituted by Münchow and carried out by his subordinates: in fact Massow was ordered to see that these officials continued to carry out the plans of their deceased master.[39]

39. *AB*, 9: 667 ff. In order to clarify the discussion of the place of the Silesian administration in Prussia, it has been called the "king's bureaucracy" in the organizational charts which follow the appendixes. After 1772 the newly acquired West Prussian province (the Polish Corridor), was amalgamated with East Prussia under one "minister president" and seemed to be another "king's bureaucracy." Occupied Saxony between 1756 and 1763 was yet a third example of a province administered for the most part outside of the regular organization of the General Directory and directly under the king—hence the use of the term "king's bureaucracy" to describe such cases. These latter developments are discussed in subsequent chapters.

VI

THE DEMANDS

OF WAR

The involvement of a sovereign state in a prolonged war seems always to have placed enormous extraordinary burdens upon its government. To appreciate the nature of these difficulties one must constantly compare and contrast the histories of such states with one another and also contrast the routine of peacetime with the emergencies of wartime. The shadow of past wars hung over the governments of the major western European powers during the eighteenth century; indeed, the unsolved financial problems of the reign of Louis XIV played a significant role in the sequence of governmental crises in France that led to 1789. The experiments of John Law and of the South Sea Company in England, the famous funding scheme of Walpole, and other fiscal projects reflect the obvious fact that eighteenth-century governments, even the most important and prestigious, experienced great hardship in maintaining public credit through regular repayment of previously issued bonds. The fiscal acrobatics necessary for the outfitting of armies to fight new wars, of which there were many in this period, placed an additional strain upon public finance, a strain that the relatively primitive tax collecting systems could not meet. Due to the cautious foreign policy of King Frederick William I as well as to his efforts in the realms of improved tax collection and better administration, Prussia in 1740 did not carry a burden of debt for past wars. The campaigns of the War of the Austrian Succession were fought with the aid of the treasury surplus left by Frederick William I. Despite the absorption of Silesia and a diligent attention to fiscal responsibility, Frederick II could not possibly strengthen Prussia to the point where that state could fight a Seven Years' War against three powerful enemies, each of which possessed superior resources in manpower and material, without straining the fiscal system. One basic test of the effectiveness of any government is its fiscal power as reflected in the ability to raise new taxes as well as to collect old ones. The emergency demands of prolonged war therefore proved to be a new testing ground for the core bureaucracy in Prussia as headed by the General Directory. For the key to the momentous administrative changes that occurred in Prussia after 1763, we must search the history of the bureaucracy during the war as well as the various projects initiated by Frederick and others before 1756.

Two important factors must be kept in mind in trying to assess the performance of the core bureaucracy between 1756 and 1763. This organization had been conceived and constructed by the monarch of a second-rate power whose ambitions were realistic and modest. It had not very much altered in size or function by 1756. Frederick II brought Prussia onto the stage of big power politics in 1740 when he ordered the invasion of Silesia. Prussia, a state with a population not much larger than that of Holland or Sweden, was now required to play the role of the great power.

Disruption of the General Directory and the Boards during the War

For the General Directory itself, the demands it was forced to meet between 1756 and 1763 must have seemed virtually unendurable. Although Frederick had isolated himself from much of the routine work of high administration since 1748, when he took up residence in Potsdam, the ministers had been able to contact him quickly and to secure prompt decisions on problems which they forwarded to him. Frederick instinctively realized, perhaps, that he would not really have the time or energy to "keep a watchful eye" on the activities of his officials while he was concerned with the pressing and exhausting requirements of military leadership; therefore on August 24, 1756, shortly before he dispatched his army into Saxony, and thereby triggered the Seven Years' War, he issued a general order to the ministers of the General Directory in which he outlined administrative plans for the coming war. This thoughtful decree, remarkable both for its brevity and for its implications, reminded his ministers first that they were "exactly and dutifully" to comply with the *Instructions* of 1748. In addition, they were not to plan for any economic developmental projects during the war, or for any unusual change in the routine of administration.[1]

That the major thrust of this decree was to collect revenues and leave everything else in abeyance is made increasingly clear by a study of its other provisions. The treasuries were to be carefully maintained and the "revenues promptly and correctly" placed in them. In East Prussia the military commander, Field Marshall von Lehwaldt, was to have *plein pouvoir* and all authority over the monies of that province, as well as supervision of the two boards. The General Directory was specifically warned to leave East Prussian affairs alone. Regular financial reports would be submitted by the ministers to the king.[2]

General policies regarding employment and administrative personnel were mentioned and again emphasized. These did not constitute any radical break from established practice. No university students or civilian clerks were to be appointed to minor offices, only invalided soldiers. Frederick, well aware perhaps of the need to provide for the large number of invalided soldiers in the coming campaigns, mentioned that he would send to the General Directory a "specific list" of such suitable veterans from time to time. The ministers were then sternly warned, not for the first time, to keep an eye on their subordinates in order to prevent disloyalty, "corruption, and such things that might damage His Majesty." Special precautions would have to be taken to prevent the leakage of military information to the enemy through these clerks. The ministers, in reply, undertook to do their best.[3]

1. *AB*, 11: 6–9.
2. Ibid.
3. Ibid.

Frederick, as he later explained, did not intend to "be pestered with unimportant matters."[4] The General Directory, he complained, should not report "trivial" problems to him, but should take care of them itself. Included in the category of unimportant bagatelles were proposals for the promotion and placement of officials and questions regarding their salaries. Frederick again and again reminded his ministers that they could not consider important changes during the war: all policy decisions and changes in the performance of routine business were to be postponed until peace was restored.[5] Naturally the implications of this edict were not immediately apparent either to the king or to his ministers. In effect, Frederick told these veteran members of the collegial system that they would have to run the shop without close supervision from the owner–manager, who would be absent on other business.

But the collegial system, which worked on the basis of collective harmony and division of responsibility, was to prove itself sadly lacking. Any committee needs a chairman or the presence of a strong-willed usurper of the chairman's duties and functions, otherwise the equalitarian sentiments of the members tend to prevent the adoption of a straightforward course of action on a given issue. It is possible on rare occasions to secure universal agreement to a proposal without the presence of a chairman or other individual to promote and to encourage its adoption, but how important are such proposals? In the case of the General Directory after 1756 one finds that once the hand of the king was withdrawn the ministers seemed to lose the capacity of decision making and, more importantly, to lose the direct as well as the indirect and charismatic authority of the king. The committee without a chairman found that it could not effectively organize the civilian population for the demands of war. As a result,

---

4. Ibid., p. 180.
5. The key documents cited in previous notes are truly remarkable because they reveal a great lucidity in the thinking of Frederick. Doubtless he remembered how difficult it had been to direct domestic and internal affairs in the midst of the pressing demands of a military campaign. Frederick may have lacked certain warm and redeeming human traits, but he had a flexible mind and remembered to correct errors.

it lost decision-making power to other individuals and groups. Several perplexing problems impeded the performance of these ministers: the personalities and influence of the ministers themselves, the need for quick and competent handling of financial matters, the establishment of militia organizations in the provinces, and, finally, the flagging morale of the hardpressed civil service in the provinces. The General Directory possessed an opportunity to justify the collegial system in this crisis, but this agency and the administrative organization of which it was a part had been constructed during the peaceful years of Frederick William I in order to govern a second-rate European power under routine conditions. The collegial system was simply not flexible enough to change its ways sufficiently to handle the demands of war.

Concerning the ministers themselves, one notes that they were all veterans of the system of Frederick William I. During the course of the war almost all of these officials who collectively formed the General Directory in 1756 died. These gentlemen had faced the sometimes uncomfortable administrative changes that Frederick had instituted during the first half of his reign, and, when they died, the last remnant of the executive leadership developed by Frederick William I died with them. Adam von Viereck, the disgruntled aristocrat who had suffered defeat at the hands of Cocceji in the great judicial reorganization, died in July, 1758 and left his duties in the charge of a colleague, Reuss. Happe, who found that he could not establish the sixth, or military provisioning, department independently of his colleagues in 1746, died on July 2, 1760. The influential Blumenthal, who maintained until the end a tight grasp on the administration of East Prussia from which he came, died on December 4, 1760. The former bourgeois, Boden, perhaps the most able of this group but a man aged and tired after 1756, died on March 11, 1762. Katt, a successor to Happe in the Military Auxiliary Department, died on December 4, 1760. His duties had been taken over previously by the Silesian minister, the Saxon minister and other members of the General Directory even before his death. The postmaster, Gotter, of whom little is known, died on May 28, 1762. By the summer of 1762 only three ministers remained: Reuss, who was a jurist with one foot in the General Directory and the other in the Department of Justice; Borcke, the disgraced former head of the Saxon Field Commissariat; and a former general, von Wedell, who had been appointed by Frederick to succeed Katt.[6]

When these veterans departed, their duties were taken over by second-echelon officials until the end of the war, in accordance with Frederick's desire to postpone important appointments. One onerous responsibility of Boden, the supervision of the central treasuries, was assumed by his subordinate, Privy Councillor Köppen. Another privy councillor, Hagen, assumed seat and voice in the Directory as chief of the second department on December 29, 1760. To the sixth department, Frederick appointed General Wedell, the only man raised to ministerial rank by the king during the war. Between 1756 and 1762 certain duties of the General Directory came to assume greater and greater importance while others seemed to diminish, at least temporarily. Köppen, a competent accountant and a completely loyal official, had been sending reports direct to the king from Berlin, showing income from taxes and disbursements from the treasury. Besides this financial supervision, the importance of which can not be overstated, the supervision of military auxiliary services, of forage, horse procurement, etc., rapidly became a major concern. It is safe to say that by 1762 military auxiliary administration and the collection of revenue for military expenditures were the two primary functions of the General Directory.[7] This development was temporary but it served to illustrate most graphically the central pillars of the Prussian political order: taxation and the army.

In key areas of wartime administration the General Directory was, from the beginning, forced to share responsibility with others. Frederick began the process in August, 1756 when he first issued orders for the coming invasion of Saxony. Privy Councillor Deutsch and his subordinates were dispatched to the conquered state several months

6. *AB*, 11: 584; 12: 282, 295–96, 315, 318, 325, 336, 446, 448.
7. The best account of Köppen's role during the war is by Reinhold Koser, "Die preussischen Finanzen im siebenjährigen Kriege," *FRPG* 13 (1900): 340–51.

later in accordance with the August decrees in order to establish a
field commissariat. In addition, Minister Borcke was ordered to head
the entire Saxon civil service and to harness it to the demands of the
Prussian army and its supply system. Both Borcke and Deutsch
worked directly under Frederick and independently of the General
Directory. Deutsch possessed extensive experience with the military
warehouse system which had been built up in the provinces of the
realm before 1756 and used this background to advantage in Saxony.
Similarly, the Silesian minister Schlabrendorff cooperated with the
army in the establishment of a Silesian Military Commissariat. The
major campaigns were fought for the most part in either Saxony or
Silesia; so the importance of these two field commissariats cannot be
overemphasized. Minister Katt, as head of the sixth department of
the General Directory, was supposed to have some kind of general
direction over these commissariats but the administrative orders and
the subsequent correspondence of Deutsch, Borcke, and Schlabrendorff leave no doubt that the role of the sixth department was largely
illusory. Perhaps Frederick felt that Katt should be replaced by an
individual strong enough to coordinate all supply services. In any
event he appointed General Wedell and this masterful personality
forthwith ordered his fellow ministers to submit all reports to him
concerning the supply system, and to obey his directions in every
particular. His colleagues in the General Directory protested this
breach of etiquette and of the collegial system, but Wedell had ex-
plicit instructions from the king. 1762 thus marks the emergence of a
separate and distinct department in the General Directory and the
new sixth department that emerged under Wedell's leadership was
merely a preview of the administrative reorganization that was to
occur after 1763.[8]

Frederick II and his father had been preoccupied for years with the
problem of obtaining sufficient grain to store against the needs of

8. Merseburg. Gen. Dir., Mil. Dept., 2, pp. 2–27. The documents in this file,
of which only a few have been reproduced in the *Acta Borussica*, illustrate clearly
the masterful way Wedell obtained supreme control over military auxiliary
services in 1761.

military campaigning. To most eighteenth-century generals and their superiors it seemed impossible that an army in the field could exist without dependence upon a system which would ensure that food for men and animals was forwarded quickly and safely and in sufficient quantity. Despite his lack of success with the fifth department, Frederick felt in 1746 that he could provide this supply system adequately through the establishment of a new department, the sixth, in the General Directory. Unfortunately, the first minister, Happe, and his successor, Katt, both discovered that their ministerial colleagues would not cooperate. In fact, the old-line ministers remembered that military provisioning had previously been an additional duty of the second department and continued to bypass the new department on numerous occasions. Frederick placed the Silesian magazines under Münchow and, in 1749, appointed a general, Retzow, to take charge of the military granaries in the rest of the realm. On the credit side, one must note that Katt was able to complete about fourteen granaries throughout the realm, but this total was only sufficient to maintain the army in the field for a campaign and not enough to provide for the adjustment of the market price of grain during peace time. Some writers, including August Skalweit, have maintained that this infant price regulatory system worked on occasion, but they are forced to admit that the government sales and purchases of grain were not sufficient radically to control the market. In the face of ministerial opposition, the ignorance of the king of the realities of bureaucratic power politics, the fact that the Silesian minister, the army itself, and the second department continued to operate independently, the sixth department had not developed into a strong agency before the Seven Years' War.[9] The magnitude of the task of

---

9. Hintze, *AB*, 6:1 162–63. *AB*, *Getreidehandelpolitik*, 3: 184, 319–23, 327–28, 351, 354–55, 369–70, 385 ff., 391–92, 399 ff. According to Naude and Skalweit, *AB*, *Getreidehandelpolitik*, 3: 190, Frederick was unhappy about the flow of supplies during the Silesian campaigns. Hintze, *AB*, 6:1. 164, speculates on the rivalry of von Happe and von Boden. *AB*, *Getreidehandelpolitik*, 3: 188–92, 405–10, 429, 437–38, 444–46, 448, 459–60, 474–79, 485–89, 496, 500–4, 507–8. *AB*, 7: 21–23, 107–8, 158, 557–58, 562, 578–79, gives the *Revised Instructions* establishing the sixth department. Von Katt was given extensive authority on

grain price regulation also limited the effectiveness of the sixth department.

Nevertheless the other departments of the General Directory still possessed authority over the provinces of the realm exclusive of Silesia and the newly conquered Saxony and so in theory continued as keystones of the Prussian administrative system. But success in wartime demanded increased coordination of work between these departments as well as a closer grasp by them of the administration of the provinces. Unfortunately, in neither the area of interministerial cooperation nor in the area of provincial administration was the General Directory able to compile an outstanding record of success. Perhaps the key to this dual failure lay in the organization itself; perhaps the General Directory was impeded by the presence of built-in enervating devices.

During the war the old-guard ministers continued, if in steadily decreasing numbers, to staff the General Directory. They discovered that Frederick was too preoccupied to pay much attention to them and that the provincial boards would or could not always respond quickly to their orders. The routine of work was constantly broken by the necessity to prepare some emergency operation to handle a sudden wartime demand. A great deal of time had to be expended by these ministers in reminding the boards to forward tax receipts and reports, and often their sessions would be occupied with discussion concerning the best means of packing their own records and safeguarding the central treasuries in case of enemy threat to Berlin. Boden in 1757 and 1758 had to oversee the shipment of all these treasuries to Magdeburg, and later their return to Berlin.[10] When Blumenthal sent a pessimistic report to Frederick in December, 1758 relating the Russian occupation of East Prussia, the king, pathetically and without any of his usual cynicism, entreated him not to write about the horrors of enemy occupation because that caused him "much un-

---

paper over grain storage and allocation as well as market regulation but would have to consult with others in cases "which might encroach upon the affairs of other departments." *AB*, 7: 594 ff.; 8: 639 ff. 670, 732; 9: 30.

10. Ibid., 11: 404, 469–70. See introductory chapters.

happiness and discouragement." Blumenthal should write only details of troop movements and other useful information, and should send such reports to General von Dohna.[11] The relationship of Frederick to his ministers can be further illuminated by his reaction to what he considered to be unwarranted interference by the ministers with other departments and agencies. Perhaps Boden's colleagues were only too happy to escape the notice of the king, especially when that harassed minister was accused by Frederick of "jealousy" concerning the Silesian minister Schlabrendorff in the early months of the war. In this case Frederick wanted to emphasize the independence of Silesia from the General Directory in military supply matters as well as in routine administration. In 1759 Boden, pressed by an enormous workload, was late in submitting reports, and Frederick took time to accuse him of "caprice . . . jealousy . . . frivolous chicanery," and to restate a familiar theme: "You should know full well that I will have diligent workers and that my service must be observed with exactitude and application, and also with promptness and that all passion, jealousy, intrigues, chicanery, and private affairs must absolutely be placed aside."[12] The king expected his ministers to work without constant supervision and to avoid bickering and inefficiency.

The work of the General Directory suffered from an additional and more subtle cause: the cessation of salary payments to civil servants during the war. This action, necessitated by a fiscal emergency, probably caused deterioration in the *esprit de corps* of the bureaucracy at large. Contrary to the impression of Walter Dorn, the cancellation of salaries was not accepted cheerfully and patriotically by officials, regardless of their rank or social position. This extraordinary action was not taken until October, 1757, however, when the financial resources of the Prussian state appeared to be dwindling rapidly. The Cabinet Order of September 30, 1757 suspended all salaries and

11. Ibid., p. 649. Xaver von Hassenkamp, "Ostpreussen unter dem Doppelaar," *Neuen preussischen Provinzial-Blätter*, 3rd ser. 9 (1866): 371–72, reprints a similar letter of Frederick to Minister von Lesgewang.
12. *AB*, 12: 374, 63–65; 11: 9–11, 180.

pensions for civil servants and jurists. Only diplomatic personnel in foreign stations were exempted from the provisions of the decree. When the General Directory forwarded this news to the provincial boards it was greeted by a doleful chorus of sighs, complaints, and, probably, unrecorded curses. Some provincial presidents retorted that lower ranking officials depended upon their salaries for subsistence: "It is impossible in the present costly times for their families and themselves to live."[13] Soon both provincial officials and ministers of the General Directory became convinced that if humble clerks and porters were not paid by the State they would be paid by others, in the form of bribes. Officials claimed that they would be left in the "hands of Jews," because of the necessity for raising personal funds. In 1757 the ministers announced that "the General Directory has devised a formula for salary receipts which should serve during the period of suspension of salary payments,"[14] but of course these promissory notes, *Kassenscheine*, were not accepted by merchants at par when issued. Difficulties with this scheme finally forced the ministers of the General Directory to write a rather defiant note to Frederick, in which they claimed that the government, by 1758, had lost more through declining excise collections than had been gained by the suspension. Excise collectors were, in fact, bribed. Frederick wrote back to Boden: "I know all this myself, but I have no means with which to pay people."[15] The meager resources of the government allowed resumption of partial salaries to the lowest ranking subalterns in the service, but the rest had to be content with the promissory notes. Undoubtedly, the salary suspension scheme destroyed a great part of the *esprit de corps* of all officials and made the work of the General Directory more difficult.

The decline of the authority and prestige of the General Directory was also due to unavoidable military developments over which the ministers had no control. The fortunes of war included the salary suspension scheme, the various occupations of Berlin by the Russians,

13. Ibid., 11: 350–51. Dorn, "Prussian Bureaucracy."
14. *AB*, 11: 387–88, 636.
15. Ibid., pp. 461–62; 12: 19, 79 ff., 461.

and the departure of the king from the immediate vicinity of the city. But the ministers suffered to an even greater extent when the routine lines of communication and control between Berlin and the provinces were cut by military action. From almost the beginning of the war, and certainly since the defeat of the Hanoverian troops of the duke of Cumberland, the western provinces of the realm were geographically isolated and subjected to periodic occupation by the enemy, and the loss of East Prussia to the Russians by 1758 removed this province from the purview of the General Directory.[16] Silesia continued to be administered by Schlabrendorff, who disregarded the General Directory. Occupied Saxony was immediately, in 1756, placed under a separate and martial administration. Only the central provinces of the realm remained under the authority of the General Directory after February, 1758 since the western enclaves including Cleves and East Frisia could not be considered safely held by Prussia or by her allies. The preoccupation of Frederick with more urgent matters, various war time hardships, the declining morale of the civil service, and finally, the constant interruption of bureaucratic routine by enemy invasion of Pomerania, the New Mark, and the Electoral Mark, all contributed to the weakening of the authority of the General Directory. Apparently, no one felt that such a decline was anything more than temporary.

East Prussia, Saxony, and Silesia during the War

During the first two years of the war, Frederick developed a "heartland" geopolitical theory: the central provinces, especially the Electoral Mark, Silesia, and Saxony had to be preserved under Prussian control or the realm itself stood in danger of complete disintegration.[17] He drew up plans for the defense of East Prussia as early

16. *Oeuvres Posthumes de Frédéric II, Roi de Prusse* (Berlin, 1788), 3: 84 ff. Frederick's account of his campaigns reveals how involved he was with military problems to the exclusion of all else.

17. *AB*, 9: 361: "Les Clévois sont des imbéciles, confus et engendrés dans l'ivresse de leurs pères, qui n'ont ni des talents naturels ni de l'acquis." This statement aptly describes Frederick's belief that Cleves could be abandoned with

as 1754. Field Marshall Lehwaldt, his commander in that province, first tried to remove all peasants and their livestock from the border regions, but the Königsberg board and the provincial Superior Court opposed this scheme. Such a monumental population transfer was entirely outside the experience of both bureaucrats and jurists. The court especially defended the interests of landlords who felt threatened by the loss of their labor force. Lehwaldt, frustrated, devised an alternative scheme which called for the formation of a home defense force, a militia, to patrol the border forests. Again, the board and the court opposed him, claiming that harvest labor requirements and the organization of labor on the domains and on private holdings would be adversely affected. When the General Directory refused to take a definite stand Lehwaldt was left without any bureaucratic support. The province fell permanently into the hands of the Russians in January 1758. This conflict between the civil and military authorities was not the only reason for Prussian defeat: Lehwaldt was probably incompetent as a military commander.[18] The East Prussian estates pursued their customary policy of obstruction and mirrored a widespread indifference of the provincial society to the fate of the Prussian monarchy.[19]

Although East Prussia remained under Russian control from January, 1758 to June, 1762, Cleves and the other western enclaves suffered from only intermittent enemy occupation. But the wartime administration of both areas may have provided valuable lessons for postwar reforms. Prussian officials who remained at their posts were usually forced to take oaths of allegiance to the occupying powers. In the most lenient situation, Cleves, they actually argued with the Austrian commander before consenting to take the oath: "To Her

little loss to his State. Koser, *Friedrichs*, 3: 55 ff., discusses the abortive negotiations of 1759–60, in which Frederick tried to use Cleves as a peace pawn.

18. Hassenkamp, "Doppelaar," 6 (1860): 47–83, 107, 143, 218–50. Ibid., 7 (1861): 56–67, 361 ff. Franz Schwarz, "Organisation und Verpflegung der preussischen Landmilizen im siebenjährigen Kriege," *Staats und Sozialwissenschaftliche Forschungen* 7 (Leipzig, 1888): 160–71. *AB*, 11: 131–35, 176, 178–80, 191–94, 208–221, 223–24, 284–86, 305–9.

19. Ibid., pp. 142–51.

Majesty's [Maria Theresa's] ordained administration in the conquered Royal Prussian Lands."[20] But the Russians in East Prussia, and Frederick in Saxony forced officials to serve the ruler of the occupying power with "life and soul."[21] Regardless of such oaths, the occupying powers, backed by military force, not only speedily organized administrative systems, but made these frankly exploitive in order to milk as much material, forage, etc., as possible from enemy possessions. Frederick was able to accomplish more, perhaps, because he possessed a trained bureaucracy with Silesian experience. The Russians, French, and Austrians lacked such assistance.

The seizure of Saxony was the result of more careful planning than the earlier seizure of Silesia.[22] Frederick, after briefing Minister von Borcke of the General Directory on August 21, 1756, launched the attack on Saxony. Borcke and his able subordinate, Privy Councillor Deutsch, established offices in the conquered towns, obtained control of local treasuries, and forcibly enrolled Saxon officials under the Prussian banner. Borcke evidently felt that the occupied state should be administered with consideration for the rights of its inhabitants; Frederick, however, eagerly demanded the collection of eight million talers within four months! After fruitless negotiations with the Saxon estates Borcke was forced to report failure. His master was completely ruthless: "It is a bagatelle: the French pare much more from my provinces." Finally, Frederick bluntly announced that his requisition would be met and ordered Borcke to consider "Saxony as a conquered land."[23] Borcke complained of this policy of exploitation to Eichel, the king's secretary: "How long will a candle

---

20. Ibid., p. 381
21. Hassenkamp, "Doppelaar," 9: 374.
22. Georg Küntzel and Martin Hass, *Die politische Testamente der Hohenzollern* (Berlin, 1919), 2: 58–59. As the editors of this collection remark (p. 59), Frederick became even more interested in the "fate" of Poland in the *Political Testament* of 1768.
23. *AB*, 11: 5–6, 20–24, 33–34. *Politische Correspondenz Friedrichs des Grossen*, 13: 443, 459. Curt Jany, *Geschichte der Königlichen preussischen Armee bis zum Jahre 1807* (Berlin, 1929), 2: 361–74. *AB*, 11: 77–79, 118–19, 62–65, 78–79, 88–90, 425–26, 487.

burn if it is lighted at both ends?"[24] At least one-third of the total cost of the entire war (125 to 140 million talers), was paid from the Saxon receipts.[25]

At this point one can compare this administrative system with those instituted by the Russians in East Prussia and by the French and Austrians in the western enclaves. In all cases the occupation governments established ruthless regimes dedicated to exploitation of the conquered. Peacetime concepts of the human responsibilities of government were shoved aside. Obviously the enemies watched each other, and when Russia threatened to confiscate the property of those Prussian officials in East Prussia who refused to cooperate, Frederick retaliated with a similar edict in Saxony. Earlier we have seen how Frederick considered himself able to take money from Saxony: "It is a bagatelle: the French pare much more from my provinces." Of course, the most remarkable statement one can make concerning the Prussian occupation of Saxony was that it was an astonishing success. It was anticipated. Trained officials were dispatched to supervise it, and the total commissary workload was given to two trusted men, to Borcke the Saxon military directorate and to Deutsch the Saxon commissariat. These two officials worked fairly well together, although Borcke denied this, and, after the removal of Borcke in 1759 and the death of Deutsch in 1760, Zinnow was given charge of the total administration. The lessons were fairly clear. The Prussians obtained more from Saxony than did their enemies from their occupied provinces because they were better organized, and precisely because the whole endeavor was placed under the direct control of experienced bureaucrats and not, as was the case with the Russians or the French, under the rather inept control of a constantly changing number of aristocratic military officers. The Prussian army was given its sphere to be sure—the defense of the province at all

24. Ibid., p. 651.
25. Koser, "Preussische Finanzen," p. 371. According to de Katt Frederick admitted that his policy in regard to Saxony had been "severe . . . but if these people had been quieter, if they had not taken it into their heads to inform you the enemy of my business, I should not have demanded so much, I assure you" (*Memoirs of Henri de Katt*, tr. F. S. Flint [London, 1929], 1: 57; 2: 230)

costs—but it was not allowed to bulldoze the administrators. Apparently, then, the Prussian administrative system received its supreme vindication in Saxony and the General Directory could look with satisfaction upon the work accomplished there. But the Saxon administration was set up separately from the General Directory even before the war and seemed to resemble the independent Silesian system more than that of the rest of the realm. Significantly, when Frederick became disgusted with Borcke, he was returned to what might be considered to be a backwater of the bureaucracy: Berlin and the General Directory. As the gossipy courtier, von Lehndorff, was to state, Borcke's day of glory as a potentate had ended. It was Lehndorff who also casually remarked that the Silesian minister Schlabrendorff was another "potentate" who seemed to run his province independently of Berlin.[26] Therein lies the final key to the puzzle: Saxony was administered so well and exploited so fully, in contrast to the occupation area of Prussia's enemies, because Silesia provided a previous record of success, and Borcke and Zinnow could look eastward to find precedents.

Saxony was not, of course, merely a repetition of Silesia in terms of administrative systems. Although patterned after that remarkable apparatus of political power erected by Münchow and perfected by Schlabrendorff, the Saxon administration quickly became a pure instrument of exploitation because of the precarious situation of Prussia in the war. Shortly after his transfer back to Berlin, Borcke prepared a memorandum detailing his experiences in Saxony in which he exposed the dual nature of his administrative system. Originally, he claimed, Frederick had instructed him to treat the inhabitants well and he had thus abolished a much hated per capita tax soon after he arrived. But Borcke also realized that Frederick deliberately desired to exploit Saxony and that the Austrians and Russians would make strenuous efforts to snatch that prize from Prussian hands. The severe limits to any conciliatory policy towards the Saxons were not immediately apparent. But quickly he saw that he had to support the

26. E. A. H. von Lehndorff, *Dreissig Jahre am Hofe Friedrichs des Grossen* (Gotha, 1907), p. 416.

Prussian military effort to an ever-increasing extent, while on the other hand, he found that the increasing severity of exploitation as well as wartime destruction just steadily decreased the Saxon ability to contribute. Caught in this predicament and constantly aware of dangerous and destructive enemy forays, Borcke had no choice but to abandon his half-formed policy of leniency and fair government. Of course, he had to face a number of other difficulties, "the poor quality officials" given him by other Prussian boards in the beginning, poor harvests, the devious manipulations of "grain Jews," which caused inflation, the increasing number of bankruptcies of mercantile houses, and, finally, "the faulty establishment of the original Saxon Directory."[27] In other words, he had not known at the start how to orient his administration, whether towards the Silesian example or towards some ruthless exploitative system.

Borcke also made some valuable suggestions concerning the nature of his administration, ideas that could be used in the future in similar cases. The Prussian army soon began to expropriate grain and forage in 1757. "This action opened the eyes of the Saxons and since that time they have hidden their assets from the authorities and bought what they needed secretly."[28] Arbitrary requisitions undermined the effectiveness of civil governments; this was the plain lesson to be learned in this instance. The dual administration of the government by Borcke and by Deutsch created overlapping jurisdictions and administrative confusion. Deutsch, he claimed, would not cooperate with him. The second lesson was that provinces can best be administered by one agency with one head rather than by several. This example served to illustrate one major weakness of the collegial system. Finally, he stated that the administrative confusion allowed Saxon subordinates to sneak aid to their exiled king and encouraged local officials to falsify reports and to collaborate with Austrian agents. When an occupying regime attempts to browbeat lower ranking civil servants who had long served other masters administrative efficiency suffers. A civil service is only as efficient as its lowly

27. *AB*, 12: 204. Schrötter, *AB Münzpolitik*, 3: 33.
28. *AB*, 12: 204–8.

members permit it to be. If *esprit de corps* is lacking and if the superiors are out of touch with local conditions or unsympathetic to them, the local officials cannot and will not perform with complete loyalty.

When one turns to the wartime administration of Silesia, a great contrast to the Saxon administration becomes obvious. The Silesian minister throughout the war was Schlabrendorff. Frederick established a military commissariat in Silesia similar to that headed by Deutsch in Saxony. Unlike the Saxon case, however, the minister of the province always had a consultative voice in the affairs of the commissariat. In addition, Frederick continually reminded the General Directory to lend assistance to Schlabrendorff and to the commissariat.[29] Soon a harmonious working relationship developed between Privy Councillor von Beggerow, head of the commissariat, Schlabrendorff, and Marshal Schwerin, the military commander. As a result, the resources of the province were quickly mobilized to provide forage and foodstuffs for the army. After 1760 Schlabrendorff became de facto head of the commissariat upon the death of Beggerow, whose replacement, Reck, did not arrive from East Prussia until 1762.[30] Therefore bureaucratic rivalry with military authority was virtually nonexistent in Silesia, unlike the situation in East Prussia earlier, or Saxony.

Schlabrendorff also continued to control the Silesian military warehouses, as well as the supply system set up within the province to keep those magazines supplied with grain. In 1759 this system consisted, in part, of regular supply convoys which were dispatched under guard to the central warehouses of Glogau. All *Landräte* were made responsible for the periodic shipment of grain from their counties. When the Austrian and Russian troops came into Silesia, attempts were made by Prussian authorities to clean out their storage places before the enemy arrived. Schlabrendorff corresponded directly with Prince Henry and the other military commanders concerning these matters. Upon urging by Frederick, the Silesian minister also

29. Ibid., 11: 536–37; 12: 232.
30. Ibid., 11: 1, 186–87, 231–32.

tried to keep livestock and other resources out of enemy hands. In 1760 he undertook to transport all the grain from endangered warehouses to safety and asked Frederick for 1,500 wagons.[31]

As early as the summer of 1756, Schlabrendorff had, in truth, taken over control of the entire Silesian administration and geared it for war. He cooperated with Marshal Schwerin and other military commanders and kept his officials busy collecting taxes, forage, and food grain. He tried to preserve some kind of order among the Silesian populace by defending the serfs against renewed aristocratic attempts to impose burdens on them, clamping down on the aristocrats themselves by making them pay a direct tax which amounted to 28 percent of the provincial total, and by forcing the Roman Catholic clergy to cooperate with the war effort. Frederick considered the Silesian aristocracy to be "traitorous" and the clergy, especially members of monastic orders, to be "vermin," so the imprisonment and execution of troublemakers in both camps posed no problem for Schlabrendorff. Due also to the presence of a large military contingent in the province, and to the constant danger of invasion, harsh and repressive measures were judiciously applied to keep the upper classes of Silesia quiet. Priests, for example, were forced to administer oaths to Silesian military recruits, and the clergy in general was forced to pay hundreds of thousands of talers each year to the Prussian treasury. Periodic enemy forays into the province resulted in the capture of Prussian officials, so Schlabrendorff organized an exchange commission in cooperation with the Austrians for the repatriation of these officials. Importantly, Silesia was the only province during the war where official vacancies were immediately filled. Schlabrendorff believed that all of his officials worked to capacity and insisted on the immediate appointment of replacements for his deceased subordinates.[32] In summary, his administration was the most successful marriage of martial and civil authority under Prussian auspices in the Seven Years' War.

31. Ibid., 12: 164, 169–70, 281–82.
32. Ibid., pp. 315, 386–90, 520. L.Beutin, "Die Wirkungen des Siebenjährigen Krieges auf die Volkswirtschaft in Preussen," *VSWG* 26 (1933): 216 ff. *PKPA*, 13: 644, 663, 670–74, 686–89, 690–91, 693, 696–97, 700. *AB*, 11: 337–41, 418, 444–50, 576–78, 613–14; 12: 187, 287–9.

Schlabrendorff started, of course, with many advantages not shared by board presidents elsewhere because the Silesian Administration was an independent entity and was not encumbered by many traditional administrative obstacles. Although he had to work often in close geographical proximity to Frederick, the demands of military leadership seemed always to preoccupy his imperious master, who apparently trusted the Silesian minister to an unusual degree. True, Schlabrendorff worried at times, especially when he discovered in November, 1761 that Frederick intended to quarter in Breslau for the winter. He wrote to Eichel and that friend replied: "Believe me, the Breslau quarters were selected because they were close to the warehouses." Eichel soothingly claimed that Frederick did not intend to inflict "mortification" on Schlabrendorff. The Silesian minister, still upset, protested to Frederick, but was told, mildly enough, that the winter quarters had to be established in Breslau and he was to see that the warehouses were filled with supplies for the troops.[33] This little incident pinpoints the novelty of the Silesian ministry itself. Both Frederick and Schlabrendorff seemed to realize that they were partners, although the former was definitely a very senior partner, in the administrative direction of the province. What could serve as a better example of contrast to the ordinary collegial system than this trivial, but psychologically revelatory, episode? Schlabrendorff quite evidently considered himself master in his own house and did not wish to share quarters with his monarch. Frederick, doubtless aware of the unusual services rendered by Schlabrendorff, took care to support him and not to harass him with his usual sarcastic jibes.

The administration of Silesia seemed to be more successful than that of any other part of the bureaucracy during the war. In Saxony a similar system was established, but Borcke was unable or unwilling to create quite such a remarkable power structure. Undoubtedly the exigencies of war more or less forced Frederick to demand a complete and ruthless exploitation of the conquered state. In Silesia certainly the tax bite grew larger and the complaints of landowners and serfs went unheeded most of the time, but exploitation was controlled

33. *AB*, 12: 413–16.

because that province would remain part of the realm after the war. Certainly Frederick must have hoped that Saxony would be similarly absorbed, but he probably had no illusions after the fall of East Prussia in January, 1758. Prussia would be lucky to emerge from the struggle as an independent state. Such was the pessimistic theme that emerges in his correspondence between 1758 and 1762; therefore Saxony could be milked of her resources without scruple. But in both Silesia and Saxony, military forage and auxiliary services in general were better organized and more productive than elsewhere, internal political struggles between officials and aristocrats or the municipalities were minimized, and, finally, taxes were regularly and efficiently collected as were extraordinary levies. The final proof of the superiority of the Silesian administration can be found in the fiscal balance sheets: some 18 million talers were collected during the war while the rest of the realm, excluding Saxony, contributed a total of 25 million talers. Saxony was forced to pay 48 million talers,[34] a clear indication of the harsh nature of administration there.

Thus the worst as well as the best of the provincial administrations revealed themselves in the crucible of war. In East Prussia, before 1758, squabbling between the Königsberg board, the judiciary, and the military administration prevented that province from harnessing its resources to meet the Russians. Cleves, long a source of opposition to the Prussian state, was too small and too far away to help the rest of the realm, and Frederick considered it expendable. Its administration was custodial in nature and hampered by continual enemy invasions. On the other hand, the administrative systems of Silesia and Saxony worked extremely well because these systems were geared to work in harness with the army, were unified under one or two responsible and experienced officials, and, finally, were functional in approach rather than collegial. Duties were assigned according to evident requirements of administration rather than distributed to members of a collegium as a mixed bag to each of those who had a "seat and voice" in the sessions. For example, in Saxony, Deutsch took over the commissariat and made its headquarters in Dresden,

34. Koser, "Preussische Finanzen," p. 371.

Fielder made his headquarters in Leipzig, and Borcke his in Torgau. The whole Saxon pie was sliced three ways for better exploitation. Duties were clear and responsibilities were evident. An official was in charge *de jure* and *de facto* and did not share authority with others.

The Central Provinces

The central provinces of the realm, the Electoral Mark, New Mark, Magdeburg, and Pomerania remained the responsibility of the General Directory during the war. The central provinces, although located closely enough so that the General Directory could keep an observant eye on them, nevertheless had to adapt to the demands of war. Their boards, and the councillors and presidents, had to try to meet the increased fiscal demands of the General Directory at the same time that they tried to cope with the chaos caused by enemy forays. Lacking leadership from the General Directory, the boards seemed unable to operate very effectively.

The central provinces had to learn to work in harness with the local military commanders, or even in subordination to them. Each had, for example, to concern itself with the formation and maintenance of home guard or militia units. With the onset of the war, military garrisons had been withdrawn from countless communities and with them went a certain amount of the authority of the Prussian State, with the result that militia units had to be formed to preserve law and order, and specifically, to deter irregular bands of marauders as well as the predatory cavalry of the enemy, the much feared cossacks and hussars. Pomerania provided a somewhat better example of cooperation between civilian and military authorities than East Prussia. Within the province certain officials, landowners, and other influential persons realized that the king would not be able to spare many troops to defend the province. They pessimistically anticipated a combined Swedish and Russian invasion and decided to establish a militia to provide some protection against the cossacks. Only after this grass roots movement had been organized sufficiently to recruit peasants to serve in paramilitary units did Frederick intervene. He ordered the estates and municipalities to raise money to maintain these troops, emphasizing that he could spare no funds from his own treasuries. The militia question thus became an important test of official efficiency, provincial loyalty, and grass roots political action. In effect, the inhabitants were told that the defense of their property and lives was their own responsibility. This type of emergency was bound to illuminate the degree of political education and civic spirit. Only in Pomerania, however, were the militia units formed and maintained on a large scale for an extended period of time. Initially, the board called a meeting of the Estates and persuaded the grumbling representatives of the rural landowners and of the towns to lay aside their customary antipathies towards one another and towards the government in order to support the militia. Ultimately, with the assistance of the General Directory, the countryside raised three-fifths and the municipalities two-fifths of the militia levies. From this propitious start the relationships between the board, the General Directory, the representatives of the provincial interest groups, and the military authorities proceeded in an atmosphere of collective harmony. Occasionally difficulties occurred, as when General von Bevern was appointed by Frederick without adequate consultation with the board. But Bevern very tactfully worked with the civilians, and the militia was ultimately organized under his command. This quasi-military body, which was one of the last examples of successful use of militia in the eighteenth century in Europe, kept the Swedish army at bay, actually invaded and imposed tribute on Swedish Pomerania, and provided some needed protection against enemy cavalry. But by 1761, the resources of money, men, and material were exhausted and Frederick provided relief.[35]

Overriding the militia issue everywhere was the great fiscal problem. The government never instituted new taxes or increased existing levies without prior consultation with prominent taxpayers in Prussia. Provincial board members spent many anxious months negotiating with the representatives of provincial estates where such existed,

35. Schwarz, "Organization," pp. 60–63, 28–30. Carl von Sulicki, *Der siebenjährige Krieg in Pommern und in den benachbarten Marken* (Berlin, 1867), pp. 25–27. *AB*, 11: 109–15, 641. Schwarz, "Organisation," pp. 60–87.

or with the representatives of merchants and landowners in other cases. In Pomerania, the General Directory had hoped in early 1757 that estates would contribute 25 percent of a general provincial war loan, but so bitter was the reaction of the aristocrats who dominated this body that the levy was subsequently cut from 110,000 talers to 80,000 talers. In subsequent years the war loan levies were always less than expected by the General Directory, and in 1761 the estates convened to tell the king flatly that the province could not contribute to the war effort.[36] The experience was similar in the Electoral Mark but the municipalities remained utterly uncooperative. Before 1758 the board had been able to raise only a few thousand talers for a militia force from Berlin, for example, but when the Russians occupied the city for a week it was able to provide 248,000 talers. The Electoral Mark *Landschaft*, which was a quasi-estate, flatly refused to contribute towards the war effort in a *Landtag* held in 1760. Naturally, in both provinces the damage to crops, livestock, real estate, etc., was very considerable, and tax payers felt that they possessed a genuine excuse for opposition to the demands of the king and of the General Directory. Was war damage greater in these provinces than in Silesia? From available evidence it is impossible to confirm or to deny this point. Certainly warfare raged in Silesia continually, while the central provinces suffered grievously from enemy forays. One reason why treasury balances declined in the central provinces was the decision taken by the Electoral Mark board in 1757 to set up special funds to use for the "alleviation of poor harvests" as well as for the payment of enemy contributions. But the Electoral Mark board failed in providing a standing militia of any importance, in increasing tax collections except in the cities after 1758, and in supplying enough forage, men, and material to the army after 1758. The same must be said for Magdeburg, the New Mark, and Pomerania. But the Electoral Mark was the most populated, industrial, and commercial of these provinces, except, perhaps for Magdeburg.[37] It is not enough to say that the central provinces contributed what they could

36. *AB*, 11: 109, 233, 490, 531, 632–35; 12: 334–36.
37. Schwarz, "Organisation," pp. 140–50, 96–133. *AB*, 11: 241–42, 299–301; 12: 77, 139–140, 245–7, 363–64.

in view of wartime hardships: Silesia is always the example to serve as a contrast. The mediocre performances of provincial officials must be explained in other terms.

The collective leadership of the board in provincial administration left much to be desired. The *Landräte* posed special problems which were not immediately apparent. They were barometers of aristocratic patriotism and devotion to the crown. If *Landräte* became obstinate or otherwise difficult to manage, the board knew that their peers were unhappy and rebellious. From the standpoint of both the General Directory and of the boards these officials were the most important and tangible signs of official presence in the countryside. The *Landräte* were directed over and over again to remain at their posts when the enemy came and to negotiate in order to relieve some of the hardships of the populace in their counties. But throughout the war many would attempt to flee, despite repeated warnings from their superiors. The Pomeranian board hoped in 1759 to collect all *Landräte* and their records in well-guarded fortresses, but Frederick vetoed this local decree. The military commander of that province, Bevern, followed the king's wishes by keeping the *Landräte* at their posts; if "vassals, cities, and all subjects, including *Landräte*," came under the control of enemy authorities, orders from such authorities were to be ignored. The persons who illegally cooperated with the enemy subjected themselves to summary military justice, including forfeiture of life. Such orders, whether from the king or from the boards or military commanders, were to prove worthless in many instances. In Pomerania by 1761 the board had really lost effective control over the countryside and was openly defied by the *Landrat* von Blankensee. This *Landrat* fled his post many times and apparently had friends in Berlin and elsewhere, so that all attempts to discipline him ended in failure. The *Landräte* of the Electoral Mark persistently reflected the views of landowners when they protested the recruitment of peasants from their counties, while the *Landräte* of Magdeburg repeatedly left their posts in panic at the approach of the enemy. If this behavior, which could not be general, although widespread, was at all indicative of the thinking of the provincial "establishment,"[38] the landed aristocracy, it indicated lack of courage, lack of a feeling of involvement in the fortunes of Prussia, and generally, a passive attitude towards the State and its ruler on the part of a great number of aristocrats, who were supposed to constitute *in toto* the "soul" of the State. Quite obviously the boards everywhere experienced great trouble with the *Landrat* system. These officials were not subject to ironclad bureaucratic control and seemed to reflect only negative sides of their informal constituency. The squire–official did not prove his worthiness in war time, and this fact was noticed by perceptive administrators and would be taken into account after the war in proposed administrative reforms of local agencies.

Collective harmony could distinguish the operations of the boards and of the General Directory at times, particularly in peacetime when these agencies united internally to face a threat emanating from the king or the judiciary, for example. But in wartime, in the absence of single-minded and strong willed central direction, this collective spirit was often manifested in the form of less desirable group behavior such as panic and the common evasion of responsibility. Despite orders to the contrary, President von Bessel of the Cleves board fled before the enemy several times together with some of his friends among the councillors. The ministers of the General Directory fell victim to panic in August 1759, when news of the Prussian defeat at Kunersdorf caused Boden and Happe to leave hastily for Rathenow, Katt to go to the protection of Spandau fortress, and Blumenthal to Paretz. Since Minister Reuss was left behind, he quickly began to assume the duties of his departed colleagues. Thereupon followed a disgraceful scene. The absent ministers, now ashamed of themselves for the "tumult of August," told Reuss that he could "no longer meddle further" and that he "no longer represented the Directory."[39] Frederick then ordered all to report back to Berlin to duty. When the Russians did come they had to negotiate details of their

38. *AB*, 12: 91 ff., 249–53, 372–73, 381–86, 497–99.
39. Ibid., 9: 2–3, 31–32, 194–95, 203, 225–26, 273–79, 305–9; 12: 145 ff.

fiscal expropriation with a group of private individuals headed by the entrepreneur Gotzkowsky since all the prominent Prussian officials had fled. The General Directory was subsequently very angry about the Russian episode and accused the Electoral Mark board of desertion in time of crisis. But if the board left, so did the General Directory, and no amount of subsequent name-calling could erase the fact that both agencies had fled and left the city to fend for itself. When faced with another invasion of Berlin in 1761, the General Directory issued a decree which prohibited all agencies, public and private, except itself, from negotiating with the enemy. Such persons and associations were "not to meddle" with such problems. Finally, when the Russians placed the capital of the New Mark, Cüstrin, under siege in 1758, the entire board decamped for a safer location, and the president, von Rothenberg, relayed reports of the siege and capture, using the information provided by refugees.[40] Caught by these wartime emergencies, neither the General Directory nor the boards were able to react courageously. When the routine of collegial administration was disturbed these hapless officials fell victims to panic.

The deterioration of provincial administration in the Electoral Mark, Pomerania, New Mark, and Magdeburg during the war produced several examples of large scale fraud and embezzlement. The most egregious involving officials during the war concerned the first director of the Electoral Mark board, Groschopp. Groschopp had been the board's chief negotiator with the *Landschaft* when financial arrangements for the militia had been settled and assumed general responsibility for the collection of revenue. During the war he began systematically to sell timber from the crown lands, ostensibly to aid the war effort. As time progressed, however, he built up a corrupt network of complaisant foresters, merchants, and subordinate offi-

40. J. E. Gotzkowsky, "Geschichte eines patriotischen Kaufmanns," *Schriften des Vereins für die Geschichte Berlins* (Berlin, 1873), 7: 12 ff. Stephan Skalweit, *Die Berliner Wirtschaftskrise von 1763 und ihre Hintergründe* (Stuttgart, 1937), pp. 20–21. Jany, *Armee*, 2: 574–75. *AB*, 12: 304 ff, 366. Paul Schwarz, ed., "Berichte des neumärkischen Kammerpräsidenten über die Einäscherung Cüstrins durch die Russen in August, 1758," *Schriften des Vereins für Geschichte der Neumark* 25 (1910): 103–5. J. C. Seyffert, *Annalen der Stadt und Festung Küstrin* (Küstrin, 1801), pp. 108–15. Schwarz, "Organisation," pp. 99–101.

cials which he used to siphon off part of the profits of the timber sales. A substantial percentage of the proceeds went into the pockets of the ring rather than into the excise tax treasury of the board. In July, 1763, several months after the war ended, the conspirators were tried and convicted for these crimes.[41] The board treasurer of East Frisia, Councillor Hitjer, formed a similar corrupt alliance with an official of the estates.[42] Doubtless others were guilty of peculations, large and small, but were never caught. Undoubtedly the Groschopp crime was possible because the usual peacetime checks on monetary dispersals were no longer working very effectively, but this peculation can also be understood if one considers a particular weakness of the collegial system: the division of responsibility without a strong direction.

The Economic Boom and its Collapse

Fraud, panic, and irresponsibility appear in the history of Prussian administration at the top and in the central provinces during the war, dysfunctional ills that reflect the impotence of bureaucratic authority and a real crisis in collegialism. This ministerial incompetence was also to be revealed in loss of direction over crucial economic and financial matters. Despite the protests of Mint Director Graumann, Frederick determined in 1756 to grant exclusive specie supply monopolies to a consortium consisting of the firms of Ephraim and Sons, Gumpertz, Moses Isaac, and Itzig. Pressed by financial necessity, the king overrode Graumann's protests and began a systematic policy of monetary debasement, using the resources of his consortium to provide the direction. He tied the Saxon mints into this system so that all mints by 1760 were making thirty talers out of one fine mark of silver, whereas the accepted ratio before the war, the so-called Cleves standard, had been eighteen to one. Koser speculated that mint manipulations raised 25,617,000 talers between 1756 and 1763, but a later student, von Loehr, maintained that the English specie subsidies,

41. *AB*, 13: 127–31.
42. Ibid., 11: 540–43.

amounting to 27,000,000 talers, have to be considered part of the minting problem, because they provided a substantial part of the silver needed for the production of debased coinage; therefore, "between a fourth and a third of the war costs (about 40 million) were probably covered by the issue of debased coinage."[43] The General Directory, especially after the death of Graumann, failed to assume direction or supervision over this mint debasement, and the busy king turned over the business to his private consortium instead.

Well known to investigators of the economic effect of the Seven Years' War is the spiraling inflation that developed in the Prussian cities. This inflation was caused by the currency manipulation and also by the lucrative military contracting sponsored by the exigencies of war. In Berlin Gotzkowsky and other merchants were given the opportunity to approach Amsterdam for loans to purchase munitions, weapons, and other supplies for the Prussian army. Gotzkowsky waxed fat, and his newly enlarged fortune provided the basis for his brilliant parties and other ostentatious and parvenu displays in the capital. But Frederick, if upset by the rumors of bourgeois prosperity, had no urge to stop it, because Gotzkowsky had wide and valuable mercantile contacts in Holland and Germany and truly performed invaluable services for his king. Even the despised "mint Jews" such as Ephraim and Sons managed to improve their positions in the esteem of Frederick by handling the international negotiations for specie and for obtaining Dutch bills of exchange. So necessary were the activities of the Ephriam firm that Frederick told his officials in 1762 to allow the members of the firm to purchase landed property in war-devastated Pomerania and New Mark. Complimenting them on the "industry and skill they have provided in commerce," Frederick wanted to make sure that they did not become disgruntled and leave the realm. In Silesia in the same year he permitted the sale of landed property to commoners. Frederick realized shrewdly enough that in 1762, the war profiteers, dismayed by inflation and by material shortages, were no longer interested in investing in trade or industry,

43. C. W. Eldon, *England's Subsidy Policy towards the Continent during the Seven Years War* (Philadelphia, 1938), appendix 2. Koser, "Preussische Finanzen," pp. 340–51. A. C. von Loehr, "Finanzierung," p. 99.

but wanted to sink their profits in landed property. As long as these quasi–country gentlemen endeavored to settle peasants on these properties and to aid in the "populating" of the land, Frederick was cooperative.[44] The fifth department of the General Directory apparently had nothing to do with the control of these war profiteers.

As the war progressed, a remarkable traffic in bills of exchange developed between Berlin, Hamburg, and Amsterdam. The debasement of Prussian currency, the shifting military fortunes of the Prussian armies, and continual mercantile speculation concerning the outcome of the war,combined to provide just the right kind of atmosphere for the collection or disposal of large numbers of bills. Gotzkowsky, Splitgerber, and the mint bankers all involved themselves in this heady game: Gotzkowsky became so involved that he lost his fortune in the crash that occurred in July, 1763. Splitgerber and Daum collected the British subsidies during the war and provided other banking services, admitting Schütze and other rivals on occasion. The prosperity of these people ended with the coming of peace and with postwar administrative readjustments. The Great Crash of July, 1763 was to provide the occasion for such changes.[45] Again, the General Directory seemed to play a minimal role in a crucial wartime problem.

Administration of these important financial and fiscal matters simply did not exist in so far as the General Directory was concerned. Early in the war most of the central treasuries of the realm were placed under the direction of Privy Finance Councillor Köppen and not under the ministers of the General Directory. Köser stated "The General Directory was fully excluded from the administration of the funds obtained from the mints, so the total amount of these funds remained a secret to the whole civil service."[46] Köppen alone knew that this sum reached the total of 78 million talers. Minister Boden

44. Eichborn, *Soll und Haben*, p. 21. Stephan Skalweit, *Berliner Wirtschaftskrise*, p. 21. Koser, "Preussische Finanzen," p. 361. Otto Hintze, "Johann Ernst Gotzkowsky," *Historische und politische Aufsätze* 3 (Berlin, 1908): 118–20. Ludwig Beutin, *VSWG* 26 (1933): 230 ff. *AB*, 12: 480–81.

45. Skalweit, *Berliner Wirtschaftskrise*, pp. 39–42. W. O. Henderson, *Studies in the Economic Policy of Frederick the Great* (London, 1963), ch. 1 *passim*.

46. Koser, "Preussische Finanzen," p. 339.

had charge of the entire operation, but evidently knew less than his subordinate Köppen. Frederick continued to work directly with Splitgerber and Daum, and with Köppen concerning the details of revenue collection. In Saxony and in Silesia the military commissariats functioned without consultation with the ministers of the General Directory. The financing of the war was thus the responsibility of Köppen, Borcke, Zinnow, Schlabrendorff, Splitgerber and Daum, Gotzkowsky, Ephraim and Sons, and other assorted officials, military commanders and merchants with official connections. It was chaotic, corrupt, highly irregular, and probably outraged the ministers of the General Directory almost beyond endurance.

Ad hoc Administration in Contrast to the Old Bureaucracy

Bureaucratic efficiency differed from one province to another during the war. Pomerania was the most successful example of provincial administration, while the province which was the most intimately connected (in terms of geography and politics) to the General Directory and the Electoral Mark, did not emerge with a glorious record of achievement. The General Directory itself seemed to lose its grip on the provinces due to communication problems, the death of most of the top executives, and destructive enemy action in Berlin and elsewhere. Russian, French and Austrian troops managed to infiltrate all provinces of the realm at one time or another, but fortunately not simultaneously. One must decide, therefore, how much of the difficulties suffered by the General Directory and by the boards was due to factors outside their control, occasioned by a very destructive war, and how much was due to the inflexibility and inefficiency of the bureaucratic system itself. In Silesia, a province subject to many destructive enemy forays, administration was always tightly and centrally controlled under one minister. In the central provinces administration was not tightly controlled. The history of provincial tax collections and of the militia organizations proves this point. The provinces had to fend for themselves. Administration was not centrally administered under one executive, because the king who was president of the General Directory, had removed himself. None of the ministers of the General Directory was able to take command of the others: ministerial rivalry precluded this development. The collegial system therefore was not vindicated by the history of Prussian administration during the Seven Years' War. The contrast between a well run and effective bureaucracy and one that suffered from lack of direction, from inflexibility, and from inefficiency is completely evident in the cases of the Silesian ministry and of the General Directory.

Prussia survived the Seven Years' War because Russia withdrew from the rank of her enemies, because Frederick, Prince Henry, and others were, by and large, astute field commanders, because her enemies were unable to work together to achieve her downfall, and because her administrative system was geared to war. But the war clearly revealed that that part of administration which had been founded by Frederick William I, including the General Directory and the boards, did not play a distinguished role. The war effort was maintained flexibly by the assorted individual bureaucrats, entrepreneurs, and military officers who operated almost day to day. They kept the ship of state afloat using whatever expedients were at hand. The war was thus a defeat for the ordained, duly established fiscal bureaucracy and a victory for the Silesian system. Frederick and his most imaginative and astute lieutenants after 1763 remembered the lessons they had been forced to learn under agonizing conditions.

VII

RÉTABLISSEMENT

The Seven Years' War left many poignant reminders of its severity in Prussia: ruined crop lands, debased coinage, dislocated trade, depopulation, and a general decline in the collection of taxes. Although these problems confronted other states after 1763, they were more pressing in Prussia because so much of the war had been fought there.[1] Before the war the Prussian civil service had experienced difficulty and frustration in its struggles with the Silesian minister, the judiciary, and the king. Its greatest trial began in 1756 with the coming of the war and continued after 1763, when it had to face still another emergency: the task of rebuilding the entire realm. The strains and stresses of war helped, perhaps, to push the old-guard officials of the General Directory into premature retirement or contributed to the deaths of several of them; by 1761 only one old minister remained. Obviously the civil service had to rebuild itself at the same time that it rebuilt the economy.

There was no one period of reconstruction, with finite beginning and end, but rather a long period of administrative development after 1763. Certainly the period runs to the end of the reign of Frederick II and can be identified with that monarch. Looking at the evidence, it is equally obvious that the period of *Rétablissement* can be divided into phases: between 1763 and 1772 rather startling and radically new programs with long range goals were established, while after

1. The best survey of the *Rétablissement* in Prussia can be found in Reinhold Koser, *Geschichte Friedrichs des Grossen* (Stuttgart, 1913), 3: 169–220. Many monographs explore various themes such as the settlement programs and shall be cited later. On Saxony, see the excellent work by Horst Schlechte, *Die Staatsreform in Kursachsen 1762–1763* (Berlin, 1958), which supersedes a number of sketchy articles by others.

1772 these programs were refined until 1786. After the death of Frederick II another period begins.

Reconstruction of Property and Programs for Resettlement

Even before the end of the war, Frederick began to think about the job of reconstruction in the heartland of the realm, which consisted of the provinces of the Electoral Mark, Pomerania, and the New Mark. As early as 1763 he felt that he could not depend upon the boards of these provinces to do the enormous job themselves and therefore appointed a complete outsider, Franz von Brenckenhoff, to take charge of most reconstruction in Pomerania and the New Mark. Prior to his appointment in April, 1762, Brenckenhoff had worked for years in the service of the prince of Anhalt-Dessau. Frederick summoned him to Breslau and, as Brenckenhoff said "entrusted to me the complete *Rétablissement* of both ruined provinces." He obtained "free and unlimited authority" under the king alone and Frederick ordered "both boards to make prompt payment for the measures which shall be ordered."[2] Thus began a long and difficult career for Brenckenhoff. From 1762 to 1779 he endeavored to satisfy Frederick, but succeeded only in avoiding ultimate disgrace and dismissal.

Although able, Brenckenhoff was never given ministerial rank. Partly because he was only a privy finance councillor, board presidents resented him and did not always defer to his wishes. All the boards were already trying to cope with the reconstruction of urban and rural property, since all had suffered invasion. The Pomeranian and New Mark boards resented having to consult and follow the orders of Brenckenhoff while other boards were able to act independently. Brenckenhoff had no friend in high places, no minister to protect him.[3] His career, which might have marked a new departure

2. "Brenckenhoffs Berichte," *Schriften des Vereins für Geschichte der Neumark* 10: 38–40. See also Rehmann, "Kleine Beiträge zur Charakteristik Brenckenhoffs," *Schriften des Vereins für Geschichte der Neumark*, 22: 101 ff.

3. As a matter of fact the General Directory was ordered by the king to have nothing to do with him. *AB*, 12: 470.

in administrative history, suffered instead from all the failures of old-fashioned bureaucracy. He was stymied in exactly the same ways as had been Marschall, Fäsch, and Graumann before 1756.

Frederick first ordered Brenckenhoff to make a complete report on the state of the economy in his provinces, including a "specific, and precise accounting" of losses of property, livestock, etc., during the war. From the first Brenckenhoff obtained the full backing of the king; the General Directory and the boards were ordered to cooperate with him.[4] Indeed, when certain officials in the Pomeranian and New Mark boards failed to convince the king of their loyalty and fiscal purity, they were dismissed. Brenckenhoff was not required to enquire into past administrative errors in the provinces but, instead, to plan for future economic regeneration. 1763 seemed to be a year of preparation for massive *Rétablissement*.[5] Brenckenhoff determined, perhaps correctly, that Frederick desired the quick settlement of foreign artisans and peasants in Pomerania and the New Mark; therefore, after the middle of 1763, he concentrated his efforts on solving this problem.[6] The other alternative was to push for compliance with the king's edicts abolishing serfdom in Pomerania. Brenckenhoff wasted no time attempting this impossible task.

Although Frederick spent almost three million talers on his *Neues Palais,* when he allocated funds for *Rétablissement* projects he did so with the greatest stinginess and reluctance. Brenckenhoff could settle relatively few artisans and rebuild fewer properties with the modest grant of sixty thousand talers in the New Mark. Frederick was unhappy and expressed his "chagrin." In an effort to make his program synchronize with the conflicting expectations of the king, Brenckenhoff claimed that 12,000 families had been lost during the war; Frederick suspiciously replied that the total was 70,000. The two were

4. *PKPA*, 11: 336–38. *AB*, 12: 470, 484–85, 596.
5. *AB*, 13: 47–48, 296–97, 48–50, 115–20.
6. A considerable debate raged during Brenckenhoff's lifetime and between certain nineteenth-century historians. This problem is examined by Rehmann, "Kleine Beiträge," pp. 101–30. Rehmann portrays him as a dedicated official, a loyal servant of Frederick, and a person of probity and rectitude. Despite an investigation ordered in 1770 by Frederick, Brenckenhoff was never found guilty of corruption. He was forced to pay a considerable fine later, however.

in accord concerning the need to use force to prevent local aristocrats from mistreating settlers and the desirability of keeping these colonists immune from serfdom. But the king thought Brenckenhoff imported too many "peruke makers and comedians" and did not provide adequate housing in the new communities. "I judge people not by their words, but by their actions and methods," he warned. By the middle of 1765 Brenckenhoff realized that it cost, on the average, 15,000 talers to settle 150 textile spinners and their families: He obtained 768,149 talers over a seventeen-year period for work in the New Mark. At no time could he expect to achieve great success because of the small grants he obtained. Of all the reconstruction measures favored by Frederick after 1763, the settlement program constituted the most frustrating and one of the most expensive.[7]

Frederick blamed the General Directory, the boards of the two provinces, and the reactionary nobility for much of the failure of Brenckenhoff's program by the end of 1765. At least three times between 1762 and 1765 he warned the General Directory not to meddle in the project.[8] Preoccupied with his desire for "exactitude and order," Frederick bombarded his officials with reprimands and injunctions. Initially he encouraged Brenckenhoff to give funds first to the most impoverished and needy class, the peasantry, but found that the Pomeranian nobility was diverting funds to its own uses. "Loud confusion rules," he complained to Brenckenhoff after inspecting the program at Cüstrin and finding that houses remained in ruins and that officials and landlords remained indifferent and uninvolved in reconstruction. He seemed to have discovered a weakly directed and enforced reconstruction program.[9]

Feeling frustrated, no doubt, by the early failure of his plans to abolish serfdom in Pomerania, Frederick began to reconsider the

7. *AB*, 13: 525; 14: 659–63, 665–67. Merseburg. Rep. 92, Brenckenhoff, 3. H. Tröger, *Die kurmarkischen Spinnerdörfer* (Leipzig 1936), pp. 31–33. M. Beheim-Schwarzbach, *Hohenzollersche Kolonisationen*, pp. 275–78, describes dishonest settlers and the additional problems they created. Detto, *FBPG*, 16: 179 ff.

8. *AB*, 12: 470; 13: 314–15; 14: 661–62.

9. Ibid., 13: 527–28; 14: 667–69.

future of reconstruction work in that province and in the New Mark. The social structure and the conservative nature of bureaucratic operations combined to reduce all peasants, recent settlers and natives, to a common and most debased status. Frequently only unsuccessful peasants could be enticed to come to Prussia, and their often minimal achievement after settlement did not escape the attention of the king. Beheim-Schwarzbach, still an authority on Prussian settlements, believed that the nagging doubts about future returns made the king become more and more cautious after 1770 in approving new projects.[10] Certainly the immediate consequences of the New Mark and Pomeranian settlement programs proved disappointing by 1765.

If Brenckenhoff suffered constant rebukes from the king, his lot was far better than that of the hapless officials of the Electoral Mark board. Between 1762 and 1766 Frederick tried to make this board institute wide-ranging ameliorative programs, but the board was unable to accomplish the tasks assigned to it. Even before the end of the war, the board had suffered disgrace because of exposure to the embezzlements of its first director, Grosschop. Thereafter Frederick issued extensive directions to the president, von der Horst, concerning the preparation of statistics covering war damages. Unfortunately Horst failed to grasp the seriousness of the king's intentions and submitted an early and amazing report in which he claimed that 4,359 talers would be sufficient to restore the province to its prewar condition. By January, 1765, when the *Rétablissement* was supposed to be finished, the king wrote to Horst "nothing has been brought to complete and correct status," and accused his board of being "negligent and rotten."[11] Frederick, still angry, purged the first director and asked the Silesian minister, Schlabrendorff, to recommend a replacement. Frederick remarked; "I know the Silesians are strong in land economy and livestock." Siegroth, a former Silesian *Landrat*, was brought in as the new first director of the Electoral Mark board. Frederick then warned the General Directory that Siegroth would be obeyed in everything and that there "must be no hindrance or

10. Beheim-Schwarzbach, *Kolonisationen*, pp. 279 ff.
11. *AB*, 13: 399–400, 526–27.

chicanery."[12] The king noticed that Brenckenhoff had managed his share of *Rétablissement* work with greater efficiency and success than had the Electoral Mark board.[13] The Electoral Mark board, largest of the provincial directorates, had been shown to be inefficient and corrupt. Since it was under the close supervision of the General Directory, the board seemed to Frederick to be representative of the entire core bureaucracy. Partly because of lack of interest on the part of the king, and partly because of lack of board initiative, the *Rétablissement* proved to be of small consequence in all of the other provinces except Silesia and, possibly, Magdeburg. In East Prussia only 2,588 peasant plots were settled by 1786. Few were settled in Cleves and elsewhere.[14]

Schlabrendorff, the Silesian minister, was able to obtain better results than the board presidents, partly because he could anticipate the desires as well as the prejudices of the king. He also possessed a genuine interest in the lot of the peasants and did not wait for instructions to resume work on a prewar project to increase the hereditary rights of the cultivators so that a growing number of them could hold property in perpetuity, regardless of the changing ownership of the estate (*Rittergut*). Not much was accomplished, but the words suited the ears of the king even if results were not forthcoming. Schlabrendorff reminded him, "Your Majesty knows full well how much the land depends on the conservation of the peasantry . . . they were subjected to heavy wartime burdens such as delivery of food and forage."[15] He also promised action to resettle some 3,000 vacant plots, which will bring "profit to the cantons in time and, in time of war, will assist the army to a greater extent."[16] He was not able to satisfy Frederick by January, 1766, when he claimed that

12. Ibid., pp. 660, 686–89.
13. Tröger, *Kurmark Spinnerdörfer*, pp. 31–33.
14. Ring, "Kolonisationsbestreburgen," pp. 50–51. Beheim-Schwarzbach, *Kolonisationen*, pp. 624 ff., Walter Mertineit, *Die friedericianische Verwaltung in Ostpreussen* (Heidelberg, 1958), pp. 131–45. Gustav Aubin, *Zur Geschichte des gutsherrlich-bäuerlichen Verhältnisses in Ostpreussen* (Leipzig, 1910), pp. 183–85.
15. *AB*, 13: 92–93. J. Ziekursch, *Hundert Jahre schlesischer Agrargeschichte* (Breslau, 1927), pp. 185 ff. Büsch, *Militärsystem und Sozialleben*, p. 59.
16. Schlabrendorff, quoted in Büsch, p. 59.

two-thirds of the rural property left vacant during the war had been reoccupied. The king grumbled that everything should be in order as in Pomerania and New Mark, reflecting a temporary satisfaction with Brenckenhoff. Schlabrendorff, nevertheless, was not afraid to ask Frederick for the enormous sum of 359,000 talers to use to begin work in the cities and persisted in this demand even after the king cancelled his original grant of 50,000 talers. Frankness was an endearing quality of this energetic minister, as Frederick shortly realized when he reinstituted the original grant.[17]

Frederick began to understand the magnitude of the reconstruction work between 1762 and 1766. He obtained somewhat equivocal results in areas administered by Schlabrendorff and Brenckenhoff, but very little from the boards when left to their own initiative. The chronic ailments of the old bureaucracy manifested themselves in feeble direction, incomplete and misleading reports, the sudden dismissal for cause of high ranking officials, and a plethora of written jibes and admonitions from the king. So much should be done—the rebuilding of war-damaged properties, resettlement of vacant farm properties, continuation of the mulberry tree planting program, enticement of artisans in the textile industry, and alleviation of the lot of bankrupt and near bankrupt landowners and peasants. The list is nearly endless and encompasses widely disparate, if somewhat formless, aims. During this first phase of the *Rétablissement*, the king and some officials seemed to waste a great deal of energy trying to pursue all at the same time. The first of the aims to be forgotten was the abolition of serfdom in Pomerania and in Silesia. After the first distribution of livestock, seed, and feed grains in 1762 and 1763 in the most heavily devastated areas, the peasants and the aristocrats alike obtained precious little from the crown until after 1766. Finally, both

17. *AB*, 15: 382. Beheim-Schwarzenback, *Kolonisationen*, p. 624, gives the inflated figure of 61,652 settlers by 1786. See A. Skalweit, "Wieviel Kolonisten hat Friedrich der Grosse angesiedelt?" *FBPG* 24 (1911): 243–48, for corrections. *AB*, 13: 468–69; 14: 220–21. Schlabrendorff was concerned with the recruiting of foreign artisans to a considerable extent and submitted many reports between 1763 and 1766 concerning the results of this labor. Merseburg, Rep. 96, 426 M Fol. 114, Immediat berichte der Sch. Min. v. Schlabrendorff in Varia Retablissement, 1764–67, pp. 14–114.

Frederick and his officials seemed to concentrate on the one problem that could be handled, the resettlement program. The king could make periodic inspection trips (and he made more outside Berlin in the years from 1763 to 1766 than he had made in the entire prewar period), and he could note whether land in a particular area was being settled. Misleading reports by the board presidents could fool him for a time, but when he discovered the truth he punished those he held responsible with vigor. Brenckenhoff summed up the frustrations of the king during this period when he remarked concerning the reform edicts issued by Frederick, that "they were instituted, printed, publicized, but only seldom followed."[18] This remark suggests that the king did not know what was going on. Actually he revealed his knowledge by his increasingly irritable jibes and, finally, by his administrative changes in 1766. The introduction of the *Regie*, or French tax farming system, in 1765 and 1766, was to be one important administrative innovation.

In one important sense the first phase of *Rétablissement* did not result in failure: this period saw the continuation of many programs that had long existed in Prussia. Resettlement, for example, and especially the recruitment of foreign peasants and artisans, had been a regular duty of bureaucrats since the time of the Great Elector. All east European states hoped after 1648 to obtain larger populations, and all tried to attract people from elsewhere. Particularly important was the movement of Germans from the western and middle states to such eastern ones as the Prussian realm. It is possible that a total of 57,475 persons were settled in Prussia during the entire reign of Frederick II.[19] While the efforts of Prussian officials such as Brenckenhoff must be acknowledged, it is quite obvious that this total figure was very minor in importance; the average number per year was 1,248. Since adequate methods of accounting were lacking in most cases, and officials frequently lied, the actual number may have been much smaller. Frederick claimed that the realm lost 500,000

18. A. Skalweit in *AB Getreidehandelspolitik*, 3: 39, quotes this.
19. Brenckenhoff, "Brenckenhoffs Berichte," *Schriften des Vereins für Geschichte Neumarks*, 1: 41 42.

people in the Seven Years' War—the settlement program could not make up such a loss.[20] The *Rétablissement* settlements amounted to a small and rather unimportant phase of a traditional Hohenzollern program.

That favorite belief of textbook writers, that thousands of acres of swamp land were reclaimed by the "enlightened despot" Frederick II after 1762 is also misleading. The retrieval of crop land had been a favorite project of King Frederick William I. The draining of the Oderbruch and the Warthebruch had been started and brought substantially forward before the Seven Years' War. Even the construction of canals was a traditional project of the bureaucracy: all the important ones had been finished by 1756. The settlement of foreign peasants and artisans, the reclamation of farm land, the draining of marshes, and the building of canals were not innovations of Frederick either before or after the Seven Years' War.[21]

Civil servants, therefore, were not required to engage in any fundamentally new programs by the king in 1763, but only to accelerate their previous efforts. They were also told to increase the revenues from taxation to the 1756 level within a few years. By 1765 Frederick felt that his officials had not been able to meet either of these two fundamental demands.[22] He believed, perhaps rightly, that massive development of the realm after that year could only come about if revenues were substantially increased. Given the problem of funding expensive ameliorative projects, he was susceptible to the suggestions of persons outside the official bureaucracy.

Calzabigi and the Search for Greater Revenue

Between 1762 and 1766 Frederick became more and more aware of

20. A Skalweit, "Wieviel Kolonisten," pp. 243–8, corrects Brenckenhoff.

21. On settlement programs before Frederick II, see Gustav Schmoller, "Die preussische Einwanderung und ländliche Kolonisation," *Umrisse und Untersuchungen* (Leipzig, 1898), pp. 598–99. See also chapter 1 above.

22. Otto Hintze, *FPBG* 10: 292–94, claimed that the efforts of both the king and the bureaucracy to improve the living conditions of the peasants amounted to very little between 1752 and 1772. The chief impediment was, of course, the landowning nobility; Frederick tried to keep them happy at almost any expense. Hintze aptly commented, "Realpolitik triumphed over humanity."

a grave financial crisis in the realm. The speculative boom led by the Berlin entrepreneur, Gotzkowsky, had collapsed in the spring of 1763. The economic malaise of Prussia resulted from the war: debasement of the coinage, widespread bankruptcy of businessmen and landlords, and direct and indirect damage to property. Some of Frederick's attempted solutions were guided by his sound decision to obtain reliable statistics regarding property damage, but others were ad hoc and clumsy, based only on hunches or a defective comprehension of economics. He was never strong in matters of economic policy, possessing a rather simplistic, even naive, view of the machinery of the economy, which he doubtless obtained second hand from the cameralistic legacy. He made some serious mistakes during the *Rétablissement*. One such decision was to institute national lotteries.

A lottery seems to attract the attention of many statesmen interested in obtaining a relatively large revenue voluntarily through subscription rather than through a more formal tax system. Frederick had tried to institute one in 1755, following the recommendation of a French entrepreneur, but the war intervened, and he could not find enough private investors to provide the initial working capital.[23] By 1764 he was ready to listen again to quick money schemes and proved receptive to that proposed by an astute Italian from Livorno, Calzabigi. Calzabigi claimed that he could provide a 55 percent profit to the State if he was allowed to establish a national lottery, hire his own officials, and distribute the winnings as well as the tickets.[24] In his subsequent organizational scheme he requested the founding of seven bureaus in Berlin and three elsewhere in the realm with a total payroll of 400,000 talers. Despite the fact that this sum was equal to that of the executive corps of the core bureaucracy, Frederick was prepared to approve the plan. After all, the overhead expenses would be met with the income of the lottery. Frederick had sense enough to appoint the Berlin banker, Schickler, to handle the treasury. Schickler, David Splitgerber, and the experienced accountant, Privy Finance Councillor Köppen, all subsequently warned the king of "great

23. Merseburg, Rep. 96, 410 N, 2–6. This contains the Dehampiguy proposal and related material. For Calzabigi see subsequent notes.
24. Merseburg, Rep. 96, 410 N. 10–16.

hazards," but he resolutely persevered. Triumphantly, Calzabigi wrote to Frederick, "I am going to Berlin."[25]

The warnings of officials had resulted in two important amendments to Calzabigi's scheme; that the entrepreneur would pursue the project at his own risk, and that his treasuries would be checked periodically by a committee composed of trustworthy businessmen. Expenses exceeded income by nearly 100 percent in the first drawing. In 1764 the income of 16,006 talers met expenses, but complaints were coming from all parts of the realm. In Cleves the lottery director complained of a conspiracy of the local board and magistrates intended to frustrate operations. The powerful president of the East Prussian boards, Domhardt, and the Silesian minister, Schlabrendorff, criticized the project. The one official who endeavored to help Calzabigi set up his lottery, Privy Finance Councillor Hagen, remained skeptical throughout. Only the king continued to see much validity in the "grand design." The lottery continued to operate on a small scale for some years.[26]

In 1765 Frederick was approached by Calzabigi and Baron von Knyphausen with a "Dossier de Travail pour l'Etablissement du 5me Départment des Finances, de Commerce et de Marine." This plan was much more ambitious than the lottery scheme: the proposed department would have been organized outside the General Directory, would have been headed by a director-general responsible only to the king, and would have assumed total legal and police control over all foreign and domestic commerce, excises, shipping—in short, of all entrepreneurial activity in the realm. Suboffices would have been established in all major ports and towns and the whole organization was carefully worked out, including the number of clerks and customs inspectors needed, together with detailed cost estimates.

25. Ibid.
26. Ibid., 34, 80, 81, 82, 110, 124. Rep. 96, 410 P. Rep. 96, 410 0. Calzabigi was also placed in charge of the lottery in Silesia, and Frederick ordered Schlabrendorff to cooperate with him. When the lottery was established in Silesia, attempts were made to make it more efficient than the Cleves lottery. The latter failed to produce a profit by 1765. Rep. 46B no. 229 Lotteriewesen in Schlesien, 1763–1786, 1–87.

Frederick curiously enough did not send the plan to the General Directory for consideration, but to the Justice Department. The plan was vetoed on the grounds that it would have circumvented too many laws, not because the basic scheme was held to be unworkable.[27] Calzabigi's plan may well have remained in the mind of the king after June, 1765.

In the same year, Calzabigi had convinced the king that a "Ferme Royale de Tabac" should be established. This tobacco bureau would, in fact, be a private organization operating under government contract, a kind of fiscal "farm," and was initially proposed by a consortium consisting of Calzabigi and six other speculators. In scope the proposed organization was imaginative and broad, with central offices which would supervise judicial, fiscal, and industrial aspects of the tobacco trade. Each province would have its own large staff of inspectors of crops and customs and the importation, growth, manufacture and sale of tobacco would be subjected to extensive and intensive control. Hoping to be established as seven *Directors Généraux*, the consortium immodestly requested individual salaries equal to those of the ministers of the General Directory. Although the tobacco *Regie* was approved by Frederick and put into operation in 1766,[28] the dazzling career of Calzabigi had reached its end by that time and he and his cronies, including the curious figure of Quintus Icilius, were removed when the bureau was transferred to the consortium that had engineered the establishment of the General Excise Administration (*Regie*). After 1766 the golden age of French entrepreneurial activity was represented only by the *Regie* of taxes. The Tobacco Administration was absorbed into the core bureaucracy in 1767,[29] and became a profitable segment of the bureaucracy, administered by experienced Prussian officials of the privy finance councillor level such as Taubenheim and Magusch. Of all the schemes introduced since 1763, this and the regular *Regie* were the only lasting

27. Ibid., Rep. 9, C, 1B, 3. Fasc. 31.
28. Koser, *Friedrichs*, 3: 230–31. Merseburg, Gen. Dir., Tabacks-Sachen, Tit., C. no. 1. *Plan Générale d'Administration, 1765.*
29. Koser, *Friedrichs*, 3: 182–83. *AB*, 14: 135. Merseburg, Gen. Dir. Tabacks-Sachen, A, Tit. I, 1.

and successful innovations. The Tobacco Administration cost about 180,063 talers a year to administer after 1766 and brought in 1,286, 289 talers in profits in 1786 alone.[30]

Beginning of the Regie: Retreat of the General Directory

Frederick continued to search for ways to increase revenue. The most obvious, and most lucrative, seemed to be to increase the excise taxes. But the ministers of the General Directory felt that such a raise was "unthinkable." Frederick also felt that the machinery of collection was often inefficient and even corrupt. In January, 1766 Frederick told his ministers that he was satisfied with their financial management at the same time that he was entering negotiations with a consortium of French entrepreneurs with the object of founding a separate financial ministry.[31] The General Directory was not aware of impending change, but within a few months the ministers were to receive a great shock. As the most careful student of the General Excise Administration, Schultze, said: "The *Regie* was not a great financial innovation, but a strike against the Prussian bureaucracy."[32]

The capstone of the French entrepreneurial craze was this General Excise Administration. Frederick was inspired to establish the *Regie* by the promptings of Helvetius. He wrote to d'Argens, after the departure from Berlin of Helvetius, requesting assistance in the selection of appropriate officials. Helvetius had been a tax farmer in France until 1751, and both he and d'Argens had many friends in the French administration. It was not difficult for them to select three potential managers of the proposed Prussian tax farm: de Launay, Candy, and de Crecy. Frederick interviewed de Launay on January 15, 1766, and promptly offered to let the consortium handle all excises, tariffs, tobacco revenues, stamp, salt, and wood contracts.[33]

30. Merseburg, Gen. Dir. Tabacks-Sachen, A. Tit. V, 1. Koser, *Friedrichs*, 3: 231.

31. *AB*, 13: 732.

32. W. Schultze, *Geschichte der preussischen Regieverwaltung von 1766–1786* (Leipzig, 1888), pt. 1, p. 29.

33. *AB Handels, Zol- und Akzisepolitik*, 3: 150, includes a significant letter of

Frederick probably would never have agreed to the suggestions of Helvetius and de Launay if he had not himself attempted similar plans, although on a smaller scale, with such adventurers as Calzabigi.

From the beginning, the scale and scope of the *Regie* was conceived in the most grandiose terms, so that it overshadowed the traditional core bureaucracy. Although nominally part of the General Directory, it really remained under the control of the consortium of French entrepreneurs. The *Regie* employed about 2,000 persons, of which between 175 and 200 were French. Most of the latter were to be found in the most important offices. The roster of the *Regie* probably resembled that of the Tobacco Administration of 1766: Frenchmen dominated positions of prestige and profit, while Germans occupied the humble posts of gatekeepers, inspectors, and collectors.[34]

Between 1766 and 1768 the *Regie* found itself involved in conflict with the core bureaucracy, the judiciary, and nongovernmental associations. It constituted a radical and abrupt change in the administrative system of the realm. The *Steuerrat*, who had devoted much of his efforts to the collection of the excise taxes in the city, was now forced to relinquish this duty to a local representative of the *Regie*. Municipal boards of aldermen no longer exercised control over excise collection. In short, the *Regie* was a parallel bureaucratic structure, existing alongside the core bureaucracy and taking from the old bureaucracy a large part of its revenue raising authority. Gloger, a recent student of the Potsdam *Steuerrat*, remarked that the introduction of the *Regie* marked the end of the "classical" period in the history of that position; it also marked the beginning of decline and eventual elimination of *Steuerräte* during the Stein reforms.

Frederick II to de Launay in which the king said: "I have given a commission to the Sieur Helvetius" to find suitable French tax farmers. Schultze, *Regie*, pp. 31–4. A considerable number of documents concerning the *Regie* have been published in the *Acta Borussica* as subsequent notes will show. Unfortunately, however, the archives at Merseburg and at Potsdam do not appear to contain a great deal of additional material. In 1786 de Launay and his entire administration came under investigation and many documents were taken from the archives but never returned. (See the note by the editors in *AB*, 14: 678).

34 Schultze, *Regie*, pp. 46–48.

Naturally officials in the core bureaucracy who had previously administered the excise collection were confused and angry when told that the *Regie* would do everything. They resisted by contesting the authority of the new tax collectors in specific localities and they protested to their superiors. In Silesia, for example, the county clerks (*Kreiscalculator*) protested that the inspectors of the *Regie* knew no German and had no knowledge of the accounting practices of the bureaucracy. When the arrogant Candy arrived in Glogau in Silesia to revise local excise regulations and accounting practices, he encountered official opposition. Candy threatened the Silesian board: officials who stood in the way of the *Regie* would suffer the same fate as the unfortunate former fiscal general, Ursinius, who was currently imprisoned in Spandau. The Silesian tax quota would also be increased if cooperation was not forthcoming. Board officials later decribed this meeting as "more of a Spanish Inquisition than a conference."[35] A magistrate elsewhere complained of the presence of the *Regie*'s municipal controller: "Other cities are luckier if they are not trampled under by such a superior and have no French excise collectors within their walls, but can do their work without trouble and in quiet."[36] The core bureaucracy was faced with a direct and extraordinary challenge.

The Regie *in Conflict with the Core Bureaucracy*

Naturally the directors of the *Regie* found themselves involved in a bitter conflict not only with local officials but with the executive leadership of the entire bureaucracy. Frederick indicated, at first, that the new bureau would be responsible to the minister of the fourth department of the General Directory, Horst, and that that department would be "completely new."[37] However, that unfortunate official never had any authority over the directors of the *Regie*. His subordinate position was revealed in the salary table: he received

35. *AB*, 14: 177–82, 186–87. Gloger, "Steuerrat," pp. 148–51.
36. Schultze, *Regie*, p. 53.
37. *AB*, 14: 88–92.

one-sixth the sum paid to each of the French directors. Frederick bluntly told Horst later, when that minister was in the midst of an argument with de Launay, that he would choose the French entrepreneur and dismiss the German official if forced to make a choice. Horst occupied himself with angry colleagues in the old-line bureaucracy in the thankless task of obtaining harmony. The Silesian minister, Schlabrendorff, attempted to organize an undercover opposition to the *Regie* by asking friends elsewhere in the civil service to determine if the excise receipts declined after 1766 and to supervise a general observation of the effectiveness of the *Regie*. He hoped, quite obviously, to tell the king that the experiment was a failure.[38] Although the preliminary results of Schlabrendorff's attempt to organize this reaction proved fruitless, this development within the civil service executive leadership helped to lay the ground work for a future bureaucratic reorganization.

The *Regie*, if it harmed the authority and prestige of the old-line core bureaucracy, also provided a stimulus to increased collaboration between officials. In fact, the grizzled veterans of the civil service of Frederick William I were now outnumbered, for the first time, by younger officials who had entered the service since 1740. The Silesian minister after 1766 was a natural source of guidance to whom younger officials came when confronted with both the enormous problems of postwar reconstruction and the *Regie*. Schlabrendorff collaborated with two other key officials in providing a kind of underground leadership for this dangerous movement of opposition to the king's desires. In 1762 Johann Domhardt was appointed president of the Königsberg board, and he subsequently obtained the additional supervision of the Gumbinnen board and became minister-president of East Prussia. Between 1763 and 1769 Domhardt acquired nearly absolute authority over the Prussian administration in that province, defeating the judiciary in the course of his power struggle. Finally, in 1772, he also became president of the newly acquired West Prussia and wielded the authority of a viceroy over a tremendous land mass, acknowledging no real superior other than the king. Domhardt

38. *AB Handelspolitik*, 3: 188–89. *AB*, 14: 76–79.

fought the *Regie*, first by claiming that the French excise directors
sent to Königsberg were incompetent—were "no magicians"[39]—and
second, by keeping in contact with Schlabrendorff. These two kept up
a constant campaign of opposition, claiming that the profit-seeking
Regie tax collectors were causing hardship to merchants and to
ordinary subjects of the king of Prussia and that the new administration was not bringing forth concrete results in the form of greater
receipts. In the General Directory itself this coalition found an ally
in the powerful minister Ludwig Hagen. After 1766 when he became
the most influential member of that body, Hagen did not take an
open course of opposition to the *Regie*, but managed to reorganize
the core bureaucracy so that it could work with the semi-independent
Silesian and East Prussian presidents. The *Regie* thus caused these
three energetic leaders of the new generation of bureaucrats to work
together and to make the entire core bureaucracy function as a team
after 1766 for the first time since 1740. Even when the new mining,
banking, and engineering bureaus were organized under Hagen's
auspices after 1767, the three ministers seemed to be able to resolve
their jurisdictional problems. The judiciary, which had fought the
core bureaucracy so bitterly before the war, still fought it, but on a
much reduced scale because the jurists disapproved of Frederick's
decision to allow the Frenchmen to establish their own courts for the
trial of excise crimes. Nothing united so many potential enemies more
than the sudden appearance of a formidable outside threat.

The *Regie* served still another useful purpose: it became the scape-
goat for all subjects of the king of Prussia. To Germans, the French
entrepreneurs soon seemed to be arrogant and callous profiteers. One
of the directors-general, Candy, became involved in an argument with

39. See Erich Joachim, *Johann Domhardt* (Berlin, 1899). *AB Handelspolitik*,
3: 160–62. *AB*, 14: 79. W. Schultze, *Geschichte der preussischen Regieverwaltung,
1766–86* (Berlin, 1888), gives an impartial and intelligent account of the *Regie*.
Frederick defended the *Regie* against attacks made on it by board officials; he
told the Minden president: "You and the board are not set up as judges." When
President von Auer of Magdeburg complained that the *Regie* was responsible for
mercantile bankruptcies, Frederick replied: "Your own evil and dissolute way
of life and economy since the war" were the real causes. Even the army was told
to cooperate. See *AB Handelspolitik*, 3: 156–57.

a colleague, de Lattre, fought a duel with him, and was killed. This affair was undoubtedly greeted with joy by Prussian bureaucrats, since Candy had behaved arrogantly in Breslau and had created many enemies in an amazingly short time. In their search for contraband, the *Regie* inspectors and collectors constantly caused complaints. The General Directory charged in 1770 that foreign merchants were harassed so much when inspected at the gates of Königsberg that "many are going to Riga and to Danzig where the tax collectors are less rigorous."[40]

Ultimately the administrators of the *Regie* were forced to make certain internal changes in order to continue in the favor of the king and to avoid, possibly, even more conflict with the core bureaucracy. De Launay made one great mistake in the course of his career: he consistently opposed Frederick over the question of the employment of subalterns, gatekeepers and inspectors. The General Excise Administration soon became a large employer of such persons, the costs of operation totalling 722,968 talers by 1733, and 1,094,887 talers by 1781. In fact, so many officials were appointed to work at the gates of towns and cities that travellers were often forced to wait for hours before being cleared by the inspectors, and by the inspectors of those inspectors. For de Launay was obsessed with fraud, and in his *Promemoria* of 1766, which Frederick accepted as the basis for the *Regie*, the French entrepreneur emphasized time after time that loose administration of the excises caused fraud. He thus developed very elaborate checks and balances, including a prolific corps of accountants that did nothing except check tax receipts. De Launay wanted to have complete control of all appointments, even of the most humble persons, but Frederick insisted, time after time, that all such appointments must be made from the lists of invalided soldiers. As Schultze indicated, de Launay viewed his job as a profit making opportunity and could not understand why poorly trained and nearly illiterate ex-soldiers should be hired when more qualified persons were available. Frederick harped on this issue in 1768, six different times between 1773 and 1779, and finally in 1782. Then,

40. *AB*, 14: 225 ff. Schultze, *Regie*, p. 53. *AB Handelspolitik*, 3: 221, 188–89.

losing patience, Frederick denounced his corps of French officials from top to bottom in 1782. One provincial director was fired when the king called him "an evil rascal" and another with the parting accusation: "no good." The corrupt "pigs" who he imagined now filled the ranks of the *Regie* were to be removed. Due to Frederick's growing disenchantment with the personnel of the *Regie* and with the costs of its operation, de Launay was forced to fire some officials in 1772, and, finally, to agree to hire regimental quartermasters after 1783. The collegial structure, with its cumbersome subbureaus, was greatly simplified in 1772 when de Launay emerged as the uncontested chief executive, but this reshuffling did not lower the overhead costs. In the last three years of the reign of Frederick II, the fortunes of the *Regie* continued to decline. The aged king no longer thought his Frenchmen were better bureaucrats than his own subjects; in fact, the "good" regimental quartermasters were "ignorant" of the "subtleties of corruption" which the French had developed into a fine art.[41]

The *Regie* was nevertheless a successful administrative arrangement; the separate administration of a crucial part of taxation was shown to be practical. Between 1766 and 1786 a total of some 42,718,000 talers was collected, according to de Launay. Even if this

41. Schultze, *Regie*, pp. 53–71, 34. Schultze remarks that Minister von der Horst "had absolutely nothing to say" about the administration of the *Regie* until his death in 1774, but de Launay had been forced to modify the *Regie* as early as 1768, as stated (ibid., pp. 60–71). The disenchantment of Frederick with the *Regie* can be followed in the documents reproduced in *AB Handelspolitik*, 3: 253–54, and 265, 285–87, 291, 293, 297–99, 304–5, 312. Schultze concentrates on the economic side: he shows that the *Regie* administration ran into increasing conflict with the king and the General Directory over the tax receipts and the strong-arm measures sometimes undertaken against smugglers and merchants in general (62 ff.). The original proposal of de Launay and Candi is reproduced in *AB*, 14: 678–89. It should be noted that Frederick came to agree with the ministers of the General Directory concerning the economic harm the *Regie* caused. Schlabrendorff and others always claimed that the excessive tariff controls impeded commerce and caused great unhappiness among town dwellers in general. When one remembers that towns of any size were invariably surrounded by walls and that the gates were manned by very zealous customs inspectors it is easy to believe that town dwellers sometimes imagined that they were living in a prison.

figure is exaggerated, no doubt exists concerning the economic health of the organization and its revenue raising capabilities.[42] Curiously enough, however, Hagen, Domhardt, Schlabrendorff, and other opponents of the *Regie* succeeded in destroying the organization in the long run by accusing it of being a *French* confidence game—when they destroyed the bureau they also destroyed the concept of a separate revenue collection agency and reinforced the old collegial system. Remarkably, the conservative-minded officials of the core bureaucracy made no effort to invigorate themselves or their work until they were confronted by the *Regie;* Hagen's rise to supreme power within the General Directory parallels the rise of de Launay and of his consortium.

The Francomania of Frederick

Why was Frederick willing to adopt the various French entrepreneurial schemes? He was the only man in Prussia who seemed willing to experiment, and he had his opportunity in 1763 for the first time since coming to the throne. All of his efforts before 1756 had been directed against the bureaucratic system devised by his father; all had been devised to cope with the emergency demands occasioned by the conquest of Silesia and the desire to bring about judicial reforms. The presence of old-guard ministers had impeded

42. The figures are reproduced in *AB Handelspolitik*, 3: 335–36. The most famous critic of the *Regie* was H. G. R. Comte de Mirabeau, *De la monarchie prussienne sous Frédéric le Grand* (Paris, 1788), appendix to vol. 2. It is impossible to really determine if the revenues collected by the *Regie* were greater than what may have been collected by the old administration because the incorporation of West Prussia in 1772 would make earlier figures questionable for comparative purposes. *AB Handels-Zoll, und Akzisepolitik*, 3: 76, gives an interesting table in which the excise collection totals for the different provinces, except Silesia, are reproduced for the two months of June and July of 1765, and for the same months in 1755. By multiplying the figures for 1755, a good peacetime year, by 6, one arrives at the total of 1,298,778 talers. Multiplying this figure by 20 to give a comparable span of time to that of the *Regie*, one obtains 25,975,570 talers. Even if the Silesian revenues were included, and accounting for sums from excise collection included in other treasuries it seems more than probable that the *Regie* was a more lucrative tax collector than the boards. Of course, such comparisons are only illustrative and cannot be strictly accurate.

his prewar plans, but by 1764 he could appoint men of his own choosing to fill all ministerial posts of the General Directory. He could, and did, have the courage to dismiss officials who disagreed with him, or those who no longer enjoyed his trust. The same exaltation which seemed to grip him when he ordered the construction of his monument to the "miracle of Prussia," the *Neues Palais*,[43] seemed to motivate his abrupt and decisive efforts to remold the bureaucracy. For three years his officials were ordered to perform the task of reconstruction, but in 1765 he felt they had failed in one key area, their effort to increase taxes. Frederick favored the surprise assault in warfare, the sudden attempt to catch an enemy off balance. Is it unreasonable to assume that he used the same tactics in other, nonmilitary, campaigns?

The lifeblood of any government is money collected by taxes. Even the most unambitious and ordinary jobs of a civil service depend upon a steady flow of revenue. In the Old Regime throughout Europe the work of tax collection probably accounted for 80 percent of the time available to civil servants. An examination of archival materials leaves the modern student impressed with this unremitting concern with revenue and treasuries: most domain records of the reign of Frederick II concern finance directly or indirectly, for example. The science of bureaucratic statistics was invented and improved primarily in order to keep control of such monies. Prussia was the most efficient collector of taxes in Europe due to the reforms initiated by Frederick William I. As Schultze astutely remarked, however, "the technical establishment of financial affairs was better in the completely corrupt France than in Prussia."[44] Colbert, the supreme bureaucrat of the Old Regime and the inspiration of the

43. This palace still stands, but in a state of decrepitude. An old joke in Potsdam, which still makes the rounds, claims that the two heroic female figures perched on the top of the dome holding a gilded globe represent the two "defeated" monarchs of the Seven Years' War: Czarina Elizabeth and Maria Theresa. Presumably the globe represents Prussia. Pedantic readers should note that the term "Neues Palais" is, and always has been, the title of this structure; the marriage of French with German words was very common in the eighteenth century.
44. Schultze, *Regie*, p. 9.

cameralists in Germany, was believed to be the creator of the French fiscal system, which allowed bureaucrats to handle, as a matter of routine, enormous sums of money, thus giving them the impression that they were participating in a gigantic governmental organization. But could the French system be used effectively in Prussia? In France central control was by this time more apparent than real, with resulting inefficiency and general laxity, while the opulence of the country allowed official peculation on a fairly wide scale. Just as Frederick had long followed the cultural lead of France, so now, despite his own misgivings and the warnings of others (Justi claimed that the introduction of tax farming "was a great mistake which burdened the population unequally"),[45] he decided to follow the French economic and fiscal lead. Frederick, especially after 1763, wanted to strengthen his government, and he probably wanted to support some expensive reform movements such as the alleviation of impoverished aristocrats and the improvement of agriculture, but he doubted whether the existing bureaucracy would produce sufficient tax receipts to pay for his developmental projects. Losing patience with his own officials, a patience long strained because of prewar difficulties with them, he eventually took steps to separate a major part of their work load from them and to give it to various entrepreneurial consortiums.

Again, one should stress that the existing core bureaucracy was established to support a large standing army, the expenses of the court, and very limited ameliorative programs such as the settlement projects initiated by Frederick William I. It accomplished these difficult tasks efficiently by any standard, whether of the eighteenth century or the twentieth. The establishment of the Regie forced the executives of this service to begin to adapt to changing times. First, they devised ways to sabotage it, but, secondly, they devised ways to improve the performance of their own subordinates.

45. Justi, Staatswirtschaft, 1: 18.

VIII

BIRTH OF THE

NEW ADMINISTRATION

The success of the *Regie*,[1] the king's distrust, and the enormous weight of postwar reconstruction problems finally forced more flexible-minded officials to look for the safety and enhancement of their own careers. Naturally, much that happened after 1766 was due to bureaucratic fear of the loss of career opportunities, but much was also due to rather imaginative rethinking on the part of a particular reform group of bureaucrats of the role of a civil service in Prussia. Some officials finally learned how to work with the king, and he began to realize how the bureaucratic system might be redirected and reformed.

Curiously, the birthplace of the postwar bureaucratic reform was the fifth department of the General Directory. For years a small group of officials had labored under Fäsch in the tasks of compiling trade statistics and negotiating with various entrepreneurs. Fäsch was a good bureaucratic schoolmaster, since he possessed considerable knowledge of the complex western European economy and undoubtedly passed it on to his subordinates. One such was Ludwig von Hagen.[2] Hagen was born in Hohenstein in 1724, attended uni-

1. W. O. Henderson, *Studies in the Economic Policy of Frederick the Great* (London, 1963), p. 63, estimates that the *Regie* collected as much as one-third of the national revenue after 1766. This book provides a convenient survey in English of the economic history of the reign of Frederick II; the judgements expressed in it are usually shrewd and well founded.
2. C. A. L. Klaproth and W. C. Cosmar, *Geschichte des königlichen preussischen und kurfürstlichen brandenburgischen wirklichen Geheimen Staatsrats* (Berlin, 1805), pp. 444–45, gives a biographical sketch of Hagen.

versity, and entered the Prussian foreign service in 1744. A year's diplomatic service in 1745 was followed by entry into the civil service as a councillor for the Halberstadt board. He later served in the Cleves board before promotion to privy finance councillor of the General Directory in 1754. Hagen served as a senior subordinate of Fäsch in the fifth department until 1761. He was to be the greatest official to emerge in Prussia during the later half of the reign of Frederick the Great.

In 1761 the new minister of the sixth department, General von Wedell,[3] selected Hagen as his second in command. The sixth department, concerned with military provisioning, had not developed into a major department of the General Directory since its founding in 1746. During the Seven Years' War, however, its duties became of paramount importance, and Frederick determined to infuse some life into it by appointing a general to succeed the deceased minister, Katt. Wedell played a largely unrecognized but important role in the General Directory; he knew he was entrusted with a vital duty and determined to eliminate bureaucratic red tape whenever possible in pursuing this duty. Frederick told the surviving ministers of the General Directory that Wedell would receive all reports concerning the forage magazines and would have full charge of his department. The protests of Minister Boden, who defended bureaucratic niceties and procedure, were ignored by Wedell, who cared little for collegial administration. Furthermore, the "Ministre de Guerre" as Frederick called him, next sent a peremptory note to the General Directory (February 19, 1761), declaring that he would have complete responsibility for "all military matters," the supervision of the fifth department for the time being, the supervision of the salary charge treasury (*Chargenkasse*), and the authority to disburse from the general war treasury. In effect Wedell obtained a mandate from Frederick to unify the most important fiscal agencies of the General Directory under his immediate control. This emergency wartime development constituted a fundamental departure from the collegial

3. Klaproth, *Geheimen Staatsrats*, pp. 437. Merseberg, Gen. Dir. Mil. Dept. No. 2, 2–37.

system of the General Directory. It is quite possible that Councillor Hagen paid considerable attention to this object lesson in functional administration; the revitalized sixth department worked well during the last two years of the war.[4]

Hagen's Opportunity: Cleves, 1763

By 1763 Hagen possessed an intimate knowledge of the peculiarities of the western enclaves, particularly Cleves, much experience in the fifth department, and valuable service in the emergency administration of the sixth department. His first opportunity to wield enormous authority on his own without the immediate supervision of more senior officials came in 1763 when Frederick sent him to Cleves to head a commission to determine the extent of war damage.[5] He quickly revealed ability to handle problems as he found them, to plan flexibly, and to propose various alternative means for bringing about a revival of the economy in that western enclave. He appeared to obtain prompt results, unlike the hapless Brenckenhoff, who had been working almost fruitlessly on similar problems in Pomerania for over a year.

Hagen, for example, tried to solve the problem of agrarian indebtedness by first examining all available statistics on export–import trade and tax revenues. Secondly, he approached the local estates and obtained an agreement from them to establish a Land Credit Institute. Desperate private landowners were loaned capital at 3 percent interest and the king agreed to contribute some 105,010 talers to form

4. Merseberg, Gen. Dir. Mil. Dept. No. 2, 2–37. Curt Jany, *Geschichte der Königlich preussischen Armee bis zum Jahre 1807* (Berlin, 1928–33), 2: 212–13, maintained that von Wedell's sixth department was not "a war ministry in the modern sense" since, aside from that department, three other departments in the General Directory and the Silesian ministry continued to supervise diverse aspects of military supply, recruitment, etc. Nevertheless, the archival records clearly show that von Wedell was able to take charge of most supply matters within the General Directory during the latter half of the war, including the general war treasury which was nominally under the second department. Much of this emergency authority was given up in 1763, and Jany's statement becomes more applicable to the postwar period.

5. *AB*, 13: 222–23. Klaproth, *Geheimen Staatsrats*, pp. 444–45.

part of the loan capital. Hagen also obtained long-term Dutch loans. Although the nominal management of the institute was in the hands of a joint committee of officials and representatives of the estates, the actual administration was undertaken by an expert accountant sent from the General Directory. The whole plan had been brought to fruition as a result of considerable bureaucratic finesse and political skill. The provincial Estates and the boards both hoped to control the institute but Hagen knew that he and the General Directory would really manage it.[6] The Cleves Land Credit Institute was to be a fore-runner of the more famous plans to eliminate rural indebtedness in Silesia and elsewhere in the realm.

In fact, as happens so often, Hagen impressed his superiors more by the energy with which he tackled perplexing problems than by the questionable long-term success of his plans. The establishment of lotteries and tontines was particularly dubious: these projects proved troublesome, produced a small and uncertain income, and were a form of tax collection disguised as gambling. But Frederick demanded the tontine and lottery in Cleves, and Hagen had to include these dubious projects in his planning. After he had worked in East Frisia, Mörs, Halberstadt, and Cleves, Hagen admitted: "I know that one could bring forward better and more adequate proposals, and which would create fewer debts, but, in view of the effects of the war, little could be accomplished." A sympathetic jurist, von Raesfeld of Cleves, frankly replied to him, "that is the way of the world: one can seldom bring about even a single improvement."[7] The pessimistic resignation of these two experienced officials proved justified, since all of these measures were palliatives of little long-term benefit. Cleves suffered from economic stagnation that had existed long before

6. *AB*, 13: 158 ff., 204 ff., 222–23, 243 ff., 297 ff., 319 ff., 380, 532. See Ring, *Kolonisationsbestrebungen*, pp. 17–33, for discussion of one aspect of Cleves *Rétablissement*. Hartung ignores the rather insignificant Cleves *Rétablissement* in his "Der preussische Staat und seine westlichen Provinzen," *Staatsbildende Kräfte der Neuzeit* (Berlin, 1961), pp. 414–30. He portrays a Cleves society rent by international divisions; a society and economy unimaginatively dominated by the Hohenzollerns and their officials in the seventeenth and eighteenth centuries.

7. *AB*, 13: 373–81. For economic problems including tariff decline see *AB Handelspolitik*, 3: 1, 62–71, 84–85.

the Seven Years' War and would continue until the industrial revolution of the nineteenth century. But Frederick, if he had pessimistic thoughts, still was impressed by Hagen's efficiency. Hagen had also revealed an extraordinary ability to fathom the motives of people, whether they were board officials or local merchants or landlords, and to establish amicable working relationships with most of them.

From Chief of the Third Department to Chief of the General Directory

After subjecting Hagen to an interview, "a sharp examination, province by province," the king appointed him to the post of minister of the third department of the General Directory in June, 1764.[8] Between that date and 1767 Hagen continued to direct the activities of Cleves and other enclaves in the west in this least prestigious of the departments. Since he believed that the previous government of these isolated territories no longer sufficed, he abandoned collegialism and greatly restricted the authority of provincial presidents. His efforts took two main directions: first, he maintained constant vigilance fortified by frequent personal inspections, and, secondly, he reorganized the boards in order to make their work functional in orientation and decentralized in operation. He determined to establish the entire western administration on a new basis that would result in higher tax revenues and, generally, in less trouble with local interest groups.

Between June, 1764, and February, 1767, officials were shuffled about, new regulations introduced, and a far-ranging experiment in decentralized government started. Hagen was aided by very able lieutenants: Reichard of the General Directory, Colomb of the East Frisian board, and Derschau of the Cleves board. Working together, these officials established a new administrative bureau in Cleves, a so-called "board deputation" to administer Geldern and Mörs. This step, initiated by Reichard, eliminated a local aristocratic commission in favor of a miniature War and Domains Board technically responsible to the Cleves board, but actually independently operated under

8. *AB*, 13: 401–2.

permanently assigned bureaucrats. In one sense the board deputation represented something new; it decentralized bureaucratic control and took away some of the authority of the Cleves board. Separate board Deputations were subsequently established in the County of Mark, Lingen, Tecklenburg, Halberstadt, Hohenstein, Altmark, and Prignitz. The last two had previously been under the control of the Magdeburg and Electoral Mark boards respectively, but they were obviously established along the lines of the Geldern-Mörs board deputation when Hagen became the chief minister of the General Directory after 1767.[9] In total, these administrative innovations seemed to portend important changes in the Prussian bureaucracy itself. Decentralization and functionalism seemed to be guiding lights after 1767.

Hagen could not forget the nagging problems of reconstruction in the west completely, and he was to complain in 1768 that the "disorders and the impertinent Cleves board have greatly shortened my life."[10] But he possessed enormous reserves of energy and a restless ambition; he determined to remake his department. He rewarded his loyal subordinates: Reichard was promoted to privy finance councillor in the General Directory, Derschau succeeded the tired and semi-competent Werdre as president of the Cleves board, and the commoner Colomb became the president of the East Frisian board in 1769.[11] Reichard, a minister of the General Directory by 1768, and the other two officials spent many nerve-racking months between 1763 and 1767 negotiating with the provincial estates over *Rétablissement*

9. Ibid., pp. 471–77, 497–500, 502–13. Upon the protests of the local superior court in Geldern concerning the assumption of control by the new deputation over Protestant churches, Hagen claimed: "The Superior Court is filled with loud mouthed Catholic subjects" and should have only limited judicial responsibility in consistorial matters (Ibid., pp. 541–44). Ibid., 14: 150–56. The subsequent history of the Geldern Mörs board can be found in Rohde, "Die Reformen Friedrichs des Grossen in Geldern" (Ph. D. Diss., Göttingen, 1913), pp. 19–52. This board failed, according to Rohde, to secure support of the local estates and did not compile a great record of accomplishment. In 1794 Stein more or less turned over local administration to the estates. *AB*, 13: 185–86. 14: 278–86, 536–38, 630–36; 15; 144–55.

10. Ibid., 14: 570–71.

11. See citations of note 6 above and *AB*, 14: 491–92, 527–30, 570–71.

problems and working with their subordinates in a very weedy administrative garden.

So great was Hagen's prestige by 1765 that he could work virtually unimpeded within the General Directory. All of the other ministers were new and had not participated individually in important reconstruction work in the provinces. Because he had built up an unusual position of trust with the king during the last two years, he could now afford to ignore the collegial system to some extent. His experience in the west had convinced him that most officials in the civil service lacked training in economics or in other branches of "cameral science." This deficiency could be remedied, he believed, by streamlining the lines of command within the bureaucracy and by better on the job training. He had, in connection with the first objective, established three new tax districts in Cleves, required annual reports of progress of reconstruction from all western board officials, and reformed the excise collection system.[12] These measures did not, however, solve a deeper problem, the lack of really efficient and well-trained men.

On March 25, 1765 he ordered the placement of *Referendare* in the third department. These apprentices, similar to those *Auscultatoren* in the boards, would learn finance and "cameral science" and would remain in the provinces to establish industries and to reform local administration. "The well-being of the subjects, depends . . . on subjects who have studied well and possess natural ability, energy, strength, and accuracy, to be drawn into the service and to be taught."[13] Certainly the nearly moribund *Auscultator* program, long opposed by the king, was being revived by this edict, but on new and professional lines. The older edicts, primarily promulgated during the

12. Ibid., 13: 554–55, 572–73.
13. Ibid., pp. 565–67. Schlabrendorff tried to institute the same type of program in Silesia in an edict of March 29, 1765. The timing of the two orders implies that von Hagen and von Schlabrendorff were both thinking of the same thing at the same time; they were probably collaborating in this matter as they were to collaborate later concerning the *Regie* and mining affairs. This cooperation marks a new departure in the relationship of the General Directory with the Silesian administration. See note of the editors on *AB*, 13: 565. (The editors of the *Acta Borussica* make no comment on the issuance of these two similar orders.)

reign of Frederick William I, had simply assumed that youths could be appointed to perform various odd jobs around the board so that they could pick up knowledge of existing techniques. But Hagen stipulated that these apprentices were now to receive a special training course within each board and should subject themselves to a thorough examination in tax affairs (excise taxes in particular), commerce, and manufacturing. Examinations would be conducted by the boards and the results forwarded to the General Directory. Unfortunately, Hagen received little cooperation. Few if any *Auscultatoren* were appointed in the boards, and the examination plan did not go into operation.[14]

It is probable that Hagen could only turn his attention to the internal organization of the General Directory itself after he had attempted these preliminary arrangements within his own department. It became obvious to him that his professional reforms had failed because they had been restricted to the third department. Reform would have to embrace the entire system and not just part of it. But Hagen could not devote attention to the extensive debates with his ministerial colleagues that would have been required until he put his own house in order and placed his lieutenants in key positions where they could supervise the third department. Freed of this responsibility, he initiated an enormous number of projects between 1767 and his death in 1771.

Under his forceful guidance, the ministers of the General Directory succeeded in promulgating new local regulations for East Prussia and in obtaining tighter control over internal security in the clerical bureaucracy in Berlin. By September of 1766,[15] when he was ordered by Frederick to establish a new central bank, it was obvious that he was the one minister whom the king regularly consulted. The metamorphosis was complete; he had developed from being just another chief of a department into that of chief of the General Directory as a whole.

14. Ibid., p. 567.
15. Preuss, *Friedrich der Grosse*, 3: 69–72. Preuss, *Urkundenbuch*, 3: 453–56, gives portions of the official edicts establishing the bank in 1765 and later.

The Professionalization of the Core Bureaucracy

Once he had consolidated his position in the General Directory, Hagen was ready to tighten up the organization of the entire central administration. At first he determined to revive the moribund Superior Accounts Office (*Oberrechnungskammer*) by making it the focal point for all revenues collected by the State, with the exception of the funds collected by the *Regie*, which were no longer under the control of the General Directory. As was typical of administrations throughout Europe in the Old Regime, the revenues of the Prussian State were collected by a number of different officials and deposited in a number of central treasuries. Only under Privy Finance Councillor Köppen during the Seven Years' War had there existed one treasury chief for all of these treasuries; both the ministers of the General Directory and many cameralists feared the institution of a finance ministry because its chief would obviously dominate the entire civil service. Hagen did not go so far as to advocate such a bureau, but his central accounting office would, nevertheless, keep close watch on all accounts and would be responsible only to the directing ministers and the king.[16] Moreover, he hoped to make the *ORK* a real central information agency that would provide the kind of accurate statistics that the directing ministers needed to formulate their projections and plans.

Of course, periodic "reforms" of the Superior Accounts Office had occurred before, with little result as Hagen well knew. He therefore insisted that each province would also have its accounting board subordinated not to the War and Domains Board but to the *ORK* in Berlin.[17] Hagen thus intended to establish a completely new bureaucratic system, one independent of the entire core bureaucracy except for its directing ministers. It would be a true watchdog because it would recruit, train, and promote its own officials. The system

16. Reinhold Koser, "Die preussischen Finanzen im Siebenjährigen Kriege," *FBPG* 16 (1903): 445–76. H.C. Johnson, "The Concept of Bureaucracy in Cameralism," *Political Science Quarterly* 79 (1964): 378–402. *AB*, 14: 421–26.

17. *AB*, 14: 263–68, 421–26, 429–33, 637–38. The *ORK* offices were organized collegially.

would be functional in approach: it would be responsible only for the control of funds through efficient bookkeeping, and it would see that the provincial accounts were carefully prepared and promptly forwarded. The importance of this innovation is obvious. It aimed to correct the diversified and confused fiscal supervision of the entire service and to prevent future embezzlers from taking advantage of this confusion. It would give a clearer picture of the strengths and weaknesses of administration because it would provide reliable statistics. Modern, yes. Unprecedented, no. Again, cameralists had often stressed the importance of a centralized fiscal control.[18] The foundation of the revised Superior Accounts Office was the most important reform to be introduced into the General Directory since its establishment in 1721. It spelled the ultimate defeat of the collegial system and the beginning of a professional and impersonal approach to state finances.

To Frederick the system afforded one great advantage: it would discourage embezzlement. Probably with this thought in mind, he ordered the chancellor of justice, Jariges, to cooperate with Hagen in drawing up the appropriate edicts.[19] The presidents of the provincial boards complained bitterly. They were to have no real control over the provincial accounts office, and for the first time, they were forced to submit their accounts regularly to these agencies or suffer severe fines. Hagen also recommended the dismissal of the present staff of the ORK and its replacement by a younger, better trained, group of accountants. He intended to make a complete break from the fruitless past history of this agency. Frederick could not help but be impressed with the scope of the scheme as well as with its attention to the specific details of administration.

Hagen next persuaded the king and his ministerial colleagues to support the establishment of a centralized recruiting system for the entire executive corps of the bureaucracy. The opportunity came

18. Jacob Bielfeld, *Institutions Politiques* (La Haye, 1760–72), 2: 5–15, makes perhaps the most elaborate case.
19. *AB*, 15: 30–32. By splitting financial control functions from the structure of the core bureaucracy, the *ORK* reforms weakened collegiality.

when Frederick sent one of his periodic injunctions to the General Directory to recruit more aristocrats. Hagen, although a Junker, was not particularly interested in recruiting aristocrats; he hoped to obtain qualified personnel regardless of their social background. But, accommodating himself, he recommended a dual recruitment: aristocrats would be appointed as *Auscultator* to an experienced *Landrat* and commoners as *Auscultator* to a *Steuerrat* of the board. For half of each year the apprentices from both sources would be trained together in the board itself. This period of training would provide a pool of young candidates for vacant councillor or *Landrat* posts. The local county estates would then elect a *Landrat* from the list of the aristocratic apprentices who had passed a qualifying examination. The boards would do likewise when they needed to fill a councillor post, presumably selecting from the commoners who had worked under a *Steuerrat*. One central commission in Berlin would examine the candidates and prepare the lists of qualified appointees.[20]

The projected training program was of key importance; all apprentices would acquire a knowledge of finance and "cameral" affairs, taxes and contributions, domain revenue, agronomy, manufacturing, commerce, mathematics, "practical physics and mechanics," and all would learn the "solid interest of the landlords as well as conservation of all *Stände*."[21] On the surface, Hagen's plan called for the aristocratic apprentices to proceed up one bureaucratic

20. Ibid., pp. 240–54. See chapter 2 for a discussion of prewar attempts. Justi, perhaps the most famous cameralist of his generation, favored a bureaucratic recruitment and training program even more extensive than Hagen suggested, and without any attempt to separate aristocratic from commoner candidates. See Johnson, "Concept of Bureaucracy," pp. 393–95.

21. *AB*, 15: 240–55. Again Hagen's course of study is typically cameralistic. Joachim Georg Darjes, *Erste Gründe der Cameralwissenschaften* (Berlin, 1768), pp. 426–43, wished to see a lower and secondary school system established which would separate peasants from the urban poor and would educate each according to the "needs of the State." The peasants should be taught to "read, to write a little, and to acquire the first principles of religion" so that they would "follow the rule of reason as members of the peasant estate" and could contribute to the general welfare. The cameralists of this generation, including such men as Darjes, Phillipi, and Justi, were not radical social reformers, and Justi was almost alone in developing a theory of bureaucratic expertise. Hagen's plan is thus quite remarkable, because it dealt with the training of bureaucrats themselves and not with plans to vaguely encourage the populace to be good.

line, that beginning with local agrarian management, while the non-aristocratic apprentices would proceed up the other line from first jobs in local municipal bodies. But commoners often attained agrarian skills as *Amt* contractors, and the mastery of manufacturing processes required knowledge of the so-called cottage industry. Under the putting-out system, many peasants were also weavers, and there was not always a clear-cut division between town and country. The skills mentioned by Hagen included knowledge of physics, mechanics, and mathematics—a technical background not common to country squires.[22] The cameralists taught that the economy consisted of interdependent play of manufacturing, commercial, and

22. The nonaristocratic managers of domain properties were of three kinds: one group resembled the French entrepreneurs of the *Regie* in that they hoped to exploit the peasantry as much as possible. Frederick II instituted many plans to make the domain contractors more efficient, and these plans probably convinced them to search more diligently for a greater profit. A second group of managers probably resembled the run-of-the-mill aristocratic landlords since they were neither well educated in contemporary agronomic theories nor anxious to do more than was absolutely required. But the third group consisted of dedicated professional agricultural executives. These persons were the real experts in Prussia, and in the years 1763–1780 a select number of them were sent by the Electoral Mark board to England to study the revolutionary methods employed there. When the king ordered the General Directory to dispatch young and intelligent men on this mission, it is highly significant that professional bureaucrats and aristocratic landlords were *not* chosen. See Potsdam, Pr. Br., Rep. 2, I, Dom. Reg. D 1819, 2 ff. The old works on the domains *Beamte* do not discuss this matter. See S. Isaacsohn, "Das Erbpachtsystem in der preussischen Domänenpolitik," *Zeitschrift für preussische Geschichte*, 2: 698–736 (1879); and Franz Berghoff-Ising, *Entwicklung des Landwirtschaftspachtwesens in Preussen* (Berlin, n.d.); Rudolph Stadelmann, *Preussens Könige in ihrer Thätigkeit für die Landeskultur*, *PKPA* IX: 119–24. (1882) The merchants of Prussian cities were as much bound by semifeudal traditions and modes of thought as were the *Junkers*. They, in common with the aristocrats, were firmly convinced of the validity of inherited position and were nearly as ignorant of physics, mathematics, and western European culture as their country cousins. Nevertheless, after 1750, increasing commercial contact between the most powerful of Prussian bankers and merchants with Amsterdam and Hamburg, the foundation of the central state bank, the influence of outsiders such as Fäsch and Calzabigi, and, perhaps, the impact of the Enlightenment, helped to raise the stature of the businessman. Certainly the novels of the period from 1700 to 1810 show a changing picture of the merchant from being a petty, grasping, local profit-maker to a more cosmopolitan, affluent entrepreneur in the early stages of modern capitalism. Ernst Baasch, "Der Kaufmann in der deutsche Roman literatur des 18. Jr.," *Aus Sozial-und Wirtschaftsgeschichte: Gedächtnissschrift für Georg von Below* (Stuttgart, 1928), pp. 283–98.

agricultural production; their suggestions seem to have been followed
by Hagen. The aristocratic apprentices were thus required to learn
certain technical and managerial skills already possessed by many
commoners.

Parallel with the system of dual apprentices was Hagen's plan for
the examination of candidates for vacant provincial board presidencies and first directorships. Again, aristocratic *Landräte* would be
examined for presidential vacancies while bourgeois *Steuerräte* were
to be examined for the first directorships. On the surface, then, the
bureaucracy would be comprised of two separate divisions, one dominated by aristocrats and the other by commoners. This constituted a
retrogressive step since the civil service had long operated on the
theory that recruitment would be based on ability, not social origin.
Nevertheless, the preeminence of aristocrats in society and Frederick's
own preferences influenced Hagen.[23] The king stated many times that
he thought the aristocrats were better fitted to be policy makers and
executives than were commoners, who were inclined to specialization
and lacked ability to command.

Hagen's plan was a masterpiece because it seemed to achieve two
objectives: the fulfillment of the preferences of the king as well as the
professionalization of the bureaucracy. But, in common with many
marriages of convenience, the plan lacked cohesion and contained
certain fallacious assumptions. The plain fact of the matter was that
administration in the Prussia of the post–Seven Years' War period
required that even high-ranking executives learn many details of commerce and manufacturing, much more than even well-travelled and
well-educated noblemen were apt to have. The bureaucracy would be
professionalized, but it would be professionalized on technocratic,
not aristocratic, lines. It would not be a division of responsibility
between agrarian (aristocratic) specialists and urban (commoner)

23. Rosenberg, in *Bureaucracy, Aristocracy, and Autocracy* (Cambridge,
1958), p. 160, claims correctly that "the numerical ratio" between noble and
non-noble office holders did not change drastically in the reign of Frederick the
Great. However, as he pointed out (p. 163), aristocrats took the lion's share of
high offices after 1740. But his conclusion, that aristocratic office holders molded
the bureaucracy according to aristocratic criteria, is one that does not seem to be
in congruence with the facts of bureaucratic life after 1763.

specialists. The static and neat division of society into aristocrats, bourgeoisie (and urban classes in general), and the peasantry which Frederick described in his *Political Testament*[24] of 1752 did not exist, nor could a bureaucratic parallel to it be established.

The aim of the plan, then, was not the bifurcation of administration which it implied but the stress on an essential unity. All officials of executive rank would have to submit themselves to examination at some point in their careers. The new examination commission would perforce direct its work in different ways to fit the requirements of vacant offices, but the essential unity was present. On February 12, 1770 the Superior Examination Commission began its duties.[25] The professionalization of the Prussian civil service began.

Harnessing of the Entrepreneurs: The Royal Bank

Hagen occupied himself with three struggles during his ministerial career: with bureaucratic problems, with the *Regie*, and with economic problems. The professionalization of the bureaucracy, partly the fruit of conflict with the *Regie*, was to be further developed through involvement of officials in far-ranging mining, engineering, and banking managerial activity. All of these latter aspects of economic policy were connected with one central program: the king and Hagen both hoped to bring the entrepreneurs under control. The chaotic currency exchange business and unregulated banking activity were the first undesirable manifestations of entrepreneurial independence to be conquered. Previous to 1756, both Fäsch, head of the fifth department, and Graumann, head of the mint, had proposed the establishment of a state bank to control great entrepreneurs such as Splitgerber and Gotzkowsky. By 1763 nothing remained of these abortive schemes; the absence of governmental control over the Berlin banks was an important factor in the damaging market panic of that year. An unsigned *Promemoria* of 1764 in the Electoral Mark board drew

24. See Elsbeth Schwenke, *Friedrich der Grosse und der Adel* (Berlin, 1911), for an intelligent and brief discussion of this problem of Frederick's social philosophy.
25. *AB*, 15: 260–62.

the attention of the higher officials of that province to another danger:
letters of credit for Prussian commercial transactions in Stettin and
other border cities had to be endorsed by either Hamburg or Amsterdam banks. Only a central bank in Berlin under government
auspices could rationalize banking activity and destroy foreign control over currency transactions.

Aware of this background, Hagen ordered Kircheisen, president of
the Berlin administration, to persuade prominent local merchant
firms such as Splitgerber and Daum, Schutze, Wegely and Son, and
others, to agree to serve on the board of directors of a new state bank
as well as to subscribe funds for its capitalization. Calzabigi obliged by
supervising the subscription list and by obtaining private capital from
foreign as well as domestic investors. Frederick, already approached
by a Hamburg consortium with a similar plan, cooperated with
Hagen and signed the appropriate edict in June of 1765. In order to
heal the wounds of the Seven Years' War a government bank would
be established to "make all exchange and trade business flourish."[26]

Initially established with public funds amounting to a million
talers, the bank eventually opened seven branches throughout the
realm. The special role of Splitgerber and of the famous Breslau firm
of Eichborn continued; they remained official bankers of the crown,
but by 1772 they no longer wielded great influence. The Royal Bank
was a successful attempt to regulate commercial activity and encourage private investors to direct their interest towards trading and
manufacturing rather than towards currency speculation. The Asiatic
Trading Company of 1772, the Emden Herring Company, the Bengal
Trading Company, and other enterprises also could be funded with
greater ease than their abortive prewar predecessors.

Prussian officials did not know very much about banking prior to
1766. Graumann and Fäsch, brought into the service at high ranks
after extensive experience with west European finance, possessed
limited influence in the bureaucracy at large. But Hagen, assisted by
Privy Finance Councillor Magusch, relied on the services of both

26. J.D.E. Preuss, *Friedrich der Grosse* (Berlin, 1833), 3: 70. Schrotter, *AB
Münzwesen*, 2: 138 ff. Potsdam. Pr. Br. Rep. 30, Berlin, Tit. 23, no. 2–250.

Prussian businessmen and a Hamburg consortium to provide the technical guidance needed. A few imported Amsterdam banking experts undoubtedly supplemented this guidance. Hagen wanted the Royal Bank to control the business community by regulating speculators. His revised Bank Ordinance of 1766 struck directly at the currency exchange business by requiring that the notes of the Royal Bank were to take the place of foreign bills of exchange. Of course the prewar dream of Magusch that the government could absolutely control all important fiscal activity in Berlin would not be realized until 1786 or later, perhaps because the bank did not possess sufficient funds to assume this grandiose role.[27]

The Mining and Minerals Department

Hagen was able to establish a number of new functional agencies after he had introduced purely administrative reforms and had supervised the foundation of the Royal Bank. The Mining and Minerals Department, the Forestry Department, the Bank Commission, the Superior Construction Department (*Oberbau Department*), and other innovations seemed to resemble, as Haussherr suggested, the fifth and sixth departments of the General Directory as they were constituted before 1756.[28] But they really differed: they were established within the General Directory, not imposed from without. Secondly, they were the achievement of one important minister and were

27. Preuss, *Friedrich der Grosse*, 3: 69–72. Idem, *Urkundenbuch*, 3: 453–56, gives portions of the official edicts establishing the bank in 1765 and later. Friedrich Lenz and Otto Unholtz, *Die Geschichte des Bankhauses Gebrüder Schickler* (Berlin, 1912), pp. 125–30. W. O. Henderson, *The State and the Industrial Revolution in Prussia, 1740–1870* (Liverpool, 1958), pp. 140 ff., gives an interesting sketch of the subsequent history of the bank; see also his *Studies in the Economic Policy of Frederick the Great* (London, 1963), p. 62: "The teething troubles of the Royal Bank of Berlin . . . were due largely to the failure of the King to find administrators of the necessary caliber to take charge of them." Henderson thus puts his finger on a fundamental bureaucratic problem of eighteenth-century Prussia. See also *AB*, 14: 164.

28. Hans Haussherr, *Verwaltungseinheit und Ressorttrennung* (Berlin, 1953), p. 139. Haussherr does indicate that the postwar innovations were far more important than the establishment of the fifth department in 1740.

interrelated aspects of one, new, approach to the problems of administration. All were designed to give a new direction to the General Directory and to liberate that organization once and for all from the soul-destroying tasks of fiscal supervision and to make it a true promoter of economic development. Hagen, of course, never lost sight of the fiscal side and believed that all agencies of the government existed for the purpose of increasing the tax-paying potentiality of the subjects of the king of Prussia. But the cameralistic message had finally reached his mind: the power of a state depended upon the economic resources of its subjects. Since he had a practical, rather than an abstract or theoretical, approach, his innovations were never established on grandiose philosophical grounds or given vague general directions. The original fifth department had been established by Frederick in 1740 precisely on these theoretical grounds and its failure proved that no one agency could supervise all aspects of economic development. Hagen believed, however, that one minister, or a few ministers working in harmony, could supervise various aspects of the economy.

Both Hagen and the king realized that gold and silver deposits were not available to be exploited; the deficit in the balance of trade could not be rectified so simply. But iron deposits were large, and that metal was widely used by artisans. The exploitation of mineral resources, particularly iron, became an important aspect of economic planning because such metals, if obtained outside the realm, would adversely affect the balance of trade. The edict that established the new Mining and Minerals Department in February, 1768,[29] simply transferred all

29. The history of mining operations has been discussed rather fully, but little emphasis has been placed on the administrative framework. For a general discussion of the Malapane mining settlement see Walter Kuhn, *Siedlungs-geschichte Oberschlesiens* (Würzburg, 1954), pp. 201–18, which places mining endeavors in a wider discussion see H. Fechner, "Die Königlichen Eisenhütten-werke Malapane und Kreuz zu ihrer Übernahme durch des schlesische Ober-bergamt, 1753–1780," *Zeitschrift für Berg- Hütten- und Salinenwesen*, 43: 43, 81 ff. Hans-Wilhelm Büchsel, *Rechts- und Sozialgeschichte des oberschlesischen Berg- und Hüttenwesens 1740 bis 1806* (Breslau, 1941), gives a very complete history of mining in Silesia and includes a good discussion of the work of Heinitz. A. Zottmann, *Die Wirtschaftspolitik Friedrichs des Grossen* (Leipzig, 1937), pp. 1–49, places mining promotion within a wider context of general economic planning by the State.

matters concerned with mining to the supervision of Hagen. At first he considered this change to be merely an administrative one. Files were consolidated and officials were assigned to clerical tasks.

By the end of May, 1768 Hagen had established a separate bureau and had acquired the services of two experienced privy finance councillors. Councillor Ernst had earlier performed inspection trips in the provinces and received a promotion to privy finance councillor when he became Hagen's senior subordinate. But for some months he had to administer banking and invalided veterans' affairs in addition to his mining duties.[30] As late as November, 1769, all of the executive officials were forced to devote most of their energy to their other duties. Finally, Hagen obtained the transfer of a whole host of clerks and prepared a general ordinance for the conduct of business. In no way was the mining department a radical break from the traditions of the General Directory during this two year period. Hagen had to occupy himself with paperwork and with the recruitment of clerical staff. Frederick was not yet convinced that Hagen had a serious reform in mind, but did order the General Directory to refer all mining matters to him.[31]

After 1770, however, the Mining and Minerals Department began to develop along unprecedented lines; it acquired technical expertise and expanded its activities considerably beyond its original borders. Originally, the agency was established to consolidate existing administrative controls under one head, but the mining ordinances of 1769, issued in Berlin and in Breslau, suggested that the consolidated agency would, in fact, attempt to direct all mining operations in the realm. The Breslau ordinance was signed by both Hagen and the Silesian minister and gave to the mining department supervision of all minerals in the realm.[32] Prospectors would have to report their finds to the new department, and they, or other entrepreneurs, would

30. Hagen obtained control of all mining affairs in May, 1768. See *AB*, 14: 47; 476–77. One mining expert, Cramer, had been hired from the Brunswick service according to the editors of the *Acta Borussica*, 14: 477.

31. Merseburg, Rep. 120 I, Tit. III, I, 108, 1–7. Chancelry clerks and copyists were not trained or experienced in mining matters and were hired in the same way as other clerks in the General Directory.

32. Merseburg, Rep. 121, Abt. A. Tit. IV, Sect. 3, No. 104, Vol. I, 4–57.

receive concessions from this agency. Inspectors would check the
technical side, including "machines, whether operated by water,
beasts, or manpower, or by other means."[33] These administrative
directions, not particularly novel elsewhere in Europe, were new in
Prussia where the direction of mining had been poorly organized.

After the death of Hagen in 1771, the supervision of the mining
department passed first to his lieutenant, Schulenburg, then to Waitz
von Eschen for a few months in 1774, and, finally, to Heinitz. Although Heinitz is usually credited with the founding of the mining
department, the real credit belongs to Hagen. The successors of that
enterprising official built on his foundations. In 1774 the department
developed a research laboratory after Superior Mining Councillor
Gerhard, a lieutenant of Eschen, submitted a report stressing the
need for "metalurgical and chemical research" of the soil samples
forwarded to Berlin. Frederick, after hesitation, approved the ex-
penditure of 336 talers for chemicals and equipment.[34] The department had taken a first tentative step towards bringing about a union
of administrative authority with technical expertise. The techniques
of mining were old, the experience of Prussian officials and miners
limited, and nothing of the "industrial revolution" could be seen in
the work of the new department. But one of the most significant
foundations of the nineteenth-century technological and industrial
"great leap forward" was laid. Justi and other cameralists had vaguely
hinted that administration might be improved by official sponsorship
of technological research,[35] but this development only occurred in
Prussia after 1763.

33. Ibid. A separate Superior Mining Office was opened in Rothenburg on
December 7, 1772, as a dependency of the office at Halle. This edict marks,
perhaps, the first time the government tried to supervise the extensive coal mining
operations in this region. The *Ober-Hütten und Bergbau Rat* Unger received
typical instructions to see that shafts were prepared in accordance with safe
practice and that a program of exploratory digging was instituted and carried out.
Merseburg, Rep. 121, Abt. A., Tit. IV, Sect. 4, No. 1, 27. See same file for
Magdeburg Mining Office which was established for similar purposes in 1772,
(pp. 45–46). These offices were established as *collegia* (pp. 47–48).

34. Merseburg. Rep. 121. Abt. A, Tit. III, Sec. 4, No. 1, 18–19, 3–15.

35. Louise Sommer, *Die österreichischen Kameralisten* (Vienna, 1925), 2:
226–34, gives a summary of Justi's views on economic questions. Typically, Justi

Soon the recruitment of personnel for the new department revealed a similar concern for technical expertise. In 1778 a recruiting poster called for those who "have the necessary school science, are able to write in a good hand, to reckon adequately, and who prove themselves capable." In order to obtain such technicians, or mining supervisors, Heinitz stipulated that apprentices (*Elève*) must first work in a mine or in some other basic area of production such as smelting, "in order to make themselves aware of the practical side of all work and business." After working for two years in a *Bergamt*, or contract mine, they would become "cadets" and be paid a subsistence allowance. The most able would be sent abroad to study foreign mining and all would take an examination. The *Elève* and cadets were distributed in the central office and in provincial centers such as Breslau, Magdeburg, Rothenburg, and Hagen. Iron production, which centered in Silesia, was the most important aspect of mining in the realm: it merited its own office and was jointly managed by the Silesian minister and Heinitz. Professionalization appeared even more advanced when Heinitz and his aides surveyed the scientific literature on mining and required all officials to study Waller's *Metallurgy,* Cramer's *Advanced Soil Analysis* (*Grosse Probier Kunst*), and three others of similar nature. Heinitz expected new officials to have a solid grounding in theory acquired partly in universities and other schools, practical training in the field, and experience in mining administration.[36] He had, in summary, a well thought out and practical program of recruitment.

---

emphasized commerce and the support of manufacturing. He did, however, have a reputation as a mining expert, and was on this ground so hired in Prussia after the Seven Years' War. Justi proved a failure and was convicted of neglect of duties. He was dismissed and played no role in the establishment of the mining administration under Hagen or Heinitz. *AB*, 13: 720–21; 14: 277–78, 443–44. One biographer states that Justi met a "tragic end" as a prisoner in the Cüstrin fortress. See Ernst Klein, "Johann Heinrich Gottlob Justi und die preussische Staatswirtschaft," *VSWG* 48 (1961): 145–202, for a review of his influence on Prussia. In reality, Justi echoed the views of Frederick and many Prussian officials on economic matters, but Klein is not able to show that he possessed much influence.

36. Merseburg. Rep. 121, Abt. A, Tit. IV, Sec. III, No. 104, Vol. 1, 3–162, (particularly 102). Rep. 121 A, Tit. X, Sect. I, No. 101, I, 1–3. The mining

Heinitz and his predecessors were bureaucrats of long standing and only secondarily mining administrators. The mining department was therefore a strange mixture of well-tried administrative techniques, cameralistic theory, and true innovations. The administrative format was copied from the core bureaucracy; each mining office was collegial in nature.[37] Heinitz admonished his subordinates to do their duty in the same tone used by ministers in the General Directory for decades. His apprenticeship program resembled the old *Auscultator* program in the General Directory. The mining department revealed little new in administrative organization and techniques.

Certain characteristic goals of the later cameralists such as Justi were shared by the founders of the new department. Officials, for example, were supposed to find and exploit mineral resources and oversee the activities of the entrepreneurs and miners. Justi himself was hired by the General Directory in 1764, but remained in the Prussian service only three years.[38] Possibly both Hagen and Heinitz were influenced by Justi, but the evidence is not at hand. Both ministers were practical minded officials and not interested in theory. Heinitz, at least, thought officials needed such a preparation and was thinking along the lines of Justi.

Practically all of the cameralists thought economic policy could be determined and executed by a single all-embracing department, such as the Prussian fifth department of 1740. They had not really emphasized reorganization on functional lines;[39] that step would be taken by Hagen when he created a number of specialized departments. By establishing the mining department he made it possible for Heinitz to emphasize expertise in his officials. A superior mining councillor had to know a complex field and had to have both theoretical and

department began to subscribe to the major European economic journals by 1778: *The Hamburger Intelligenz Blatt, Hannoversche Magazin, Gazette d'Agriculture et de Commerce*, and others. Heinitz was particularly interested in Hanover and Braunschweig mining practices. Merseburg, Rep. 121, Abt. A, Tit. IV, Sect. 2, No. 2, vol I, 55–9.

37. Merseburg, Rep. 121, Abt. A, Tit. IV, Sect. 2, No. 2, Vol. I, 4–33 ff.

38. See note 35 above for Justi.

39. Justi, *Staatswirtshaft*, xxvii ff. Justi, *Policeywissenschaft*, pp. 337 ff. See Johnson, "Concept of Bureaucracy," pp. 393–95.

practical training. The functionalism of the new department and the peculiar expertise of its officials made it a revolutionary innovation in Prussian administrative history.

A pervasive theme of contemporary literature was the idea that all human knowledge could be simplified and codified so that it could be included in a rationalistic philosophical system of categories. This was a familiar theme of Diderot's *Encyclopédie*. The *Philosophe* hoped to be a gifted amateur in many fields, but a specialist or expert in none. Also many aristocrats and their admirers such as Frederick really despised individual specialization as a "bourgeois" attribute. In a modest sense, the mining department was a triumph over both philosophical *simplificateurs* and aristocratic dilettantes.

How did Hagen and his successors bring about this astonishing innovation? Hagen, well versed in the pedestrian, fiscally oriented routine of the General Directory, discovered that his training and the organization of the bureaucracy itself could not make Prussian administration in the western enclaves successful. Between 1763 and 1767 he grappled with this problem and tried many different expedients in order to improve the administration of the third department. But he finally realized, as did few of his contemporaries or predecessors, that the civil service was poorly instituted and outmoded and had to be thoroughly changed. The worst enemy of the General Directory and of the boards was neither the king nor the landed aristocracy, but the old bureaucracy itself. It was a hidebound victim of its own routines and circumscribed view of the world. Hagen's decision to create functional departments, of which the mining department was the first and most important, constituted a new attempt to grapple with the real problems of the realm. These problems included a caste-bound social system, a large standing army, and a stubborn, cynical, but intelligent chief executive. Hagen and his successors could do nothing to change these realities. But the backward economic status of the realm constituted an area for reform. Hagen and Heinitz especially wanted to orient the entire bureaucracy towards the attainment of the goal of economic development, parity with western Europe and with England. These, perhaps, were the great although unstated aims of the avant garde within the Prussian corps of officials who, however, did not understand the nature of the pervasive change underway in England.[40] Before 1760 Hagen had been an unimaginative man of routine and a respectable bureaucrat, but he underwent a metamorphosis such as few men experience. He became more and more convinced that a civil service should be a dynamic organization filled with technically qualified people. He was a Junker, a landowner, and no friend of the serfs, but his quest for technical expertise made him a true radical in an age that despised technical expertise. This Junker became, perhaps, the prototype of a new bourgeois. Without Hagen's preparatory work it is extremely doubtful whether Heinitz would have been able to pursue his particular form of *Bildung*.

Science: Captive of the State

Within a year Hagen understood the ramifications of the establishment of the mining department and was ready to apply similar techniques to other administrative problems. In the last week of March, 1770 Frederick became impatient with the performance of the civil engineers in the Electoral Mark board, threatening them with dismissal for incompetence. Hagen quickly suggested in a long memorandum that construction projects in the provinces could best be supervised by a new department of the General Directory: the Superior Construction Department (*Ober-Baudepartement*). Such a department, to be established according "to a systematic plan,"[41]

40. Hagen probably accepted the ideas and policies of the General Directory without question until he was selected to work with General Wedell in the sixth department in 1761. Between 1761 and 1764 he was already trying to devise new administrative techniques in the western provinces as described earlier in this chapter. Apparently English statesmen only began to understand the nature of industrialization after 1785. Witt Bowden, *Industrial Society in England* (New York, 1925), pp. 119 ff.

41. Potsdam, Pr. Br. Rep. 30A, 16, 13–23. This file pertaining to the affairs of the Electoral Mark board is useful because it shows how intimately von Hagen understood the need to recruit able technicians; he emphasized, in these orders, specific steps to be taken by provincial officials. The governor of Potsdam, who was also garrison commandant, was given authority to supervise building construction in that town, for example.

would incorporate the reforms suggested by the king, Hagen, and the engineering advisers of the latter (who were associated with the mining department). On April 7 he submitted his plan for the recruitment and training of apprentices for the *Ober-Baudepartement*, young people who "know building, forestry, and mining." These recruits would have to be trained at an institute which would be set up in the department. Hagen remarked that the professors of the Academy of Science were not working on important matters at present and could be used in the institute, but the universities he dismissed: "The professors from the universities are more speculative than practical." Within the institute, Professor Castillon (mathematics), Walter (mechanics and hydraulics), Rose (chemistry), Mining Councillor Gerhard (mining and minerals), and Gleditksch (forestry) would train youths to be *Bauräte* (engineers). A library would be assembled to house necessary technical books. Separate and subordinate construction departments would be established in each of the provinces. Finally, the new department would be responsible for three main administrative areas: machine construction for use in mines and elsewhere, construction of workhouses and other projects on the domains, and supervision of waterways construction. Obviously the *Ober-Baudepartement* was designed from the beginning to be a technical agency with rather precisely defined technical functions.[42]

Hagen had grasped the potential significance of his new department immediately. He noted that the Academy of Architecture, Sculpture, and Masonry already provided obvious technical services, and this agency, he suggested, should be incorporated into the Superior Construction Department. The academy was founded in 1699 in order to foster architecture in the realm, and the unique and numerous public and private buildings in Potsdam, Berlin and elsewhere erected between 1700 and 1770 provide some evidence of the success of its efforts. However, the great architects such as Knoblesdorff worked independently, and many of the artisans were imported on an ad hoc basis for elaborate building projects such as the ostentatious Neues Palais in Potsdam after 1763. The academy

42. See note 52 below; *AB*, 15: 280 ff.

existed, but its role has yet to be clarified. In any event Hagen discovered that it numbered on its staff in 1770 some twelve architects, master masons, and sculpturers. As an *Adjunctus Ordinarius,* Professor Wagener gave advice on mathematical matters (which amounted to geometry), optics, and perspective. Hagen believed the whole staff should be incorporated in his new department in order to "draw together all sciences and arts" connected with the construction not only of buildings but of machines of all kinds.[43] Experiments would be conducted on machines designed to be run by water power, wind, or manual human or animal labor. To Hagen, the Academy of Architecture, Sculpture, and Masonry was a ready-to-hand source of experts, and he wanted to put them to work in "practical" projects.

Negotiations between the General Directory and this academy continued over the next three decades. The academy remained indifferent to the approaches of the General Directory. The directors of the academy acknowledged that their work could, and should, be applied to the construction of new buildings and that art should serve as the informant of technology. But they were concerned with the problems of aesthetics: "The great masters such as Raphael, Michelangelo, Rubens, Corregio, etc., should be studied to see if they painted accurately and with proportion." Hagen replied that construction workers should be instructed in "accuracy" and "proportions" by the learned scholars.[44] Two worlds came into conflict: the practical bureaucrat with his evident intention to make the arts technological instruments and the artists insisting on the independence of art and its integrity.

Most remarkable as an example of Hagen's attitude towards science was his attempt to chain the Academy of Science to administrative and bureaucratic wishes. From 1764 onward he persuaded the Academy of Science to offer annual contests, open to its own members and to private inventors, to determine solutions to certain technical problems. One such was the construction of canals with their complicated lock systems. The mathematician Euler of the

43. Merseburg, Gen. Dir., *Oberbau Dept.*, Tit. I, No. 2, 1–7.
44. Ibid. pp., 8–9, 17.

academy had been consulted before the war on the Oder canal construction and had made various mathematical computations designed to insure accurate construction.[45] But after 1764 the academy was forced to consider specific problems submitted to it each year by the fifth department of the General Directory. Sometimes these problems were complicated applications of mathematics and physics to construction work, but most of the time they were surprisingly mundane, even simple, technological questions such as the General Directory's prize project of 1764: the invention of a stove. In that particular case the energies of the academy were spent over a period of a year examining various plans and preparing experiments to determine if a stove suitable for heating a large enclosed room could be invented. The prizewinning design attempted to utilize the heat usually dissipated through smoke from the fire. Remarkably, no one thought of the possibility of using steam, and the recommended design was based on the simple idea of having the smoke channelled through four columns surmounting the stove before it was finally discharged.[46] Subsequent prize contests proved just as questionable in value.

Considering the vast amount of time and effort expended on such proposals by persons in the General Directory and the Academy of Science, one remains astonished by the apparent lack of results. Naturally the king and his ministers had always been bombarded by elaborate projects submitted by entrepreneurs and adventurers:

45. Adolf von Harnack, *Geschichte der Königlichpreussischen Akademie der Wissenschaften zu Berlin* (Berlin, 1900); I.I. Detto, *FBPG* 16: 179 ff. Euler was also ordered to check on Calzabigi's lottery scheme of 1763 and was subsequently placed on a lottery supervisory commission, but resigned later. *AB*, 13: 206 ff., 346 ff.

46. Berlin, Zentrales Archiv der Deutschen Akademie der Wissenschaften, contains files recording requests from the General Directory as early as 1746 to examine plans submitted to it of improved forges and other devices. Apparently this did not become a regular practice until 1764, the year when von Hagen and others succeeded the Old Guard of the General Directory. The director, Formey, was ordered from 1746 onwards to test devices of various kinds, despite his protests that the scientists lacked the facilities to perform them. Specific files include: 1:5. 15; 1:6. 2, 80, 82, 142; 1:5. 10. Description of the prizes awarded by the General Directory for practical machine designs annually after 1764: 1:3, 84.

Calzabigi and his career mark one successful approach. Other entrepreneurs believed that they had invented "a machine which would uproot trees, launch ships, and move cannon easily," or a double-barrelled cannon which would increase the firing power of artillery units. Most of their proposals were fraudulent enterprises and fooled no one, but occasionally a promising technological proposal would have to be studied. One such was a new pump invented by Bertrand, formerly chief engineer to the Margrave of Hesse-Darmstadt, in 1769. The General Directory habitually sent such plans to the Academy of Science for investigation.[47] But a basic divergency of interest and technical backgrounds prevented the General Directory from turning the Academy of Science into a research laboratory, since neither the bureaucrats nor the scientists were really capable of solving problems of technology.

How does one explain this curious interplay of bureaucratic, entrepreneurial, and scientific ambitions? First, Hagen and his colleagues, including the veteran of the fifth department, Fäsch, had no expertise in tool design or other engineering problems, and they really could not separate the worthless proposals of cranks from the promising proposals of inventors. Secondly, none of the prize contest proposals, either the proposals of the ministers or the projects submitted by inventors, constituted revolutionary technological innovations. In contemporary England the application of machinery to the textile industry and the stumbling experiments in the use of steam served as a true prelude to modern industrialization, but on the continent, particularly in France and Prussia, few thought about division of labor, mass production, and the replacement of human labor by machines. Frederick II believed that the introduction of machines would displace the labor market and paid little attention to a curious experiment, a steam ship, launched on the Oder in the 1780's by some English entrepreneurs. To Hagen, or even Heinitz, the English innovations seemed unimportant. Therefore the schemes that bureaucrats in Prussia seriously consdiered were modest improvements on previous designs. For example, Bertrand's pump apparently did not

47. Ibid., 1:5. 15, 50–86.

use steam power but was a more efficient design possibly powered by a windmill. To the members of the academy, technological problems were of little interest. In 1772 the academy announced that its most famous member, the mathematician Euler, was offering a prize for the best explanation of the problem of floral transplants: how could trees and other flora be taken from one environment and placed in another successfully?[48] Even in this case no attempt was made by the scientists to help the Prussian silk industry, the dubious venture so highly prized by Frederick. Bureaucrats wanted quick solutions to minor technical problems, entrepreneurs wanted money to develop vague projects, and the academicians probably cursed both groups and preferred to contemplate the puzzles of "pure" science.

Nevertheless, a curious relationship existed for many years between the General Directory and the Academy of Science. Shortly after its reinstitution in 1746, the academy was ordered to prepare annually a massive calendar and almanac to be printed and distributed by the government. This clerical task, which the resentful scientists could never avoid during the reign of Frederick II, actually took up most of their time and energy. When Hagen and his colleagues began to consider the academy a cheap research and testing laboratory, Euler and his colleagues became even more discontented. Euler eventually left to take service under Catherine II. The forced marriage of science and industry nevertheless was a revolutionary insight on the part of Hagen and Fäsch, but only because of its nineteenth-century evolution, not because of the ideology that underlay it during the reign of Frederick II.

Introduction of "English" Agronomy

As early as 1764 Prussian officials began to interest themselves in English methods of farming. An apprentice to the Electoral Mark board, Neuhaus, had recently been sent to England and on his return was assigned to investigate certain domain properties in the Altmark,

48. Ibid., 1:6, 10, 8–13. Conrad Matschoff, "Friedrich der Grosse als Beförderer des Gewerbefleisses," *Technik Geschichte* (1912).

Uckermark, and Prignitz to see if "English agronomy (*Wirtschaft*)" could be introduced. He was supposed to check both methods of cultivation and problems of forest management. The General Directory and Frederick decided to send several "outstanding young men" to England to learn more about the new agronomy. These men were drawn solely from the families of domain managers in Pomerania, the New Mark, the Electoral Mark, and Magdeburg, one from each province. They left in 1764 for a year of research.[49]

An English farmer, Joseph Wilson, was given a contract in 1767 for the cultivation of some domain land in the Electoral Mark. Unfortunately, he was assigned land he considered "extremely Barron and very inconveneant" and claimed that efforts to cultivate it "will be attended with an Extronery Expense." He nevertheless obtained funds and permission to erect the necessary buildings. The Wilson project or others like it apparently continued until 1774, when a financial accounting was made of the various attempts to introduce "English agronomy." These expenses seem high: some 63,657 talers to work domain plots in various counties of the Electoral Mark. Little evidence remains of results, but apparently they were insignificant. Despite this record, Robert Williams obtained a contract in 1780 for a similar project. By 1780 officials were more cautious and offered to grant Williams a regular domain (*Amt*) managership. He was then equivalent to other domain contractors and under the same rules and regulations.[50] Results from Williams's experiment have apparently not been noted. The land selected for such experiments usually was of poor quality: Neuhaus had earlier warned that it was uncultivated and sandy.[51]

Obviously Hagen knew something of the earlier attempts to improve agriculture on the domain lands, since he signed some of the decrees concerned with the Wilson project and with the plan to send agronomists to England. But Frederick played a more important

49. Potsdam. Pr. Br. Rep. 21, Dom. Reg. D1819. 1–32.
50. Merseburg. Gen. Dir. Kurmark. Tit. LXVII, Sect. b, no. 15, includes material on the Wilson project. The Williams project is to be found in Potsdam. Rep. 2, D1801.
51. Potsdam. Pr. Br. Rep. 2, I Dom. Reg. D1819, 1–32.

role, and the actual supervision of work was left to board officials. The domain contractors were probably the most able farm managers in the realm and were more likely to respond to the introduction of new methods than private landowners. Nevertheless, they enjoyed considerable latitude in operations during the contractual period; only at the end of a contract period was any official attempt made to assess their performance. No concerted program was ever devised to encourage agricultural improvements. Prussian officials vaguely knew that turnips and soil enrichment were keys to English success, but they lacked reliable information on England and were preoccupied with a multitude of other problems. The potential importance of agronomy was not understood by the king or by his officials. In fact it is quite possible that much money was wasted because officials believed that the "English System" would greatly improve uncultivated and poor land. The agronomic improvements in England may well have been introduced on much better land, land that had been productive and might be made even more profitable. Wilson tried to warn his employers in 1764 that agriculture depended upon climate, humidity, and the basic quality of the soil. He was expected to transmute lead into gold and failed. It is also quite possible that these abortive schemes reflected a basic misconception of agrarian economics. Hagen might have profited, if he had been able, from the later analysis of Ricardo: the amount of land placed into cultivation was largely dependent upon the prices of farm produce, and where prices were low only the best available land would be used by farmers. Where prices were high, said Ricardo, less desirable land would be used in order to increase productivity. The international demand for German grain continued to be reasonably good throughout the eighteenth century, particularly after the American Revolution. But, as Skalweit suggests,[52] the capital necessary for cultivating new domain or private land was relatively limited, and peasant work traditions were relatively inflexible.

Hagen apparently never grasped the lesson that the experienced English farmers such as Wilson were trying to teach: that more could

52. Skalweit, *AB Getreidepolitik*, 3: 23–30.

be obtained from improving land that already was productive than from land of poor quality. This error was obvious in the entire program for division of common land which Frederick initiated and Hagen and his colleagues in the General Directory tried to promote. In 1765 the sons of domain managers were sending reports back to the General Directory from England where they had been sent to learn English agronomy. Naturally they mentioned the enclosure movement. Frederick quickly ordered Hagen to work out a plan for division of common pasture, forest, and other land belonging to villages and towns under both private and governmental control. Since any change in the status of common land involved difficult questions in feudal and manorial law, Hagen conferred with the Justice Department. The jurists expressed doubts about the legality of abolishing common land which presently was providing the wood and supporting the sheep which the peasantry needed to sustain itself. Hagen then temporized, saying that the king intended only to abolish such common land that was being used by a particular individual or which could be made more productive than before.[53] The result was an agreement between the General Directory and the Justice Department providing for joint commissions composed of board officials, jurists, and expert agronomists. Such commissions would investigate each sizeable common land section, work out the legal problems, secure the rights of the landlord and of the peasant, and encourage the latter to place the land under cultivation. Frederick remained enthusiastic, especially when he interviewed the four domain managers' sons after their return from England; he wished to order Brenckenhoff to begin to incorporate division of common land in his *Rétablissement* work.[54] By the end of 1769, however, Hagen and his colleague, Minister von Derschau of the General Directory, reported that the few experiments promoted in the Electoral Mark over a five year period had achieved only small success. "People were so dumb that they would not understand it was to their own advantage and utility."[55] Frederick, disgusted, ordered reports every

53. *AB*, 13: 711–22; 14; 84; 199–200.
54. *PKPA*, 11: 368.
55. Stadelmann, *PKPA*, 11: 124, includes this quotation.

three months from the General Directory after December, 1769 on the progress of this plan. The divisional program apparently was not funded, and bogged down in intricate local legal and manorial disputes.

Agricultural improvement projects under Frederick II seemed to fail mostly because neither the king nor his officials were willing or able to work to destroy the agrarian social order. Secondly, private capital was available in large amounts in England and was frequently used by enterprising landowners to buy out peasant plots and to incorporate common land in a new commercial farm system. Neither private nor public capital was available in Prussia to be used for the same purpose.

Hagen and the New Administration

Hagen failed to change the core bureaucracy overnight into a technically oriented corps of reformers, but he did infuse it with new vitality. In 1763 the General Directory and the boards were floundering about trying to solve the massive fiscal problems of reconstruction, but by 1770 the new Mining and Minerals Department, the Superior Engineering Office, and the Forestry Department were becoming technically oriented within the pre–industrial revolution context, and the whole shape of the bureaucracy had changed. Procedures, methods, even personnel were taken from the old system, but they were adapted to suit the needs of the new. What constituted the major change between the bureaucracy of Frederick William I and that established by Hagen and Heinitz? Formerly officials were preoccupied with routine jobs such as collection of revenues and managing the domain lands; afterwards officials were concerned with making the civil service the fountainhead of economic reform. Unfortunately for the future of the civil service, the ideology of bureaucratic reform centered around certain fallacious concepts, such as the belief that major economic advances could be made without disturbing the existing social structure or without abandoning the precepts of cameralism. Foreign visitors sometimes caught a glimpse of error. Mirabeau, for example, caustically criticized a busybody government that regimented entrepreneurs and forced everybody to work in a closed mercantilistic organization. After 1780 disciples of Heinitz such as the youthful Stein and rebellious professors and students in the universities began to look more closely and sympathetically at Adam Smith, or at least to question official economic planning.[56] Thus, despite some novelties introduced by Hagen, the Prussian civil service remained too rigid, too uncompromising, and too routine oriented to lead the State through the revolutionary decades ahead.

Hagen left a civil service revitalized in leadership, more confident in operation, and more responsive to changing conditions and demands than it had been in 1740. Yet his important innovations have, by and large, been overshadowed by the more colorful story of the *Regie,* and by the history of the judicial reforms under Cocceji and, later, Carmer. If Hagen hoped to achieve for himself a prominent mention in subsequent histories of Prussia he would have been disappointed, for over all the work of countless bureaucrats and jurists lies the shadow of Frederick II. The reputation of such a formidable historical protagonist has, of course, left the impression that the famous king was the only molder of events in the realm. Yet when Hagen died, Frederick wrote a gracious letter to his widow and ordered a portrait of his late minister placed in the lobby of the General Directory, presumably as a reminder to others that the king paid homage to a man he considered truly important, "this upright servant of the State."[57] Many other ministers had received marks of distinction such as the Order of the Black Eagle, but Cocceji was the only other civil servant to be honored with a royally sponsored portrait. Frederick perhaps felt that Cocceji had modernized the judiciary and Hagen the core bureaucracy.

---

56. Max Lehmann, *Freiherr vom Stein* (Leipzig, 1902), 1: 21 ff., 30 ff. Henri Brunschwig, *La Crise de l'Etat Prussien* (Paris, 1947), p. 125. H. G. Mirabeau, *De La Monarchie Prussienne sous Frédéric le Grand* (London, 1788), 1: 120 ff.
57. Preuss, *Urkundenbuch,* 3: 315, 320, 483.

IX

LIMITS OF REFORM

An important problem confronting the governments of developing countries in all epochs is lack of investment capital. Besides lacking this fiscal support, eighteenth-century Prussia did not have an all-important human resource: a pool of skilled entrepreneurs, managers, and technicians. If Hagen had a dream which informed him of the possibility of grandiose economic development, reality would have shown him the fragility of his hopes. Where were the imaginative administrators, the daring entrepreneurs, the capital and labor? All official programs and policies had to be limited because of universal poverty.

Reformers were also hampered by the nearly universal attitude of pessimism and fatalism of Prussians of all classes. Frederick, seeking consolation from the urbane stoicism of Marcus Aurelius, could never become a dedicated reformer or a builder of an economic autarchy. This overall conservatism reflected the fact that society throughout the century was not in the midst of violent change. The aristocrats and the higher *bourgeoisie* sometimes found their lives and social positions altered by economic changes. But, if individuals within these classes gained or lost, the classes overall were not sufficiently endangered. No class in Prussia contemplated the overthrow of the existing government.

Obstacles in the way of administrative reform included the presence of conservative-minded officials in the bureaucracy, the stultifying effect of the army, the opposition of the judiciary, and Frederick's own beliefs. Reform which attempted to build the economy was possible, despite these factors of retardation. The *bourgeoisie* increased in numbers, prestige, and affluence. The aristocracy, on the other hand, was in a state of general decline. Since bourgeois officials predominated in the bureaucracy, some reforms were initiated.

Frederick's Policies Regarding the Prussian Society

Frederick consistently held to certain beliefs concerning the nature of society. In the *Political Testament* of 1752 he expressed a preference for aristocrats in high military and civil posts: they were his "vassals," and could bring the necessary sense of honour and obligation to his service. The bourgeoisie were supposed to be money-grubbing, narrowminded, and suitable only for providing the bureaucratic expertise and initiative in commercial and industrial enterprises. Urban artisans and peasants were "dumb" and capable only of performing the hard labor necessary to keep the State functioning.[1] In his letters to d'Alembert he likewise expressed a rather typical eighteenth-century elitism: a small minority in his State were "literati" capable of appreciating the agnosticism and radicalism of the *Philosophes*, but the vast majority were ignorant children who should be permitted to indulge in their superstitions.[2] Naturally, since Frederick was highly intelligent, he also expressed views which really contradicted these overriding opinions. He despised the universities for example, but wished that the professors would teach Locke to their aristocratic and bourgeois students. Frederick believed that an "equilibrium" should be maintained between aristocratic landlords and their serfs, and presumably, that the bourgeoisie must be protected. He contradicted this "politics of equilibrium" by actively sponsoring the reforms of Hagen. Hagen, Heinitz and the more alert of bureaucrats recognized that government policies had to be adapted to changing conditions, but Frederick, in common with Canute, tried sometimes to stop change.

The fortunes of the Prussian nobility declined stedialy after the Seven Years' War. Penurious nobles sold their property to com-

1. *AB*, 9: 361–63.
2. *Oeuvres Posthumes de Frédéric II, Roi de Prusse* (Berlin, 1788), 11: 62–67.

moners despite official prohibition. By 1806 Koselleck estimates that out of 20,000 aristocratic families in the realm, only 4,034 owned *Rittergüter*.[3] Both propertied and unpropertied nobles could obtain military commissions: the size of the officer corps increased from 3,116 in 1740 to 5,511 in 1786, and nearly to 8,000 in 1806. Penurious nobles could often obtain commissions, but their chances in civil employment were poor. The civil service, for example, provided about 100 *Landrat* positions and places for about 100 other aristocrats. The *Landräte* and the vast majority of aristocratic civil servants were customarily owners of *Rittergüter*. Fearful of loss of status most aristocrats did not seek careers in businesss. It is clear, as Martiny maintained concerning the nobility of the Electoral Mark, that a large "aristocratic proletariat" existed. Frederick's attempts to entail property, to prohibit the sale of *Rittergüter*[4] to commoners, and to safeguard property rights in general applied only to one-third of noble families that owned property and to the eldest surviving sons of such families. Moreover, it is almost certain that the unemployed, unpropertied, aristocratic proletariat had always existed in Prussia: its numbers were simply increased after 1763 because of the increased financial troubles of property owners. Frederick's idealized portrait of his "vassals" was but a caricature of reality.

The royal policy of equilibrium was a static conception. Frederick's concept of a docile bourgeoisie was fallacious. Throughout his reign the number of businessmen increased as commerce and industry developed. The increase in looms in the textile industry is but one indication. Much of this growth was obviously a byproduct of the economic policies of Frederick, Fäsch, Splitgerber, Hagen, Heinitz, and other promoters of industrial development. So prosperous did the class of businessmen become that they could, and did, buy *Rittergüter*: some 79 out of 608 in the Electoral Mark were in the hands of commoners by 1806.[5] This problem was not understood by either

3. Koselleck, *Reform*, pp. 80–83.
4. Büsch, *Militärsystem*, p. 83. F. Martini, *Die Adelsfrage in Preussen vor 1806* (Stuttgart-Berlin, 1938) pp. 29 ff., 76 ff.
5. Ibid., p. 35.

the king or the General Directory. Following his consistent policy, Frederick issued a decree in February, 1775 prohibiting the sale of aristocratic properties to commoners. But the requests from hard pressed nobles continued to pour in. He vetoed one such petition: "No, this doesn't go, there are already so many in burgher hands, and, if I permit, 100 properties would go in burgher hands each year— I cannot approve of this." A similar answer was given in another case: "He should put his money in trade and commerce, therefore he will accomplish more than if he had a property. Burghers should not have noble properties—they don't need them. Commerce is their forte." The first petitioner replied later that he was offered 34,000 talers by an aristocrat and 42,000 talers by a commoner. Would the king make up the difference?[6] Frederick tried to stop these sales but failed.

The General Directory, moreover, told the king as early as 1769 that all owners of country property possessed the same legal and economic problems on their *Rittergüter*. Therefore, they argued that all owners should be able to have "seat and voice" in county estate meetings. They should even be able to participate in the election of *Landräte*. This was totally unacceptable to Frederick: "No, the nobles should not be limited in their privileges to any extent. They alone vote."[7] This attitude was totally unrealistic, since property was held by both nobles and commoners as well as the king himself and by various municipal governments. To the General Directory it was inconceivable that lack of aristocratic status by a particular owner should prevent that owner from voting on important county business. Frankly, the core bureaucracy quietly shelved the king's decision. In 1777 the ministers told a county director in the Old Mark that all owners would possess "seat and voice" in meetings.[8] As Bassewitz noted, the Electoral Mark *Landschaft* included all *Rittergut* owners, clerical owners, and bureaucratic representatives of the *Mediat* and

6. *AB*, 16:1. 384.
7. Peter Baumgart, "Zur Geschichte der kurmärkischen Stände in 17. und 18. Jahrhundert," Diëtrich Gerhard, ed., *Ständische Vertretungen in Europa im 17. und 18. Jahrhundert* (Göttingen, 1969), p. 148.
8. *AB*, 16:1. 445. Baumgart, "Geschichte," p. 148.

Immediat cities. Commoners were theoretically excluded in the county estates, but were present in the *Landschaft*. This provincial *Stände* had to supervise the Land Credit Institute, the Property Registry (*Landbuch*), military forage, fire protection services, and poor and military invalid affairs. By 1806 this body doubtless included many former bourgeois who had obtained property before 1786 and titles after that year.[9] Some 71 were ennobled between 1786 and 1804 in the Electoral Mark alone; most were officials and army officers, but many probably owned property.[10] The bourgeoisie, enriched by wartime speculation by 1763, determined to obtain social access to the nobility: first through acquisition of property, secondly, through acquisition of titles.

The improved position of the bourgeoisie is revealed also in recruitment to the judiciary. Some 1,755 apprentices were appointed in the Prussian judiciary between 1786 and 1800, but only 178 were aristocrats. Since such positions carried no pay it seems logical to suppose that these would-be jurists were being supported by their families. Most, if not all of them were university graduates: the number of law graduates from Prussian universities increases after 1770. The Superior Examinations Commission handled 795 candidates between 1770 and 1806 of which 447 were bourgeois affluent enough to afford the 20 talers individual fees.[11] Relatively few bourgeois families could afford such expenditures. Finally, Baasch has shown that the position of bourgeois characters in German fictional literature improves slowly throughout the eighteenth century; the prevailing image of the small city petty merchant so common earlier changes to a more flattering artistic representation of the great banker or wholesale merchant. Some of the bourgeois characters by 1800 were considered important enough by novelists to be major protagonists in their works. The wealthy businessman became respectable and no longer was a figure of fun: *le bourgeois Gentilhomme* was now to be taken seriously.[12] Again, the proportion of the bourgeoisie which

9. Bassewitz, *Brandenburg*, pp. 148–88.
10. Martini, *Adelsfrage*, p. 76.
11. Brunschwig, *Crise*, pp. 146–55.
12. Ernst Baasch, "Der Kaufmann in der deutsche Romanliteratur des 18.

falls into this category of importance remains small by 1800 (in reality as well as in fiction). Frederick stymied these entrepreneurs and social climbers by attempting to restrict their entry into important governmental positions and by forbidding them to buy *Rittergüter*.

Needless to say, Frederick also possessed a static view of the peasantry and of the artisans. He did periodically decree that serfs were not to be exploited by landowners or urban workers by their employers. At no time did he institute a determined effort to improve their conditions. His educational policy, for example, remained rudimentary because he refused to allocate necessary funds. Frederick never believed that the lower classes could profit if they were made literate and exposed to unusual ideas. While the guilds were often supported by him, he sometimes agreed to the hiring of non–guild members in industry in order to increase production. A very limited protection to peasants was provided by edicts which tried to make their holdings hereditary. But the property of aristocrats was protected to a limited extent by mortgages granted by the land credit institutes—not so that of the peasants.[13] Similarly, the judiciary kept careful note of property transfers between aristocrats but apparently had no provision for recording peasant transfers. There existed considerable numbers of people who had little or no recognized status: the unemployed urban proletariat, the freeholding peasants, and, presumably, a considerable number of former peasants who had no employment. Such persons were supposed to be cared for by local authorities: the *Landrat* in the countryside and the *Steuerrat* and his *Bürgermeister* in the towns. The new police directories established in Berlin, Königsberg, Breslau, Potsdam, and other cities during the reign of Frederick II reflected, perhaps, a gradual increase in a restless proletariat without employment or hope of employment. "Police" work in the eighteenth century partly consisted of regulation of these masses.

Frederick failed to understand the changing problems of the aris-

---

Jr.," *Aus Sozial- und Wirtschaftgeschichte* (Festschrift for Georg von Below) (Stuttgart, 1928), pp. 279–98.

13. The land credit institutes will be described in section 4 of this chapter.

tocracy, the bourgeoisie, and the proletariat: his policies aimed to protect an ideal society of static aristocratic, bourgeois, and peasant orders in an age when such a concept was becoming increasingly false. Because of his preoccupation, the revolutionary work of reform-minded bureaucrats was imperfectly supported.

Social and Numerical Composition of the Core Bureaucracy, 1740–1786

The General Directory and the provincial war and domains boards, which constituted the leadership of the core bureaucracy, grew slowly. Most of the growth of the General Directory occurred because of the increase in the number of departments from four to six, and the addition of personnel concerned with mining, forestry, and economic development after 1763. The size of this top level agency varied: 5 ministers and 19 privy finance councillors in 1740, 6 ministers and 11 councillors in 1748, 6 ministers and 18 councillors in 1754, and 6 ministers and about 18 councillors in 1771. By 1786 the General Directory numbered 6 ministers and 24 councillors. Only after the death of Frederick II did the first major change occur, resulting in the growth of the privy finance councillors' group to 54 by 1806. This modest variation in size becomes even more striking when one finds that the General Directory numbered only 4 ministers and 18 councillors in 1722[14] when it was established. Neither Frederick William I nor Frederick II encouraged the growth of this top executive group.

In the provinces the war and domains boards were also forced to maintain the same numerical strength, with minor variations, between 1722 and 1786. The Magdeburg board included 15 councillors in 1755, 12 in 1786, and 13 in 1800. The Electoral Mark board included

14. See the appendixes of this work for analysis of the core bureaucracy. The information contained therein was taken from the *Acta Borussica* and archival sources as mentioned in notes 13, 14, and 15 of chapter 1. Appendices 6 and 7 of Brunschwig, *Crise*, give information of the Magdeburg board in 1786 and 1800 and the Electoral Mark board in 1806. See also *AB*, 15: 438 ff. H. Haussherr, *Verwaltungseinheit und Ressorttrennung* (Berlin, 1953), p. 140. F. Hartung, *Staatsbildende Kräfte der Neuzeit* (Berlin, 1961), p. 221, note.

26 in 1740, 29 in 1753–54, and 14 in 1806. With the addition of West Prussia in 1772, new offices were created. The total number of board presidents and councillors, including *Steuerräte,* rose from a long established level of about 200 in 1771 to 300 by 1806.[15] Only in the number of subaltern personnel in both the top level and provincial agencies was growth to be seen between 1740 and 1786. Subalterns increased from 45 in 1740 to 80 in 1754, and to 110 in 1786[16] in the General Directory. Some 200 served in 1786.[17] A similar growth occurred in the size of the subaltern group in the boards in the provinces.

Hagen was hamstrung in his reform efforts because he could not increase his executive staff. He had to limit bureaucratic expansion because it was only possible to expand the subaltern groups in the Superior Accounting Board, the Mining and Minerals Department, and the Superior Building Department. In practical terms this severe limitation insured that the reformers were always outnumbered by veterans who had spent many years patiently waiting turn to fill the limited number of executive slots available. The organization was completely rigid and gave no opportunity for the displacement of executives to make room for young blood. Only death or the king's displeasure could create a vacancy. Executives also had to squeeze whatever new projects they devised into an already heavy routine work load. Hagen, for example, tried to supervise the western provinces, the royal bank, salt affairs, the Mining and Minerals Department, the Superior Building Department, and the Forestry Department at the same time.[18] His case was extreme, but other

15. Hartung, *Staatsbildende,* p. 221. note.
16. Haussherr, *Verwaltungseinheit,* p. 140.
17. Hartung, *Staatsbildende,* p. 221, note.
18. The heavy workload of Hagen is indicated in *AB,* 15: 440–41. Some 16 technicians were employed in the Academy of Construction (*Baukunst*) in 1772. Merseburg. Gen. Dir. Ober Bau Dept., Tit. I. no. 2. The executive personnel was drawn from the General Directory and the Electoral Mark board: Privy Finance Councillor Struve, Board Councillor Voss, councillors Haerlem and Naumann, Superior Construction Councillor Bornmann. They all had additional duties in their respective *collegia.* Potsdam, Pr. Br. Rep. 30A, 16. Privy Finance Councillor Ernst supervised the clerks of the Superior Mining Department in 1770, in addition to involvement in banking and "invalid" affairs; he supervised 6 newly

ministers were burdened excessively. Only the removal of responsibility for excise tax collection through the establishment of the *Regie,* the institution of the Tobacco Administration (really outside of the General Directory), and the creation of other, self-funding and administered agencies could free officials so that they could concentrate on reform.

Unfortunately, the work load of the General Directory was again increased after 1768, when the Tobacco Administration was returned to its supervision, and after 1786, when the *Regie* was dismantled and its tax collection staffs and facilities were incorporated. Even before the latter development ministers such as Hagen were overburdened. Very probably the majority of officials welcomed the return of responsibility for excise collection after 1786. Routine tax collection was easier to administer than new programs of economic development: the bureaucracy had originally been constructed to accomplish this duty.

In 1772 the new General Directory and the boards included old-line aristocrats, aristocrats ennobled by Frederick William I or his predecessor, and bourgeois. Despite his well-known antipathy for

---

appointed clerks. Merseburg, Rep. 120 I, Abtl. A. Tit. III, I, 108. Some 9 mining councillors worked in the Berlin headquarters between 1770 and 1775. Merseburg, Rep. 121, Atb. A, Tit. IV, Sec. 2. no. 1. The volume of their work loads shows that they no longer had other duties. The Lottery Administration of Calzabigi employed about 11 executives and 35 subalterns in Berlin, 34 in the Berlin lottery, an administrator in East Prussia, and an administrator in Cleves. Each of the provincial administrators had 5,000 talers to use in employing subordinates. Merseburg, Rep. 96, 410, 0. The General Tobacco Administration was a large operation: it included 7 directors, including Privy Finance Councillor Magusch, and about 55 executive officials who earned salaries comparable to war and domains councillors in the boards. Well over a hundred subalterns helped raise the total salary bill in 1770 to 143,476 talers. It was one-fourth the size of the entire core bureaucracy! Merseburg, Gen. Dir. Tabacks-Sachen, A. Tit. V, I, Gen. Sal. Etat, 1769–70, 1–8. About 75 of the estimated 2,000 employed in the *Regie* were executives comparable to board councillors or high officials in the core bureaucracy. Schultze, *Regie*, pp. 46–48. It is interesting to note that those agencies which were self-funding, such as the Tobacco Administration, the Lottery Administration, and the *Regie*, were able to hire large numbers of executives and subordinate personnel, while the technical agencies established by Hagen had great difficulty in growing because the salaries of employees had to come from the regular treasury sources.

the aristocracy, Frederick William I appointed all of his first ministers from that class. Three of the four had been newly ennobled, however. Similarly, Frederick II appointed aristocrats, with the exception of Michaelis in 1777, to ministerial positions throughout his reign. He refused to ennoble officials except in the case of Domhardt, the president of the East and West Prussian provinces. Domhardt was never made a minister. All except one of the board presidents under Frederick William I were nobles, and Frederick II continued to exercise this preference afterwards. Lenz and Colomb were rare bourgeois exceptions as presidents of the rather minor East Frisian board at different times. After 1786 aristocrats continued to command practically all of the top General Directory and board positions. With the institution of new provincial administrations after 1806 they occupied between 25 percent and 50 percent of posts in each provincial *Oberpräsidium* between 1818 and 1901.[19] The consistent Hohenzollern policy of preference for the nobility in the highest bureaucratic offices was not changed throughout the nineteenth century, only modified.

Naturally the composition of such "aristocratic" groups would be modified if a particular king decided to ennoble promising bourgeois officials. Frederick William I pursued this policy as did the successors of Frederick II. But analysis of the structure of the core bureaucracy between 1722 and 1806 reveals that a policy of ennoblement had an effect only on the very top levels of officialdom: the 5 or 6 ministers and the 11 board presidents. Bourgeois such as Marschall and Boden might be given titles by Frederick William I, but their careers seem to be stories of accommodation to the new aristocratic status as well as to the responsibilities of high office. In any event, only a handful of commoners ever obtained such plums of office. Indeed, since some 16 or 17 offices were restricted to nobles, it is obvious that 20,000 other aristocrats would not obtain them. The post of minister of the

19. Hintze, *AB*, 6:1. 283–84. On Friedrich Gottlieb Michaelis see Preuss *Friedrich der Grosse*, 3: 137. Koselleck, *Reform*, appendix 4, 681 ff., gives tables on the period after 1818. See other tables at end of this work on social composition of core bureaucracy under Frederick II.

General Directory and even the post of board president were positions which automatically made their incumbents important. Salaries for the former ranged, in 1740, between 3,000 and 5,000 talers and, for board presidents, 1,000 to 3,000 talers.[20] Salaries increased during the reign of Frederick II. Since there probably were no more than 5,300 *Rittergüter* with more than 5,000 talers in tax evaluation,[21] it is obvious that the vast majority of aristocrats would stand to gain financially by accepting any governmental post which paid more than 500 talers a year. Since a much larger number of aristocrats lacked property, it is equally obvious that they would take even lower paid employment. Aristocrats and bourgeois *both* wished to obtain bureaucratic positions, and aristocrats were favored only in the highest 16 positions.

The second rank bureaucratic positions in the core bureaucracy were almost as important as the class of ministers and board presidents. In the General Directory the privy finance councillors numbered between 18 and 24 during the reign of Frederick II. By the end of the reign of Frederick William I, only 3 out of 18 were aristocrats. In 1748 only one aristocrat held this position. These officials were the lieutenants of the ministers, and sometimes were nothing more than chief clerks. But, during the reign of Frederick II, some, such as Fäsch who headed the fifth department and Magusch who headed the Tobacco Administration, really performed ministerial functions. In fact, Fäsch probably had a more important job than the luckless Minister von Borke, the nominal head of the *Regie,* after 1766. Appointment of a board president to one of these positions meant that the bureaucrat had to sacrifice a small amount of salary during the reign of Frederick William I, but after 1740 the average salary amounted to 2,500 talers and was thus more than some board presidents obtained.[22] In many respects the post of privy finance councillor in the General Directory was equal in importance

20. Hintze, *AB*, 6:2. 285.
21. Koselleck, *Reform*, pp. 80–81.
22. A typical salary table for the General Directory can be found in Merseburg. Gen. Dir. Gen. Kassen Dept. no. 24, 65–89.

to that of board president. Both officials had to work within the confines of the collegial system, and that system had its headquarters in the General Directory. While nobles possessed a near monopoly of board presidencies, bourgeois possessed a near monopoly of privy finance councillor posts.

In the ranks of the war and domain councillors of the provincial boards an increase in the proportion of aristocrats occurred between 1722 and 1806. Prior to 1740, about 17 percent of them were nobles. Between 1740 and 1786 the proportion rose to between 25 percent and 32 percent. It remained about 36 percent between 1786 and 1806. Finally, equivalent positions were filled by nobles to the extent of about 25 percent between 1818 and 1901. During much of the Nineteenth century the proportion tended to reach 40 percent or more. These important provincial posts were always filled by a combination of aristocrats and commoners, with the latter predominating. Many times the post of first director of the board was filled by a commoner when the president was an aristocrat.[23] War and domains councillors obtained salaries between 500 and 1,200 talers during the reign of Frederick II. Did aristocratic councillors have a greater opportunity for promotion than their bourgeois colleagues? The number of higher positions in the entire core bureaucracy was only about 36. Thus, nearly 200 provincial councillors could theoretically compete for higher office: a few aristocrats would get board presidencies, although Frederick II chose all of his board presidents from the ranks of the Landräte between 1773 and 1781. Half of those presidents were former Electoral Mark and New Mark Landräte and four were chosen from Silesian Landräte. Out of a total of 41 presidents appointed during his reign, Frederick promoted only 11 to ministerial posts.[24] As a consequence of this preference for the Landräte, aristocrats who had

23. See, for example, Silesia in 1754. Von Schlabrendorff was minister-president of the Breslau board, but Cautius was first director. Merseburg, Rep. 96, 411g, 45, 6. On social composition of board executives see Hintze, AB, 6:1. 283–85, for period prior to 1740. The period 1740–1786 is analysed in the appendices of this work. Brunschwig, Crise, appendix 6 and 7 and pp. 147–48, discusses the period 1768 to 1806. Koselleck, Reform, appendix 4.

24. Hass, "Friedrich der Grosse," pp. 206–7.

served in the boards for many years were not able to move upward. Bourgeois officials could hope to become board directors and privy finance councillors in the General Directory, but their aristocratic colleagues had more limited opportunities. It is not true to say that aristocratic bureaucrats were tremendously favored over commoners through promotions.

Between its inception in 1770 and 1786, the Superior Examinations Commission examined 110 nobles and 181 commoners for possible appointment in the future to vacant *Landrat* and board councillor posts.[25] 33 percent of these applicants were aristocrats, but since *Landrat* applicants were all aristocrats, it is possible to claim that the commission was working with the traditional 30 percent in mind (for appointment of nobles as board councillors). Such applicants, of course, were previously recommended by board presidents: they had to have some kind of entrée in the bureaucracy before they could even take the examination. Between 1787 and 1806 the proportion of nobles appointed to board councillors was about 36 percent and constituted a very moderate increase. Only in Silesia, under Minister von Hoym, was the proportion increased to 60 percent. Ziekursch rightly states that the aristocracy benefited from Hoym's benevolence. In Silesia between 1740 and 1781 the percentage of aristocratic councillors amounted to 42 percent: higher than elsewhere in the realm.[26] Even Münchow and Schlabrendorff had favored the nobles. Despite Silesia, the records of the Superior Examinations Commission do not show an increased preference for aristocrats under Frederick II and his successors.

If all of the *Landräte* were aristocrats during the entire period up to Jena, and the overwhelming majority continued to be nobles throughout the nineteenth century, it is equally true to say that the vast majority of *Steuerräte* and their *Bürgermeister* were commoners throughout. This fact mirrored the social predominance of the aristocratic landowner in the countryside and the mercantile families in the cities. About 100 *Landräte* positions existed up to 1772, while the number of

25 Brunschwig, *Crise*, appendix 6.
26. Ziekursch, *Beiträge*, pp. 8 ff.

Bürgermeister of equivalent salaries, about 300 to 500 talers, was probably as great. To the ranks of the bourgeois-dominated *Bürgermeister* must be added the 500 domain contractors, who were always selected from the bourgeoisie.[27] Moreover, the middle rank of bureaucrats, the so-called "subaltern," were nearly always commoners in the General Directory and the boards: there were usually about twice as many of them as executive personnel in both levels. By 1786, 500 persons drew salaries between 150 and 300 talers.[28] Nobles were not often appointed to the menial clerical, police, and tax collecting posts. The lowest positions were filled by a combination of retired noncommissioned officers and soldiers, bourgeois university "dropouts," and others representing the lower town and country classes.

It is thus only partly correct to say that commoners predominated at the bottom of the bureaucratic hierarchy and nobles at the top, since bourgeois bureaucrats shared many high offices with nobles. The social balance which Frederick William I had established was, in fact, maintained by his sucessors. Bureaucrats were selected from the highest bourgeois and noble groups, but not often from the penurious aristocracy or the *petite bourgeoisie*. Peasants found their way into the civil service at the lowest level through intermediate service in the army.

Was the army increasingly important as a source of recruitment of officials in the civil service after 1740? The evidence does not verify this interpretation. Some 120 war and domains councillors and *Steuerräte* served in the Electoral Mark, Cleves, Königsberg, Gumbinnen, and Pomeranian boards, as well as the board deputations in Altmark, Mörs, Hamm, and Cöslin between 1768 and 1771.[29] Some 25 percent

27. Stadelmann, *PKPA*, 11: 123, note 2, on domain *Beamte*. See the Appendix of this work for statistics on *Landräte*.

28. *AB*, 8: 190–221, reproduces the salary tables for 6 boards in 1748. See appendixes of this work.

29. The analysis of these boards is based on conduct reports reprinted in *AB*, 15: 489–505; 16: 426 ff., 433–38. In appendix 2 of this work a comparison can be made between the boards of 1754–55 and those of 1768–71. A slight increase in the number of former army officers appointed to councillor posts occurred: from 5.66 percent to 8.5 percent of the commoners, and from 8.33 percent to 21.4 percent of the aristocrats. Although the percentage increase for nobles seems large it was small in actual numbers: 3 out of 36 compared to 6 out of 28. Signi-

of these councillors were aristocrats. The bourgeois officials were recruited in the following proportions: 50 percent promoted from lower bureaucratic positions, 22 percent from the ranks of the regimental quartermasters and auditors of the army, 9 percent from the army officer corps, and the remainder from other sources. It is obvious that about 62 of the 92 bourgeois councillors were not products of the army. The recruitment system was mainly directed towards internal selection. This policy was an obvious continuation of that established by Frederick William I. Neither under that monarch nor under Frederick II was the policy designed to "militarize" the civil service.

Concerning the aristocratic minority of this group of 120 councillors, about 33 percent had formerly been army officers, and only 4 out of the 28 had been promoted from lower bureaucratic offices. The remainder was recruited from administrative interns in the boards, directly from private life, and from other sources. Aristocratic officials tended to have some kind of military background. Significantly, 25 percent of the aristocrats had been forced to work as administrative interns before receiving their positions, despite the fact that many of these persons had previously served as army officers. The *Landräte* were all aristocrats and are not included in the group surveyed; many veteran officers obtained such posts upon retirement in accordance with a very long-standing tradition. The bourgeois councillors predominated in numbers and possessed greater experience in administration than their aristocratic colleagues.

---

ficantly the percentage of former regimental quartermasters and *Auditeure* declined from 31 percent to 21 percent of commoners in the period. Therefore, in view of the fairly large sample studied in both periods, it seems clear that the civil service was not flooded with former military personnel in executive ranks. This conclusion is confirmed by table F of appendix 2. Commoners were increasingly drawn from lower bureaucratic positions and from the judiciary, but this trend is moderate. The *Auscultator* post seems to have been important for nobles, but not for commoners; generally this form of recruitment seems to have declined overall. In any event, it is safest to say that the majority of councillors were recruited by promotion from within the structure or through some type of apprenticeship such as the *Auscultator* system. Johannes Ziekursch, *Beiträge*, 8. *AB*, 16: 18–19 gives information on the East Frisian board in 1772: all 6 war and domains councillors were commoners under the bourgeois president Colomb.

Were the boards "flooded" with former aristocratic and bourgeois officers after the Seven Years' War? Again the evidence does not support this conclusion. In the period covered by this analysis, 1768 to 1771, some 33 out of the total 120 were 35 years of age or younger. All of these officials were appointed after the Seven Years' War. 33 percent were promoted from lower positions, and 24 percent were former regimental quartermasters, auditors, and army officers. But 27 percent of the total had served as administrative interns. As a result, the recruitment trend was definitely in the direction of in-service training as expressed in the apprentice program and promotion from lower bureaucratic ranks. Recruitment from the army remained at about the same level as previously.

The core bureaucracy was initially constructed as a kind of consensus of the important noble and bourgeois classes in society, and this consensus was maintained quite rigidly throughout the entire period from 1722 to 1806. Moreover, the actual size of this executive group in the General Directory and the boards did not increase to a considerable extent. The core bureaucracy was thus relatively stable, inflexible, and remained tied to traditional sources of recruitment during the period. Hagen did succeed in making some progress towards professionalism through the institution of the examinations system and expansion of the *Auscultator*, or administrative intern, system. But bureaucrats recruited their favored subordinates whenever they could, the king peremptorily appointed former army officers and regimental quartermasters when he remembered to do so, and the total service continued to move in the well-worn ruts it had contrived for itself in the days of Frederick William I. This massive conservatism, this resistance to accommodation to the new demands of a newly created first rank State, kept true innovation at a minimum. The reformers always worked with tight budgets, insufficient personnel, and their efforts were continually frustrated by the heavy old-fashioned routines which they also had to perform. Stability and an obstinate spirit of opposition to change in the very ranks of the bureaucracy impeded reform. Hagen ran into opposition from the traditionalists headed by Minister Blumenthal, and Heinitz ran into opposition from Görne.[30] Western Germans such as Stein looked with disgust at the intrigues which involved his chief, Heinitz, as a consequence of the determined opposition of old-guard bureaucrats.[31]

The Judiciary: Guardian of the Landed Aristocracy

The judiciary reinforced the traditional, consensus-minded leadership of the Prussian State. Reorganized under Cocceji, it obtained control of the Silesian judiciary in 1768, and supervision of the important land credit institutes thereafter. Its growth after 1763 is paradoxical: the majority of jurists were recruited from the bourgeoisie yet the main thrust of its work was directed towards the preservation of the status of the nobility in the countryside. Bourgeois jurists were not necessarily aware of this peculiar circumstance of their work: Carmer and his young protegé, Svarez, wished to strengthen the role of the judiciary in the cities, but did not think that the courts should give up their role of leadership in the countryside. The judiciary, a radical example of professionalization, was a conservative upholder of traditional society. Bourgeois candidates constituted about 88 percent of those examined and appointed to positions in the *Kammergericht* in Berlin between 1785 and 1800. Previously, the proportion of aristocrats in regular positions, excluding the apprentices, remained about 33 percent.[32] As in the core bureaucracy, the nobles obtained a percentage of high offices throughout the reigns of Frederick William I and his successors.

Obviously the innovations of Hagen did not change the overall social composition of the core bureaucracy, nor did the reforms of Cocceji change that of the judiciary. But these great bureaucratic leaders did professionalize their subordinates by introducing new concepts of work performances, by requiring a better educational background, and by instituting examinations for recruitment. So impor-

30. See Stein's comments in Erich Botzenhart, ed., *Freiherr vom Stein* (Stuttgart, 1957), 1: 135. Görne was cashiered.

31. Ibid., p. 272.

32. Brunschwig, *Crise*, appendix 2 and 6.

tant did educational qualifications become that after 1763 and up to
1806, some 106 board apprentices or interns in Silesia were university
graduates out of a total of 108 appointed. All except 4, who had
studied "cameral science," were law graduates.[33] After 1763 the proportion of students in the theology faculties of Prussian universities
tended to diminish in favour of an increase in those in the law faculties.[34] The judiciary, through its hold on Prussian universities, dis-
couraged the establishment of "cameralistic" studies and promoted
the study of law. Perhaps an unintentional result of Hagen's stress
upon education was the tremendous rise in recruits who had been
prepared by the judiciary. The judiciary, in fact, was training the
future administrative interns of the core bureaucracy. After 1770 the
officials who shared the technocratic interests of Hagen must have
been displeased to see that their recruitment reforms were not working. Frederick, meanwhile, continued to believe that university education was of small benefit to future bureaucrats: they needed "practical" training.[35]

The judiciary was a stronghold of conservatism despite the work of
Cocceji, Svarez, and Carmer. Svarez and Carmer were "reformers"
only in a limited sense: they wished to codify the law, to "rationalize" it, and to make the conduct of justice more efficient. Perhaps they
were inspired by the Enlightenment and, particularly, by Beccaria. It
is more probable, however, that they looked backward to Justinian's
Code and never abandoned the conservative natural law tradition of
Pufendorff and his predecessors. At times the jurists seemed to en-
dorse humanitarian ideals, but, finally, they opted to support the
conservative social structure and its mores. It would have been
strange if Svarez and Carmer had behaved differently. Therefore, the
capstone of their work, the *Allgemeine Landrecht* of 1794, embodied
provisions designed to protect a threefold division of society: the
nobility, the important bourgeoisie, and the peasantry. Artisans,
vagabonds, and other categories of persons were regulated by a mass

33. Ziekursch, *Beiträge*, p. 4.
34. Brunschwig, *Crise*, pp. 146–47.
35. *AB*, 16: 1, 256.

of guild statutes, and labor and workhouse instructions, and possessed little in the nature of legal rights. The nobility (*Adelstand*) was
guaranteed, insofar as members of the order possessed *Rittergüter*,
patronal justice, and police authority over serfs, the right to participate in the elections of *Landräte*, and the right to belong to the
county estates.[36] It is possible that a recent writer, Koselleck, is right
in saying that the regional and particularistic rights of nobles, burghers, and peasants were subordinated to a general and overall regulation by the Prussian State,[37] but such a development was an
outgrowth of natural law doctrine and the theory of sovereignty
incorporated in it. Also, the rulers of Prussia had traditionally worked
to achieve such uniformity, albeit with limited success. In attempting
to isolate certain parts of the *Allgemeine Landrecht* and to identify
them as fruits of the Enlightenment, Koselleck suggests some interesting, but dubious, interpretations. For example, there exists a
tendency to consider *all* inhabitants of the state as being "members"
or "citizens" and therefore a tendency to consider all equal before the
law.[38] But, elsewhere, the code seems clear enough when it describes
the *specific* rights and obligations of each order: *Adelstand, Bürger-
stand*, and *Bauernstand*. The code merely reflects the traditional three
fold division of society common in the writings of the seventeenth and
eighteenth centuries as well as an artificial distinction between city
and countryside. The *ALR* also attempted to prohibit the sale of
noble properties to commoners, following in the footsteps of Fred-

36. Koselleck, *Reform*, p. 81. Koselleck attempts to develop a different interpretation of the *Allgemeine Landrecht*: he believes it to contain certain innovations which make it a liberal departure from the older legal tradition. The code's
endorsement of the existing society seems, however, to relegate his conclusions
to the status of conjectures.

37. Again, the natural law theorists had always talked of the subjects of a state
in a twofold way: all persons are members of the State (the principle of equality),
but they differ from one another depending on where they stand in the social
hierarchy (the principle of inequality).

38. Koselleck, *Reform*, pp. 81–83. J. Süssmilch, *Göttliche Ordnung in den
Veränderungen des menschlichen Geschlechts* (Berlin, 1775–76), 1: 427–28, was a
true humanitarian and social radical, unlike the cautious jurists of Prussia: he
frankly recommended the abolition of serfdom, the division of landed estates
into plots which would be given to peasant families, and the expansion of state-
supported medical services in the countryside.

erick II. It was a conservative, even a reactionary document; even if a few parts of it seem to herald a new liberalism.

The conservative bent of the judiciary, besides being evident in the codes, was also reinfored by its leadership of the new land credit institutes after 1769. After the Seven Years' War, Frederick became more and more concerned about the prevalence of aristocratic poverty as manifested in increased sales of estates to commoners. Frederick, although influenced by the *Rétablissement* work of Hagen in Cleves, determined to entrust the judicial department with complete charge of the mortgage institutes he funded to alleviate the distress of rural landowners. The first of these was the Silesian Credit Bank, established in 1769 as the result of planning by Carmer and his protege Svarez. Carmer later rose to greater heights than Silesian minister of justice as a result of this work: he worked for years on the *Allgemeine Landrecht*. This Credit Bank was a great success, lending 1,462,000 talers in 1771 and as much as 8,870,000 talers in 1806. Ziekursch claimed that the result was the "best example of early capitalist accumulation of Capital"[39] in Silesia. Unfortunately, much capital was used to fortify the property titles of aristocrats, not to advance trade and industry. In fact, Carmer mortgaged his property so that he could rebuild churches in his peasant villages.[40] The obvious intent of the Credit Bank was to safeguard the nobility, not to stimulate economic development even on the land. Also, neither the Silesian board nor the General Directory had any say in the mode of mortgage distribution.

Because Frederick was always anxious to limit expenditures, the introduction of land credit institutes elsewhere came gradually: in Pomerania in 1771, in Magdeburg-Halberstadt in 1780, in the Electoral Mark in 1777, in West Prussia in 1787, and in East Prussia in 1788. In the Electoral Mark some landowners used their funds to

39. *AB*, 13: 297–304. See the following notes on the Silesian Land Credit Institute. *AB*, 14: 130–31, 221–23, 290–93. Preuss, *Friedrich der Grosse*, 3: 74. Adolf Stölzel, *Carl Gottlieb Svarez* (Berlin, 1885), p. 86. AB, 15: 65–66. Ziekursch, *Agrargeschichte*, pp. 7 ff., 95–119.
40. Preuss, *Friedrich der Grosse*, 3: 76–77.

improve crops,[41] perhaps because they were influenced by the "Anglo-mania" of the board. Most landowners everywhere simply hoped to return to a prewar standard of prosperity.

Because of the increasing involvement of the courts in mortgage problems and in other efforts to protect the existing social structure of Prussia, it is unreal to expect any jurists to have become interested in programs of economic improvement or of social justice. After all, as many of them would say, their business did not encompass such concerns.

The Army: Impediment to Reform

Hagen, Heinitz, and other bureaucratic reformers had to combat the army as well as the judiciary and the landed nobility. The army, in common with the civil service, mirrored, in consensus form, the ideals and interests of different portions of Prussian society. Otto Büsch recently described brilliantly how the army reflected the important economic, political, and social relationships of the aristocratic landowners and their serfs. In fact, as he states, the serf on the land could be readily absorbed into the cantonal system as a dependent military "serf." Similarly, the landowner was encouraged by his military obligations to carry over his peacetime attitudes toward the serfs into his military organization.[42] The army as well as the cantonal reserve was thus really conservative since it represented an extension of the hardened social structure of the countryside.

The cantonal system was a means of recruitment and training of a reserve force for the army. Originally, Frederick William I had hoped to exempt only those of the "aristocratic estate" and the wealthy few of the bourgeoisie,[43] but Landräte and board officials had frequently

41. Stadelmann, *PKPA*, 11: 129–30. F. Martiny, *Adelsfrage*, pp. 10–11. Basse-witz, *Brandenburg*, 169–88. Skalwcit, *AB Getreidepolitik*, 3: 23, 29–30. *NCC* 4: 6647–52, 7391–49, 7403–4. Ziekursch, *Agrargeschichte*, pp. 7 ff.

42. Büsch, *Militärsystem*, pp. 67–74, 161–70.

43. Arnim, *Über die Canton-Verfassung in den Preussischen Staaten* (Frankfurt, 1788), p. 7. Arnim faced an official investigation as a result of this book (Mer-

tried to limit the number of conscripts, especially peasants, taken from the counties. Landowners and domain managers disliked losing a part of their labor force during the spring when the annual maneuvers were held. Frederick II quite frequently supported such exemptions on an ad hoc basis and further weakened the cantonal system by exempting students of theology, artisans in the wool industry, and others. He also limited the authority of regimental commanders and company chiefs by requiring that enrollment coincide with the "welfare of the land." After 1763 he authorized the *Steuerräte* to exclude artisans whom they considered essential in the municipal economy.[44] By 1788, when a royal commission was established to review the cantonal system, it was clear that the overwhelming majority of conscripts came from the peasantry.

Hagen and his lieutenants believed that the cantonal system was a constant threat to their plans for the development of the economy. Since they were mostly concerned with nonagricultural sectors of the economy, they found it easy to encourage the inspector general in charge of the cantonal system, Mollendorff, to draw his quotas from the countryside. However, when shepherds were extensively conscripted between 1766 and 1769, the General Directory protested and obtained "furlough" for them.[45] After all, the most important step in the production of wool, the shearing of it, occurred at exactly the same time as the spring maneuvers. Frederick thus continued to support the weakening of the cantonal system during the time of Hagen. Unfortunately, the system still operated primarily to the detriment of agricultural production and was a real obstacle in developmental plans.

---

seburg, Rep. IX, A, 20 Fasc. 4), since he published letters written by various *Bürgermeister* protesting the cantonal enlistments.

44. Arnim, *Canton-verfassung*, pp. 10–11. *NCC*, 4: 5035–38, grants miners exemption also. The cantonal system was not generally applied in the western provinces, but military recruiting was pushed, despite the protests of local authorities. General Wolfersdorf obtained royal permission to obtain cantonal conscripts from Cleves and ran into conflict with the board president. Frederick ordered the general to work with the director to improve the system since the president was a "dumb devil." *AB*, 16: 1. 23–24.

45. Merseburg. Gen. Dir. Kurmark, Tit. CCLXVII, no. 5, Militaria.

The regular army was a similar problem for Hagen. It rose in strength from about 100,000 men in 1740 to 194,000 men by 1786.[46] In peacetime the soldiers were quartered in garrisons in most towns of any size. Most were placed on extended "leaves of absence" because the government tried to economize on wages. They sometimes found employment in government concerns, particularly in the spinning and weaving of cloth. More often such indigent soldiers were employed as night watchmen, pedlars, servants, and in other lowly positions. Since one-third of the population of Berlin after 1750 was composed of soldiers and their families, it is clear that the part-time employment of many of them had an effect on the city. Nevertheless there is little evidence that they dominated the ranks of the artisans. Certainly when Brenckenhoff and others tried to develop industry they always assumed that weavers and spinners should be exempt from military service and could not produce effectively if they could only work part of the year. Also, soldiers often elected to become night watchmen because each military commander could obtain funds to pay for such services, and the employment was not as demanding as that found in industry.[47] The General Directory was not interested in creating a part-time industrial proletariat out of such poorly qualified if desperate, people.

It seems clear that Hagen had as little regard for the army as for the cantonal system: neither provided assistance to his plans for mercantilistic development. He mirrored the opinions of practically all those in the civil service as well as the views of city dwellers. Military garrisons created great housing and police problems. The "soldier proletariat" may well have been more of a burden than an asset because it was not, really, a free labor force.[48] The *Steuerräte* found their jobs complicated by the necessity of working with garrison problems as well as all their other duties.[49]

46. Quoted in William O. Shanahan, *Prussian Military Reforms* (New York, 1945), pp. 33, 56.

47. Horst Krüger, *Manufakturen*, pp. 278–84. Kurt Hinze, *Die Arbeiterfrage zu Beginn des modernen Kapitalismus in Brandenburg-Preussen* (Berlin, 1963), pp. 171–80.

48. J. Ziekursch, *Agrargeschichte*, pp. 10–61. Krüger, *Manufakturen*, p. 371.

49. Gloger, "Steuerrat," pp. 159–78.

Every successful attempt to increase the powers of local, urban self-government, to increase the wealth of city dwellers, and to make cities important industrial and market centers would weaken the role of the army in Prussian society. The judicial reorganization enabled local authorities to cope with peace and order issues involving the military. Improved industrial and commercial conditions created a true proletariat and subordinated the part-time soldier–worker after 1750. The continued expansion of the urban economy, the decreased efficiency of the cantonal system, and the increasing indebtedness of rural landlords, despite the land credit institutes, accelerated this decline after 1763. Both the army and the cantonal system remained static bequests of the State of Frederick William I and of its agrarian society. The army became a permanent auxiliary of the agrarian society and thus mirrored its weakness.[50]

The Social Conservatism of King and Subject

The overriding conservatism of the king and of his subjects really retarded the modernisation of Prussia. Often reforms simply reinforced this conservatism; the land credit institutes, for example, were designed to fortify the small elite of aristocratic property owners but did not provide enough funds to enable these owners to introduce radical changes in cultivation. The rigid core bureaucracy, filled with routine-minded bureaucrats, was no effective instrument for leadership in ambitious economic projects. It was an impediment to change of any kind. Moreover, the core bureaucracy continued to represent a consensus of important elites in society, and because of this could only reflect a conservatism that dominated the thinking of these elites. Finally, both the judiciary and the army acted as protectors of the old society and neither supported economic reform.

50. Peter Paret, *Yorck and the Era of Prussian Reform, 1807–1815* (Princeton, 1966), pp. 16, note 27; 266.

X

THE BUREAUCRATIC COMMONWEALTH

With the closing of Hagen's career in the Prussian civil service in 1772, a long era of experiment, reform, and bureaucratic readjustment also ended. Although the entire development occurred between 1713 and 1786, the most important changes in the civil service came after 1740 and before 1772. The accession of Frederick II and the death of Hagen stamp these latter dates with significance. Since the changes were multitudinous, varied, and at times seemingly incomprehensible, some attempt must now be made to survey the entire spectrum of decisions, innovations, and alterations, that have filled the preceding pages.

Before 1740 the entire civil administration, except for the judiciary, was incorporated in a cumbersome collegial structure that included the General Directory and the provincial boards. In this study this administrative structure has been called "the core bureaucracy." Established by Frederick William I, this system was to continue to exist until the time of Stein. It did not change its basic form throughout the entire period since the new departments established after 1740 were, in one sense, mere additions to something which already existed. This indigenous bureaucracy was a natural outgrowth of the governmental tradition in Brandenburg-Prussia even though it incorporated the collegial organizational scheme which was to be found in all other Old Regime states in more or less recognizable forms after 1400 and before the nineteenth century.

Four New Bureaucracies after 1740

Four bureaucratic organizations developed as rivals of the old line core bureaucracy after 1740. The Silesian ministry was a separate entity and may be called, for discussion purposes, the "king's bureaucracy" because it was responsible only to the king. Secondly, the influx of French, Dutch, and west German bureaucrats resulted in the construction of several new and independent agencies (such as the *Regie*); they were components of a "cosmopolitan bureaucracy" because they represented foreign influences. The business community cooperated with the king to found an "entrepreneurial bureaucracy," and Cocceji presided over the construction of the new "judicial bureaucracy."

The separate administrations of Silesia, wartime Saxony, East and West Prussia were established independently of the General Directory. At first each of these organizations was filled by officials drawn from the core bureaucracy. But each was really molded by powerful and intelligent ministers: Silesia by Münchow and Schlabrendorff, Saxony by Borcke, and the combined East and West Prussian ministry after 1772 by Domhardt. In addition to having responsibilities greater than any board president enjoyed over civil affairs, each minister devoted much time and attention to military auxiliary services; each worked harmoniously with the local garrison and troop commanders. The Silesian administration was originally established to provide military support for Prussian troops as was the Saxon administration. Domhardt, the enterprising director of the Königsberg board first earned the support of Frederick in the closing months of the Seven Years' War when he succeeded in shipping considerable grain from his province to the middle provinces. Domhardt had earlier specialized in the collection of horses for the cavalry. The new organizations were set up to administer particular provinces by officials who worked independently of the General Directory and directly under the king. Frederick considered efficient civil administration and military auxiliary services essential in these provinces, which were peripheral and would face enemy troops earlier than the "heartland" provinces. Such bureaucracies were more exploitative then their equivalents in the core bureaucracy; each presided over a populace suspected of disloyalty. Each territory occupied by Frederick II for any length of time between 1740 and 1786 was administered according to the Silesian formula.

In a sense the separate administrations of these provinces represented the highest achievement of the work of Frederick William I. All of the personnel, policies, techniques, and rules were taken from the old-line core bureaucracy; the Silesian administration, for example, did the same chores that the core bureaucracy had always done, but because it operated in a less constrained atmosphere it was able to do these chores better. In fact, able bureaucrats were taken from all over the realm to work in the Silesian administration after 1740; they would learn the advantages of working in an organization outside of the world of the General Directory. Frederick II, by extending the resources of the bureaucracy that he inherited, was really changing the structure of the core bureaucracy; no longer did it possess a monopoly of civil administration. Even more interesting is the value of the Silesian ministry as a measuring stick that could be used to determine the effectiveness of administration elsewhere. Evidently, Frederick found the General Directory lacking in such comparative tests and could afford to ignore the protests of conservative ministers who claimed, "the tax limit has been reached and the State can do no more," or, "we can not make the king's subjects produce more goods because we do not have enough incentives to make them work." In short, he could find alternate and informed opinions regarding policy proposals outside the General Directory. When Frederick discovered the degree to which Saxony could be exploited during the Seven Years' War, it is quite possible that he began to see that his other provinces contained hidden and potentially taxable resources; they certainly paid much more to the State after 1763.

Since Frederick was deeply interested in western European culture, particularly that of France, it should not surprise one to discover that he was receptive to foreign influences of other kinds as well. But prior to 1749 he did not in fact think that he could learn lessons in administration from abroad. In that year he lost Marschall, was moved to issue new instructions to the General Directory in which he paid particular attention to corruption and inefficiency, and determined to

bring in the Amsterdam commercial expert, Fäsch. Fäsch and Graumann brought into the realm new and valuable administrative techniques, particularly some pertaining to the use of statistics and of
mint resources. They also brought in considerable knowledge of the
complicated international trade structure of the west European economy in general. Frederick did not really owe his success with these
imported experts to his connections with the *Philosophes*; he had
listened to Councillor Hille while crown prince. Characteristically, he
allowed them great flexibility when they assumed office, following the
precedent he had established with the Silesian ministry. Fäsch and
Graumann represented the highest type of mercantilistic thinking of
the age; they were well chosen to do their work. If neither official was
able to reform the entire core bureaucracy before the Seven Years'
War, they both, nevertheless, helped their colleagues see how to
handle the new entrepreneurs and to make intelligent use of the fiscal
resources of the State. Frederick did not stop at this point, but continued to listen to a multitude of French and even English bureaucratic entrepreneurs of whom de Launay was only the most famous.

After 1763 the king really attempted to devise ways to make the
whole civil administration more flexible and more imaginative. He
gave that rascal Calzabigi great latitude in setting up lotteries and in
planning even more ambitious projects, not because he himself was
overly gullible, but because that dubious promoter possessed verve,
courage, and imagination: qualities he valued in his own personality.
But Calzabigi was only a catalyst for others, and the *Regie* was the
final fruit of twenty-six years of royal interest in the advanced administrative and mercantilistic techniques of western Europe. The General Excise Administration or *Regie* was the center and culmination
of the cosmopolitan bureaucracy. At its height the *Regie* employed
two thousand persons, two-thirds of the total employed by the core
bureaucracy. It increased the revenues of the State enormously and,
even if the overhead expenses were large, it succeeded in giving the
king, for the first time, the opportunity to release funds from the essential services of military maintenance, internal police, etc., and to
devote them to the developmental projects. The *Regie* enabled the

core bureaucracy to devote its attention to nonfiscal matters. But the French bureaucratic entrepreneurs did not work alone; Frederick subsidized several English agronomists who wished to bring the agricultural revolution to Prussia; and he listened carefully to promoters of all kinds, crackpots and geniuses alike. Always open to suggestions, always flexible in approach, Frederick never ceased to question, examine, and to speculate about his consuming interest: the development of his realm to a position of economic parity with the advanced states of the west. A hopeless dream?

All of these foreigners may be considered members of a great, if ill-defined organization, which one might call the cosmopolitan Bureaucracy. Its members sometimes worked in the General Directory, sometimes, as in the case of the English agronomist Wilson, under the supervision of a board,[1] or they might work together in the Tobacco Administration or the *Regie*. All represented an invigorating influence on the hidebound and narrow-minded bureaucratic class of the realm. But the *Regie*, if it forced the homegrown officials to rethink their work roles, was always resented and attacked. Curiously enough, the destruction of this agency following the death of Frederick II may well have been a serious setback in the fortunes of Prussia. When fiscal affairs were again united under the General Directory, they probably tended to monopolize the attention of officials and the core bureaucracy slipped back into the same rut from which Frederick II had labored so long to dislodge it. A conservative, fiscally oriented civil administration was no great source of strength to the State during the Napoleonic wars: Stein realized the validity of this opinion. The cosmopolitan bureaucracy represented a vital and energetic source of stimulation and ideas for others and its demise, if greeted with relief by Prussians, was not altogether to be celebrated.

Because of Frederick's own interest in sponsoring mercantile activity and because of his close connection with David Splitgerber and Johann Gotzkowsky, the Berlin business community received extraordinary royal attention. Even though individual entrepreneurs existed before 1740 and worked contractually with the government,

1. Merseburg, Gen. Dir., Kurmark, Tit. XIX, no. 1, vol. 20.

these individuals did not obtain real decision-making influence in the State until after 1740. Under the often divided leadership of Splitgerber and Gotzkowsky this group grew in numbers, its members organized themselves into consortiums, and it achieved by 1763 real autonomy as a new, albeit unrecognized and informal, entrepreneurial bureaucracy. Those accustomed to the identification of organizations by legal statutes and tables of organization may hesitate to accept this title, yet it is quite evident that the entrepreneurs did more than achieve solidarity by operating under common interests with a common profit-making goal. Frederick II recognized its existence by incorporating its members in all kinds of committees and councils and by frequent and direct consultations with its leaders. This entrepreneurial, elitist bureaucracy, however, was only tenuously connected to the king or to any other governmental agency and could pursue an independent and nearly irresponsible path until after the economic crisis of 1763.

Finally, under the leadership of Cocceji, the moribund judiciary was organized into a judicial bureaucracy by 1756. The administrative reforms introduced in the courts, including the recruitment of judges and other personnel, served as models for other governmental agencies. In common with the "king's" bureaucracy, the cosmopolitan bureaucracy, and the entrepreneurial bureaucracy, the judiciary was established independently of the core bureaucracy headed by the General Directory.

The importance of this proliferation of governmental agencies can scarcely be overemphasized. All represented attempts to establish administrative controls as well as to develop particular projects; all had to be established outside the old-line bureaucracy. Only when Prussia became a major European state and made her debut in great power politics could these changes occur. They were linked directly and indirectly to the conquest of Silesia. The establishment of the Silesian ministry led to the growth of the entrepreneurial bureaucracy when the merchants of Berlin and Breslau consolidated their efforts. In his attempts to integrate Silesia into the realm economically Frederick had to use the services of Graumann, Fäsch, and their lieutenants. In his attempts to integrate the province within the Prussian judicial structure, which also meant within the ordained social structure, Frederick utilized the services of Cocceji and his lieutenants. The first motivating factor behind the development of these four new bureaucracies was military conquest of a large and prosperous province.

With the conquest of Silesia Prussia became the focus of long-standing international power plays involving France, Austria, Russia and Sweden. Two long and expensive wars resulted. Frederick undoubtedly felt that he had to try to make his state an equal of his formidable neighbors. Lacking the population and resources of the great powers, Prussia could survive only if it utilized whatever resources it possessed more efficiently than did its potential or actual enemies. Besides the often cited buildup of military strength, Frederick set about to "westernize" his economic base, using whatever techniques that gave promise of success. Foreign experts were imported, great projects were launched, and much money was devoted to the achievement of economic parity with western Europe before 1786. Frederick would have endorsed Colbert's opinion that international trade was war; he believed in aggressive mercantilism.

Why did he decide to forward these ambitious objectives through organizations separated from the General Directory and the regularly constituted boards? The core bureaucracy before 1765 failed to support the fifth department, failed to help Fäsch, failed to help Graumann, and failed to realize that administrative conditions had permanently changed after 1740. As each innovation appeared the old-line ministers attacked it because they thought it constituted another attack on their prerogatives. If the ministers and their lieutenants had been other men, men that Frederick did not associate with his father, it is quite possible that most of the administrative changes after 1740 could have been introduced under the umbrella of the General Directory. After all, the cameralists never dreamed that separate and parallel administrative organizations could build a state; they thought only in terms of a unified structure.

Thus the five primary bureaucracies operated at cross purposes, in opposition to one another and recognized only the king as a common master. In one sense only can this development be termed "centralization" of authority: it resulted in the organization of larger and larger public spheres under a general aegis. But this is not the interpretation given by the advocates of a *Gesamtstaat*; they maintained that centralization meant the *rationalization* of governmental functions under a single pervasive bureaucratic system. No single bureaucratic system existed after 1740, and functions were not divided up logically and assigned to persons placed in a bureaucratic hierarchy. The Prussian government obviously became more and more decentralized; it was divided into mutually antagonistic parts as it evolved after 1740. But the decentralization was not merely one which came about because specific departments such as the fifth or sixth were invented, or because the General Directory suddenly lost its collegial structure. Collegialism remained, and a true cabinet structure did not emerge until after the Stein reforms. The General Directory itself did not change; it resisted change and held fast to its old-fashioned ways. Similarly the view that Frederick strengthened the claims of independence of provincial presidents by working directly with them is true only if one claims that he caused confusion in the ranks and made the work of the General Directory more difficult. Until such presidents were divorced entirely from the old core bureaucracy as led by the General Directory and placed under the king in the same way that the Silesian ministry was organized, no real and permanent alteration in the core bureaucracy as a whole was possible.

Hagen and the Reconstruction of the General Directory

The development of the five primary bureaucracies was more or less complete by 1766, when Minister von Hagen became the dominant figure in the General Directory. Hagen observed that the core bureaucracy had been shouldered aside by others during the previous two decades and determined to rectify this error. One central concern of the old-line bureaucrats, the stultifying obligation to collect excise taxes, had been removed from their work load and transferred to the *Regie*. Hagen decided to reestablish the supremacy of the General Directory by subordinating some of the rival bureaucracies to its supervision.

With the establishment of the Royal Bank the foundations were laid for the conquest of the entrepreneurial bureaucracy. The professionalization of mining and mineral administration and construction work also aided in recruiting technically qualified officials who could, for the first time, work with the entrepreneurs and try to make them operate in harness. Hagen approved of some aspects of the contributions of the cosmopolitan bureaucracy; he had formerly been a lieutenant of Fäsch and was intimately acquainted with the west European economy because of his long-standing administrative responsibilities in Cleves. But he resolutely opposed the *Regie* and the schemes of Calzabigi. Thinking eclectically, Hagen believed that foreign, particularly Dutch, English, and French, administrative ideas could be incorporated into the core bureaucracy. Thus the real key to all his reforms was the establishment of a new recruiting system which would give preference to those who had training in needed technical fields. Hagen was chiefly responsible for introducing a west European and bourgeois criterion into the selection and promotion of officials. He actually succeeded in undermining the foundations of the separate entrepreneurial and cosmopolitan bureaucracies, but did not live long enough to see the demise of the *Regie* or the final surrender of the businessmen.

Hagen did not try to engage the judicial and Silesian "king's" bureaucracies in combat. He worked well with Schlabrendorff and Domhardt; the three intelligent and ambitious officials did not see the need to rival one another. The judiciary was well entrenched, although Hagen did make a few efforts to undermine its authority by claiming responsibility for the allodification of land in some provinces. Again, the existence of the *Regie* served to unite all rival organizations since each had to fight to prevent the upstart agency from undermining its authority.

The administrative task facing Hagen was one of reconstruction of the core bureaucracy. But in order to reconstruct, he found he had to extend the limits of competence of his organization. Especially important was the problem of finding duties and functions for about half the officials of the General Directory and the boards who had lost revenue collection authority to the *Regie*. Hagen tried to make the core bureaucracy an efficient, technically qualified collection of specialists in economic planning and development. He could establish his mining department and his construction department as loci of even more ambitious attempts to harness the entire economy of the realm and to force feed it, guide it, regiment it to achieve the goals of contemporary cameralists: the achievement of a higher standard of living for the subjects of the king and the buildup of a taxation base which could support Prussia's status as a great European power. How modern appear these goals! The final desired result, parity with the great states of western Europe, could come about only if the core bureaucracy dedicated itself to the task.

Hagen actually began to construct a "bureaucratic commonwealth": a state administered by experts, wherein the routine tasks of government were delegated to the provincial war and domains boards, the judiciary, and the separate organizations in Silesia and East and West Prussia. Parallel to these organizations would be erected agencies specializing in different areas of economic development. If each province were to have one or more construction offices and mining offices alongside the board, the totality of administration would be achieved in the General Directory itself. When the foremost *collegium* met, it would include old-time bureaucratic ministers responsible for routine tasks and other new bureaucratic technocrats who would handle nonroutine and extraordinary programs. Hagen was the head of the entire system. Naturally this half-developed plan, frustrated because of Hagen's early death, could only succeed if particularly imaginative and expert officials supervised it. It relied on the presence of an intelligent and flexible chief executive in the person of the king. This great mercantilistic state-building scheme marks the true beginning of modern civil service in Prussia: everything preceding it was relatively nonprofessional, impromptu, and weakly oriented and directed.

Ironically, Hagen found only one true successor, Heinitz, and that successor was never able to achieve the unique opportunity needed to fortify the infant professionalized bureaucracy which would, presumably, replace the old-fashioned core bureaucracy. Heinitz expended a great deal of energy upon his mining department, but was never able to supervise the entire bureaucratic system. While he developed one or possibly several technically oriented departments, the other ministers of the General Directory relapsed into the old-fashioned routine of the core bureaucracy, aided by the demise of the *Regie* in 1786. With the death of Hagen in 1772 the really active period of bureaucratic reform ended.

But the legacy of the reform period was considerable. First, it was evident by 1786 that the key to enlarging the authority of the civil service was not to be found in simply enlarging the core bureaucracy. Decentralization of function, or, to use Adam Smith's term, division of labor, was the key to growth. This decentralization had nothing to do with a supposed change from a "collegial" to a "cabinet" system, but rather with the construction of new agencies outside the core bureaucracy which were headed by bureaucratic entrepreneurs who fought one another, and the core bureaucracy, in true competition. Hagen succeeded in establishing supervision over several of the key bureaucratic structures, but he wore himself out in the process. The foundations were laid for the future development of an entrepreneurial bureaucracy which would, in the next century, work hand in glove with the government. The mining, construction, and forestry departments became models for similar governmental agencies in other states in the next century and possibly gave the Prussian bureaucracy a pervasive technical expertise in fields that officials in other states had little knowledge of. The reformed judiciary assumed significant control over the educational and religious sectors of the realm. It is possible that the subsequent division of Prussian higher education into two spheres, one composed of the universities and the other of the *technische Hochschule* or technical institutions, was a fruit of the division of legal and "humane" studies under the judiciary and engineering studies under the new technical departments of the government.[2]

Perhaps the greatest innovation of the reign of Frederick II was the establishment of the *Regie*. The general excise administration proved that finance need not be the major task of bureaucrats and that it had to be separated from other functions in order to foster the development of these other functions. One ailment afflicted the relatively weak governments of all Old Regime states, the constant, nagging, requirement to increase revenues. When the *Regie* was established it became clear that many officials could now work on long range developmental projects. The separation of finance from other functions of government is an absolute prerequisite for the development from preindustrial, old-regime forms of bureaucracy to modern forms. Unfortunately, the lesson was not permanently learned in Prussia or elsewhere before 1800.

The Prussian Reforms Considered in a European Setting

The bureaucratic innovations of the reign of Frederick II may well have had equivalents elsewhere in Europe: this question obviously can not be resolved here. Frederick William I created the General Directory and the war and domains boards, but these organizations were only rationalizations of the existing offices and did not result in the creation of a new, professionalized organization. In fact, the same aristocratic and bourgeois officials manned posts under the old and new organizations. Certain prominent families acquired almost hereditary rights to offices in the civil service from the time of the Great Elector on: the Dankelmann, Blumenthal, Bismarck, Borck, and Görne dynasties were represented in high executive posts each

2. Wilhelm Treue in "Das Verhältnis der Universitäten und Technischen Hochschulen zueinander und ihr Bedeutung für die Wirtschaft," in *Die wirtschaftliche Situation in Deutschland und Österreich um die Wende vom 18. zum 19. Jahrhundert,* ed. F. Lütge (Stuttgart, 1964), pp. 233–38 explores the mid-nineteenth-century development.

generation. Lack of impersonal recruiting standards encouraged these families to regard high civil service jobs as almost their right since senior members of the dynasty were in a good position to bring in the junior members as apprentices. As a consequence, and remembering that the high executive posts numbered no more than two hundred until 1763, the core bureaucracy came to resemble, *roughly*, the robe nobility of France. The difference between the Prussian system and the French may have been one only of degree and development: both were entrenched strongholds of privilege. Many of the robe nobility, for example, held hereditary posts in the *Chambre de Comptes* and other governmental bodies until 1789. It is probably true to state that modern bureaucracy simply did not exist in any European state before the French Revolution: all civil services were intimately connected with the great aristocratic and bourgeois families of the different states. Briefly, then, many of the changes in the civil service of the reign of Frederick II may have been attempts to escape this old-fashioned system of patronage; they were not only revolutionary in a strict administrative sense but also, potentially, in a social sense.

In France the parallel system of administration developed by Richelieu and his successors was an attempt to circumvent the hidebound and old-fashioned bureaucracy. But the intendants often became associate members of the old system; the Turgots were exceptions rather than rules. Similarly, Hagen's attempts to start a new technocratic bureaucracy were aimed at supplementing, not replacing, the old Prussian bureaucracy. Why was it necessary to retain the services of the old nonprofessional bureaucrats in Prussia and France? The answer can only be that they were considered indispensable, despite their flaws. Aristocratic officials mirrored the views of the aristocratic class; bourgeois officials mirrored the views of the old bourgeoisie. Both aristocrats and bourgeois were ensnared in a complex network of privilege everywhere. The established London guilds represented strongholds of bourgeois privilege as much as the East Prussian estates represented strongholds of aristocratic privilege. In England the guilds did not prove strong enough to contain the new merchants and financiers; they worked outside of them. But England was exceptional in Old Regime Europe since elsewhere the old dispensers of patronage remained firmly entrenched in society and in the executive offices of governments. No government can afford to break from the bonds of the society that it rules so it was perfectly natural for public bureaucracies to be mirrors of their society.

Nevertheless, change was in the air everywhere in the eighteenth century; the enormous growth of French governmental power under Louis XIV influenced rulers elsewhere and later. The two "super-powers" of the age, France and England, stimulated their smaller competitors to imitate their mercantilistic and bureaucratic schemes. Greatness might be communicated. Despite the basic conservatism of society in Prussia, therefore, Hagen and Frederick began to think of superimposing a new type of bureaucracy on the State. This corps of officials would be recruited carefully from the ranks of persons educated in the business and administratives techniques of the more developed states of the west. The new bureaucrats working, for example, in the mining department, would stir the mixture of society in order to stimulate the development of the economy. Unfortunately, both the king and his greatest minister never discerned that such innovations were "hot house" growths that rarely grew in an inhospitable social atmosphere. Patiently the old-line bureaucrats waited to resume control when the innovators left; they emerged triumphant in 1786. Only a residue of reform remained as the humble foundations of a great bureaucratic development in the next century.

The dream of the latter-day cameralists, and of Hagen, of the creation of a bureaucratic commonwealth remained half-formed. This State could not be reformed administratively because society was not ready for it and could not understand it, and because too few persons of importance were willing to fight for it. What was the dream? As Justi claimed, the ideal State could be governed by experts who knew the technical and material resources of the society and con-sciously guided that society into the paths of economic development. As jobs were created, new tax payers would become available. As the standard of living of the people rose the standard of power of the government would rise.

Frederick II and his Role of Leadership

Finally, the role of Frederick II must be clarified. He came to the throne lacking experience in administration aside from that gained when he worked under Councillor Hille. Throughout his reign he was primarily occupied with diplomatic, military, and intellectual pursuits and, despite the time he devoted to details of administration, could hardly be said to have considered these aspects of rule fascinating. Frederick felt, however, that he was obligated to pay close attention to domestic administration; his interest was grudging and is not often reflected in his multitudinous writings. Curiously enough he found it possible to break rather thoroughly with the policies of his father in other matters: the conservative, no-risk, preferences of Frederick William I in military and diplomatic affairs contrast markedly with the son's iconoclasm. The pietistic anti-intellectual was succeeded by the dilettante *Philosophe*. But in administrative matters Frederick's touch was unsure.

The chief policies of administration that Frederick devised owed their origins to the proposals and plans of a number of subordinates. Of all these policies that of economic integration around the nucleus of Berlin was the most important; it was learned from Hille. Although Frederick established the fifth department, he found that he could not obtain service from it because it was bypassed by other agencies. Therefore, he began to use a flexible approach to administration. He listened to Fäsch, Graumann, Splitgerber, Gotzkowsky, Hagen Domhardt, Münchow, Schlabrendorff, Calzabigi, and others; he allowed these individuals to develop programs and rewarded them on the basis of performance. Intensely pragmatic, Frederick never ceased to listen to the experimenters. The Prussian administrative scheme became one of excitement, rivalry, and conflict; it became alive. Frederick arbitrated between rivals, encouraged rivalry, and rewarded the executives he respected with extraordinary authority, increased salaries, and other more prestigious signs. But he did not dictate nor determine what was to be done according to some blueprint.

Frederick was perhaps the most successful monarch of the eighteenth century. He succeeded partly because he remembered to maintain ties with the agrarian social order, particularly with the landed aristocracy. The Junkers obtained favorable tariffs, credit institutes, and the award of prestigious jobs in the army and the civil service. But the old core bureaucracy was the stronghold of aristocratic officials and even there they had to share work with bourgeois colleagues. In effect, as the technical bureaucracy established by Hagen began to grow, the aristocrats in the old line found themselves shouldered aside within the General Directory itself. But the core bureaucracy worked with society and had to be maintained. The other competitive bureaucracies were professionalized along bourgeois lines, even the judiciary. Frederick used the civil service inherited from his father to continue the routine tasks of administration but fostered the growth of new agencies to handle nonroutine problems.

If Hagen tried to consolidate bureaucratic activity under an umbrella that one could call the "bureaucratic commonwealth," Frederick never had quite the same vision. Prussia was not just a state which had to be governed efficiently, as Hagen believed, but a congeries of interests and classes which had to be led in an ad hoc fashion. Neither rule by an absolute despot nor rule by a monolithic bureaucracy existed in Prussia between 1740 and 1786.

APPENDIX I

SIZE OF THE CORE BUREAUCRACY

1. The General Directory in 1740.

Departments	Ministers	Privy Finance Councillors (Geheime Finanzräte)	Subalterns
First	1	5	4
Second	1	7	3
Third	2	3	2½*
Fourth	1	4	1½
Accounting Office	0	0	17
Post Office	0	0	5
Medical College	0	0	12
General fiscal	(omitted because it was more connected to judiciary)		
TOTALS	5	19	45

*A clerk divided his time between the third and fourth departments in 1740. Thus the total amounted to 69 persons in Berlin. The "subaltern" category includes subordinate officials such as privy postal councillors and the six privy councillors of the Central Accounting Office who earned less than the privy finance councillors and were really glorified clerks. In addition, this subaltern category includes all registry clerks, secretaries, messengers, porters, etc., for whom information is available.[1]

2. The General Directory in 1747–1748.

Departments	Ministers	Privy Finance Councillors (Geheime Finanzräte)	Subalterns
First–sixth	6	11	83

The number of executive personnel in the General Directory has declined

1. See footnotes 13, 14, and 15 of chapter 1 for documentation for this analysis. Also footnote 41 of chapter 2, and footnotes 21 to 34 of chapter 9.

but a considerable increase in the subaltern personnel has occurred. This reflects the fact that the organization of the Central Accounting Office permitted the hiring of many technicians and clerks. But, significantly, the addition of the fifth department did not result in a great increase of officials. The same can be said of the sixth department (for military provisioning), added in 1746. All that had happened was an internal reorganization. Of course, the number of subaltern personnel is specified clearly in the archival source from which this information for 1747–1748 was drawn but Hintze, whose figures are included in *1*, above, made no effort to find out how many total officials there were in 1740 in this broad category. In summary, the total personnel of the General Directory amounted to about 100 persons by the latter date.

3. The Royal Household in Berlin and Potsdam. 1747–1748.

Cabinet secretaries (including the famous Eichel):	4
Royal chamber servants: (including Fredersdorff)	15
Royal pages:	8
Other pages: (these and persons below were *Diener*)	19
Lackeys:	22
Royal barber:	1
Royal huntsmen:	4
Fourier:	1
Maître d'hôtel:	1
Kitchen staffs	51
TOTAL:	126

4. The War and Domains Boards in the Provinces in 1740.

Boards	Presidents	Steuerräte and War and Domains Councillors	Subalterns in Board Hqs.
Electoral Mark	1	26	? probably 30
East Prussia, Königsberg	1	17	? probably 20
East Prussia, Gumbinnen	0	13	17
New Mark	1	12	9
Pomerania	1	18	23
Magdeburg	1	21	13
Halberstadt	1	10	8
Minden	1	8	? probably 8–10
Cleves	1	8	27
	8	133	157 (estimated)

5. The War and Domains Board in the Provinces in 1753–1754.

Boards	Presidents	*Steuerräte and War and Domains Councillors*	*Subalterns in Board Hqs. 1748*
Electoral Mark	1	29	57
East Prussia, Königsberg	1	?/about 17	48
East Prussia, Gumbinnen	1	13	36
New Mark	1	13	36
Pomerania	1	20	38
Magdeburg	1	20	38 (estimated)
Halberstadt	1	14	36 (estimated)
Minden	1	13	36 (estimated)
Cleves	1	20	24 (estimated)
East Frisia	1	? about 4	15 (estimated)
Silesia, Breslau	1	14	36 (estimated)
Silesia, Glogau	0	9	20
TOTALS	11	186	420

The main increase in executive personnel (presidents and war and domains councillors) came as a result of the creation of two new boards in Silesia after 1741, and one new board in East Frisia after 1744. Subaltern personnel increased quite remarkably, while executive personnel increased 20 percent.

6. Recapitulation, 1740–1754, of number of officials plainly hired as public officials, excluding those below the boards and those whose duties and salaries came from other sources primarily.

Year	Ministers	Privy Finance Councillors	*Presidents and Board Executives*	Total
1740	5	19	142	166
1754	6	18	197	221

7. Subaltern personnel, 1740–1756 and totals of all public officers aside from the judiciary, the foreign service, and those in local government.

Year	*Subalterns in General Directory*	*Subalterns in Boards*	*Executive Personnel*	Totals
1740	45	157	166	368

1754	80	420	221	641

Naturally these figures are tentative since they are based entirely upon information given in previous tables. They include all officials from ministerial rank down to the most minor copyists and junior clerks in the least significant of boards. The latter earned no more than 40 talers a year salary individually: this was near, if not below the level of subsistence according to some sources.

  8. Local Government.

    a. Number of *Landräte* in realm exclusive of Silesia, 86

    b. Subaltern personnel of *Landräte*, based upon the view that each *Landrat* had the services of a county assessor (*Kreiscalculator*) and a rural policeman (*Polizeiausreiter*), 172.

    c. It is impossible to determine the number of municipal employees in the towns of various sizes and legal status; Hintze estimated that the larger towns had about 10 councillors and clerks each, and the smaller, about four to six each. All of these except the two or three *Bürgermeister* were part-time employees in towns of substantial size, including the largest, Berlin and such smaller towns as Stargard in Pomerania or Wesel in Cleves. Exact figures may be obtained perhaps by the study of the numerous local archives; the General Directory apparently never bothered to count these municipal employees. A very tentative guess would be: 200 persons in all of the cities together except Berlin, where 43 worked (not counting city watchmen, guards, and the most humble employees). For the smaller towns and hamlets, there were some 350 visited by *Steuerräte* in 1753. Each probably had at least four employees.

Personnel in	*Personnel in*	*Total*
Major Towns	*Minor Towns*	*as of 1753*
300	1750	2050

These figures are only rough estimates based upon published and some archival material in Merseburg and Potsdam. Probably only 500 of these persons were civil servants such as *Bürgermeister*.

    d. Personnel in the Domain Administration (*Beamte*). Approximately 500.

    e. Total number of officials, subalterns, domain contractors, clerks, porters, etc.

  Since adequate information on the domain contractors is lacking it is impossible to give a fixed figure for the total. The domain contractor almost always was a commoner, had taken over the management of his farms from his father, and was training his sons in his craft. He was at once a foreman over an agrarian labor force and a businessman; he obtained a salary of about 150 talers a year. These persons were awarded five year contracts by a provincial board and were directed by a councillor.

Quite remarkable is the fact that the central archives of the Prussian state apparently have never included precise information on the number of *Bürgermeister*, other municipal employees including tax collectors, the employees of the *Landräte*, and the *Beamte* and their subordinates on the domains. Clearly these persons were hired by the boards or by local agencies in cooperation with the boards; Frederick II and the officials of the General Directory often complained about the quality of such workers, but did nothing to improve it.

9. It is thus possible to count and to identify those persons considered by the king and his ministers to be key personnel in the civil service: those hired and directly supervised by the State. The rest, including all of the persons mentioned in the last paragraph, were *not* part of the bureaucracy, but subordinate to it and subject to local influence and a certain degree of control by the boards.

a. Persons included in the official bureaucracy: all employees of the General Directory itself, all employees of the boards within the headquarters of each board. This group, which numbered 641 by 1754 (paragraph 7 above), has been called the core bureaucracy.

b. All *Landräte* and the key officials of the important towns; approximately 586 in all. These were probably part-time, locally recruited amateur officials. The *Landräte* were, of course, much more important, individually and collectively, than the others. One might term this group the "feudal bureaucracy" providing one does not equate "feudal" with discreet types of medieval political systems but rather with the admittedly loose definition employed by modern Marxist historians.

c. The personnel employed as contractors and subcontractors on the royal domains. In 1786 there were about 500 *Ämter* (domain units) and possibly between 500 and 1,000 major and minor contractors working them. They were a kind of bureaucratic work force. They were the contract bureaucracy. In some ways the Berlin entrepreneurs who obtained mint contracts, as well as the French excise tax farmers, belong to this general group also.

d. Finally, the mass of porters, copyists, minor clerks, etc., in the entire structure. Those employed directly within the boards and the

General Directory are included in the core bureaucracy, *1*, above. These humble persons were hired by municipal *Bürgermeister*, *Landräte*, and others at a low level; it is impossible to give a precise figure since records apparently were not kept even at the board level. This bureaucratic proletariat numbered, perhaps, 500 to 1,000.

e. Grand Total: 2,100 to 3,100. Hintze states that the total salary budget in 1740 was 150,000 talers: quite obviously this sum paid only the core bureaucracy above (641 persons approximately).

10. Social Structure of the Core Bureaucracy.

Ministers: All aristocrats. Two of the six had been ennobled by 1740.

Privy finance councillors: two aristocrats, sixteen commoners in 1754.

Board presidents: ten aristocrats, one commoner in 1754.

War and domains councillors (including *Steuerräte*): about 28 percent aristocrats.

Subalterns in General Directory and boards: two hundred and twenty commoners. Only in very rare instances was an aristocrat to be found in this class.

Landräte: eighty-six in realm exclusive of Silesia, all aristocrats.

"Bureaucratic proletariat": all commoners as nearly as can be determined.

Bürgermeister and other municipal officials: nearly all commoners.

Resumé: Aristocratically dominated, ministers and board presidents, *Landräte*.

Bourgeois dominated: privy finance councillors, municipal officials, and higher subalterns in General Directory and boards. Peasants dominated the bureaucratic proletariat, which was filled very largely from the ranks of retired soldiers. These soldiers in turn usually came from the peasantry. It is thus perfectly clear that all major social groups were represented in the core bureaucracy: social mobility existed in the sense that some peasants ultimately became urban workers, and doubtless some of these persons became minor clerks in the bureaucracy. Practically all of the clerks in the bureaucracy in the General Directory and the boards came from the urban middle class, however. Many of them had some university education, even certain copyists.

APPENDIX II

SOCIAL COMPOSITION

OF THE CORE BUREAUCRACY

a. Social composition of the boards in 1740 is estimated at 17 percent aristocrats in *AB*, 6:1. 285.

b. Social composition of the boards, 1753–1755—totals for following boards: New Mark, Magdeburg, Gumbinnen, Pomeranian, Electoral Mark, Minden, Breslau, Glogau, Halberstadt, and Cleves (*AB*, 9: 727–44; 10: 4–12, 26–33, 67–71, 118 ff., 155–62, 171 ff, 178–82, 202–10). No figures exist for the Königsberg and East Frisian Boards for these years apparently.

1. Total number of presidents: 9 (all aristocrats).

2. Total number of directors and war and domains councillors excluding *Steuerräte*: 175 (28 percent were aristocrats).

c. Social Composition of the Boards in 1768–1771—totals for following boards and board deputations: Electoral Mark, Cleves, Königsberg, Gumbinnen, Pomeranian, East Frisian, Altmark, Mörs, Hamm, and Cöslin (*AB*, 14: 433–38, 426 ff.; 15: 489–505; 16: 18–19). Ziekursch notes that 29 board councillors were appointed to fill vacancies between 1752 and 1771. Some 12 (41 percent) were aristocrats. No figures exist for the Magdeburg, New Mark, Halberstadt, and Minden boards.

1. Total number of presidents: 6 (all except 1 aristocrats).

2. Total number of directors and war and domains councillors including *Steuerräte*: 125. Some 27 (21 percent) were aristocrats. (Silesian boards were excluded because information on the number actually serving in that period was not available.)

d. Social composition of the boards between 1786 and 1806—totals for following boards: Magdeburg (1800), New Mark (1791), Cleves (1800), Minden (1800), County of Mark (1800), Petrikau (1793) (Brunschwig, appendix 6, 7. Bussenius, *Urkunden*, pp. 90 ff). Ziekursch notes that 33 board councillors were appointed to fill vacancies in the Breslau board between 1781 and 1806. Some 20 (61 percent) were aristocrats. No figures exist for other boards in printed sources apparently.

1. Total number of presidents: 6 (apparently all aristocrats).

2. Total number of directors and war and domains councillors including *Steuerräte*: 84. Some 29 (35 percent) were aristocrats.

e. Social origins of war and domains councillors, 1754–1755: The conduct reports for the Halberstadt, Cleves, New Mark, Minden, Magdeburg, Gumbinnen, Pomeranian, and Electoral Mark boards were analyzed. Unfortunately, reports from the Breslau, Glogau, East Frisian, and Königsberg boards were not available. The social composition of these probably followed the pattern established by the surviving conduct reports for other provinces. Silesian practices differed, of course.

1. Total number of war and domains councillors in selected provinces: 142. Some 36 (35 percent) of these councillors were aristocrats.

2. Sources of recruitment into councillor positions of bourgeois officials:

    A.   From lower bureaucratic positions: 43 (41 percent).

    B.   From regimental quartermaster and auditor posts: 33 (31 percent).

    C.   Former army officers: 6 (5.66 percent).

    D.   *Referendar* or *Rat* in judiciary: 6 (5.66 percent).

    E.   *Auscultator* or *Referendar* in boards: 10 (9 percent).

    F.   From foreign bureaucratic positions: 3 (2.8 percent).

    G.   Other and unknown: 5 (4.7 percent).

3. Sources of recruitment into councillor positions of noble officials:

    A.   From lower bureaucratic positions: 6 (16.6 percent).

    B.   Former army officers: 3 (8.33 percent).

    C.   *Auscultator* or *Referendar* in boards: 17 (47 percent).

    D.   Other and unknown: 10 (27.7 percent).

f. Social origins of war and domains councillors, 1768–1771: The conduct reports for the Electoral Mark, Cleves, Königsberg, Gumbinnen, and Pomeranian boards and for the board deputations of Altmark, Mörs, Hamm, and Cöslin were analyzed. Unfortunately, reports from the Breslau, Glogau, Magdeburg, East Frisian, and New Mark boards were not available. The social composition of these probably followed the pattern established by the surviving conduct reports for other provinces. Silesian practices differed, of course.

1. Total numbers of war and domains councillors in selected provinces: 120. Some 28 (25 percent) of these councillors were aristocrats.

2. Sources of recruitment into councillor positions of bourgeois officials:
    A. From lower bureaucratic positions: 46 (50 percent).
    B. From regimental quartermaster and auditor posts: 20 (21.5 percent).
    C. Former army officers: 8 (8.25 percent).
    D. *Referendar* or *Rat* in judiciary: 10 (10.5 percent).
    E. *Auscultator* or *Referendar* in boards: 4 (4.35 percent).
    F. From foreign bureaucratic positions: 2 (2.17 percent).
    G. Unknown: 2 (2.17 percent).
3. Sources of recruitment into councillor positions of noble officials:
    A. From lower bureaucratic posts: 4 (14.28 percent).
    B. Army officers: 6 (21.4 percent).
    C. *Referendar* of judiciary: 1 (3.57 percent).
    D. *Auscultator* and *Referendar* of boards: 7 (25 percent).
    E. From foreign bureaucratic positions: 2 (7.14 percent).
    F. Direct appointment from *Rittergut*: 3 (10.7 percent).
    G. Unknown: 5 (17.8 percent).
Some of the noble *Auscultator* were recruited from among former military officers, so it is possible that about 33 percent had formerly been officers. Only 21 percent were actually appointed councillors directly from the army. Significantly, 39 percent had previously served in lower positions in the boards or as *Auscultator*.

4. Aristocratic and bourgeois councillors aged 35 or younger by 1771 (sources are same as given for 2.–3., above):
    A. Total number aged 35 or younger by 1771: 33 (out of 120).
    B. Sources of recruitment for all these councillors:
        1. From lower bureaucratic positions: 10 (30.3 percent).
        2. Regimental quartermasters and *Auditor*: 4 (12.12 percent).
        3. Army officers: 4 (12.12 percent).
        4. *Referendar* in judiciary: 2 (6.06 percent).
        5. *Auscultator* in boards: 9 (27.2 percent).
        6. Foreign bureaucratic positions: 0.
        7. Direct appointment from *Rittergut* or domain: 4 (12.12 percent).

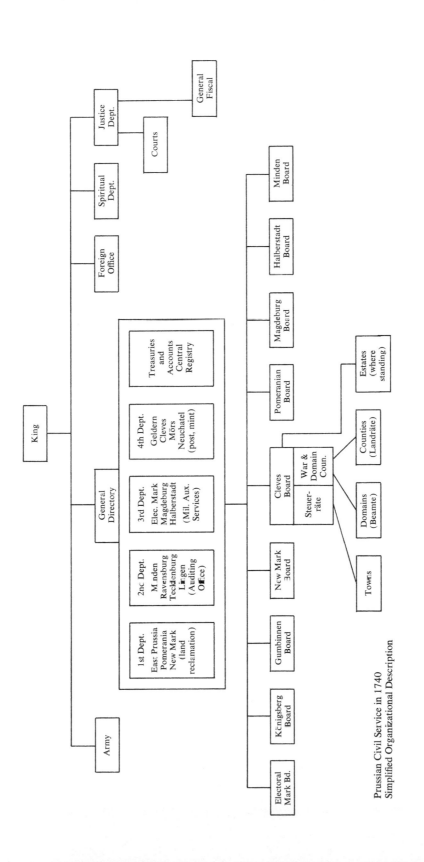

Prussian Civil Service in 1740
Simplified Organizational Description

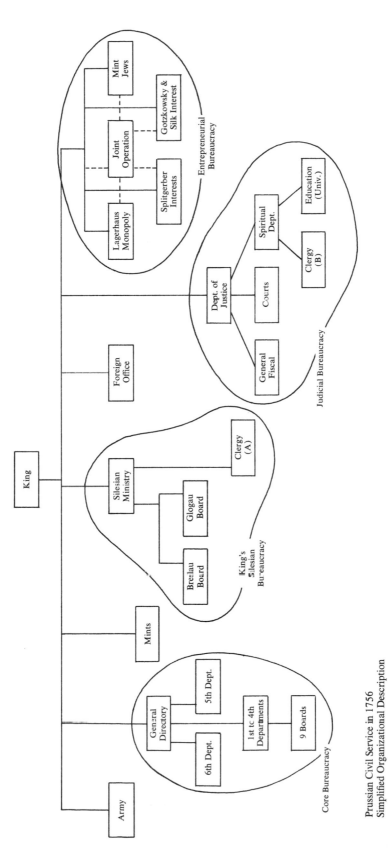

Prussian Civil Service in 1756
Simplified Organizational Description

Clergy A: Roman Catholic hierarchy in Silesia.
Clergy B: Predominantly Protestant outside of Silesia.

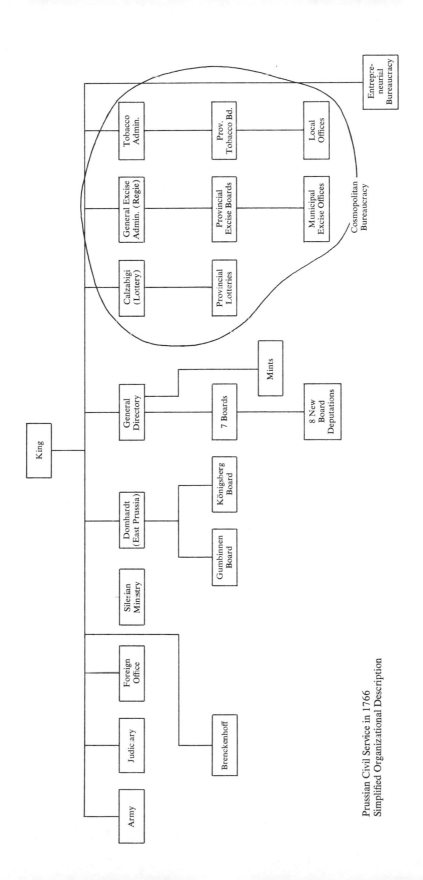

Prussian Civil Service in 1766
Simplified Organizational Description

King

Army — Judiciary — Foreign Office — Silesian Ministry — Domhardt (East Prussia) — General Directory — Calzabigi (Lottery) — General Excise Admin. (Regie) — Tobacco Admin.

Brenckenhoff

Gumbinnen Board — Königsberg Board

7 Boards — Mints

8 New Board Deputations

Provincial Lotteries — Provincial Excise Boards — Prov. Tobacco Bd.

Municipal Excise Offices — Local Offices

Cosmopolitan Bureaucracy

Entrepre-neurial Bureaucracy

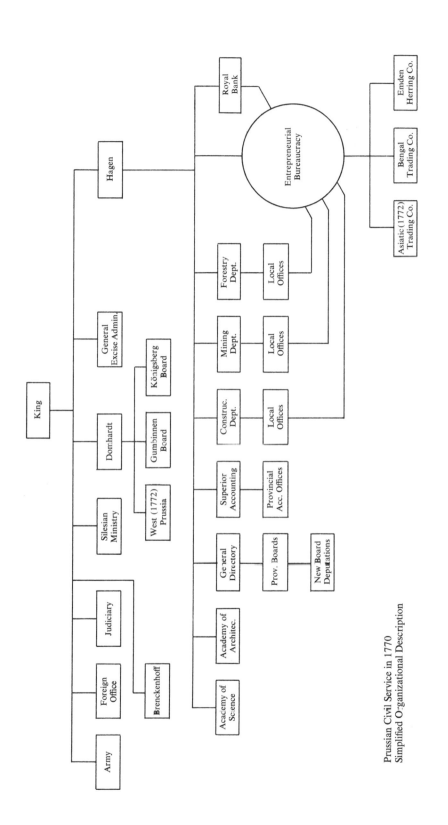

Prussian Civil Service in 1770
Simplified Organizational Description

BIBLIOGRAPHICAL NOTE

Students of Prussian administrative history have split into two main camps since 1786. One group accepts the *Staatsbildung* thesis, and the other rejects it. The mercantilistic theory associated with Schmoller has had a long history. In Germany it can be traced to the cameralists, the commentators on natural law, and to the public writings of Frederick II. It was not until the nineteenth century, however, that this thesis became an essential support to the theories of the "national economists" such as List and Wilhelm Roscher. Schmoller[1] adapted this preparatory work to his particular purpose. His theory glorifies the Hohenzollerns as the founders of industrialized Germany and excuses their despotism on the ground that it was necessary to prepare the way for progress. To several generations of German scholars the Schmoller thesis established a criterion for scholarly work. They believed in it because they admired the Hohenzollerns as the founders of the German national state.

The Schmoller thesis exercised considerable influence on the work of administrative historians in Germany. The rise of the General Directory after 1723 was viewed by many of them to be an important factor in the development of the *Gesamtsstaat*. The professionalization of the bureaucracy after that date many interpreted to mean the eclipse of local and *Ständestaat* institutions. They assumed that the civil service was a monolithic organization completely loyal to its master the king. Both king and official collaborated in the common task of benevolently ruling Prussian society. Implied also in this theory was the belief that the Prussian bureaucracy actively fostered German industrialization, and that this dedicated corps of officials was governed by mercantilistic assumptions. Among the nineteenth-century historians who actively supported this view of the role of the bureaucracy was Isaacsohn.[2] For the judiciary, the equivalent of Isaacsohn was Conrad Bornhak,[3] who, as a jurist, glorified the role of Cocceji and of the reformed courts in the formation of the *Gesamtsstaat*.

1. Gustav Schmoller, *Umrisse und Untersuchungen zur Verfassungs Verwaltungs- und Wirtschaftsgeschichte besonders des preussischen Staats im 17. und 18 Jr.* (Leipzig, 1898), pp. 1–70, passim.
2. Siegfried Isaacsohn, *Geschichte des preussischen Beamtenthums, vom Angang des 15. Jahrhunderts bis auf die Gegenwart* (Berlin, 1874–84).
3. Conrad Bornhak's *Preussische Staats- und Rechtsgeschichte* (Oberlin, 1903),

Two of the best works on the judiciary were written by Stölzel[4] and Holtze.[5] Both writers recognized the existence of conflict between the judiciary and the core bureaucracy and described the career of Cocceji with real insight.

Otto Hintze accomplished a great deal towards removing some of the worst exaggerations of Prussian historiography. In his article on Frederick's agrarian policy[6] which appeared in 1897, he exposed the errors of Stadelmann and arrived at the conclusion that Frederick's policy was based upon consideration of *Realpolitik* rather than upon humanitarian impulses. In an exhaustive study of Prussian administration in 1740, which served to introduce the volumes of the *Acta Borussica* concerned with the reign of Frederick II, he carefully described the administration of the various provinces and showed that the Hohenzollerns had had different objectives in mind in their policies towards these provinces. Aside from this, volume 6, part 1 of the *Acta Borussica* presents a rather rigid description of the administrative system during the last years of the reign of Frederick William I. Nevertheless the work remains the most complete survey of the Prussian bureaucracy for the time it covers. In other writings,[7] Hintze continued to treat the Prussian bureaucracy as a monolithic organization, while indicating in scattered places that Frederick's actions did not necessarily always follow from a desire to promote the centralization of effective authority under a few ministers.

The Schmoller thesis did not dominate all of the writing on the Prussian administration during the eighteenth century. Mirabeau[8] was the first critic of importance of Frederick and his domestic policy. Writing

---

pp. 236 ff., 212 ff. Bornhak's *Geschichte des preussischen Verwaltungsrechts*, 3 vols. (Berlin, 1884–86), concentrates on the judiciary.

4. Adolf Stölzel, *Brandenburg-Preussens Rechtsverwaltung und Rechtsverfassung* (Berlin, 1888–94), vol. 2.

5. Friedrich Holtze, *Geschichte des Kammergerichts in Brandenburg-Preussen* (Berlin, 1890–1904), vol. 3. Herman Weill, *Frederick the Great and Samuel von Cocceji* (Madison, 1961), presents a rather uncritical summary of the interpretations expressed by Stölzel, Bornhak, Holtze, and others.

6. Otto Hintze, "Zur Agrarpolitik Friedrichs des Grossen," *Forschungen zur brandenburgischen und preussischen Geschichte* 10 (1897): 275–309 (Subsequently referred to as *FBPG*). "Einleitende Darstellung der Behördenorganisation und allgemeinen Verwaltung in Preussen beim Regierungsantritt Friedrichs II," *AB*, 6: pt. 1. (Berlin, 1901).

7. "Der Ursprung des preussischen Landratsamts in der Mark Brandenburg," *FBPG*, 28 (1915): 357–422. See also his *Staat und Verfassung* (Leipzig, 1941), pp. 38 ff.

8. Honore G.V.R. Comte de Mirabeau, *De la Monarchie prussienne sous Frederic le Grand* (London, 1788).

with a Physiocratic bias, Mirabeau could find little of benefit in the quasi-mercantilistic state of Prussia. Johannes Ziekursch[9] claimed much later that Prussian administration in Silesia was unmitigated despotism. In addition, he was one of the first to show how Frederick systematically crushed the rights of the local Silesian *Burgher* and imposed an oppressive garrison administration upon them. After exposure to so much of the "Prussian school" of history, Ziekursch comes as a refreshing change.

Hass[10] investigated the relationship between Frederick II and the board presidents and discovered that Frederick often bypassed the General Directory to deal directly with these lower echelon officials. His article was one of the first attempts to show that Frederick's administrative policy was not monolithic. In 1931 Walter Dorn published an article entitled "The Prussian Bureaucracy in the 18th Century,"[11] which has enjoyed a justly favorable reputation over the years. He disclosed the existence of a "silent contest" between the king and his ministers. Unfortunately, Dorn placed too great emphasis on the supposed technical competence of the bureaucrat in all spheres and failed to discern the existence of different factions within the civil service.

Hans Haussherr[12] wrote a comparative study of the administrative systems of Europe in the eighteenth century in an effort to trace the evolution of the collegial system to the ministerial organization. In Prussia this evolution, which culminated in the reforms of Stein, began early in the reign of Frederick II.

One of the deans of contemporary German Historians, Fritz Hartung,[13] has recently published a collection of essays dealing with Prussian con-

9. Johannes Ziekursch, *Beiträge zur Charakteristic der preussischen Verwaltungsbeamten in Schlesien bis zum Untergange des friderizianischen Staats* (Breslau, 1907). *Das Ergebnis der friderizianischen Stadteverwaltung und der Städteordnung Steins* (Jena, 1909). *Hundert Jahre schlesischer Agrargeschichte* (Breslau, 1927). Ziekursch did not venture to analyse the office of the Silesian minister. See notes in chapter 5.

10. Martin Hass, "Friedrich der Grosse und seine Kammerpräsidenten," *Beiträge zur brandenburgischen und preussischen Geschichte: Festschrift zu Gustav Schmollers 70. Geburtstag* (Leipzig, 1908), pp. 219 ff.

11. Walter L. Dorn, "The Prussian Bureaucracy in the 18th Century," *Political Science Quarterly* 46 (1931): 403–23; 47(1932): 259–73.

12. Hans Haussherr, *Verwaltungseinheit und Ressorttrennung vom Ende des 17. bis zum Beginn des 19. Jr.* (Berlin, 1953), pp. 121–49, 189 ff. Walter Mertineit, *Die Fridericianische Verwaltung in Ostpreussen* (Heidelberg, 1958), p. 22 ff.

13. Fritz Hartung, *Staatsbildende Kräfte der Neuzeit* (Berlin, 1961), pp. 198–206. The essay entitled "Studien zur Geschichte der preussischen Verwaltung," of which these pages form a part, is an admirable survey of German constitutional history from 1600 to 1920.

stitutional history. Hartung maintains that the General Directory instructions of 1748 were permeated with "Enlightened Absolutism" in contrast with the original instruction of Frederick William I. Hartung's views are similar to those of Hans Haussherr, Dorn, Hintze, Schmoller, and Hass. On the one hand he argues that Frederick promoted "Enlightened Absolutism," but on the other hand he states that Frederick tried to decentralize administrative responsibility among his subordinates and that he held somewhat anachronistic views concerning the nobility. In no sense does he swallow the whole of the "Enlightened Despotism" mythology, but he never reconciles the contradictions evinced in this essay as well as in the celebrated essay on "Enlightened Despotism (Absolutism)."

Hans Rosenberg's book *Bureaucracy, Aristocracy, and Autocracy*[14] is not a study of the bureaucracy per se, but an analysis of the process by which certain members of the middle class infiltrated the bureaucracy and combined forces with the aristocrats who had previously monopolized high offices to form a bureaucratic elite. Otto Büsch in his *Militärsystem und Sozialleben im Alten Preussen, 1713–1807*,[15] compliments Rosenberg's work in discussing the attempts of various Prussian rulers, including Frederick II, to use the army to administer civilian society in general.

Although all of these studies have contributed to this work, none of them has given a clear picture of the relationship of Frederick to his civil service and his judiciary. They have sometimes been guilty of flagrant exaggerations: a Prussian equivalent of the French *Reaction feodale* simply did not exist, nor was Prussian society "militarized." The statistical analysis of the bureaucracy which has been presented in chapters 1 and 10 of this work (see the tables in the appendix also), indicate that the civil service was small, not large, that the proportion of nobles and bourgeois officials does not change remarkably during the entire period from 1722 to 1806, and that recruits from the army officer and quartermaster groups remained fewer than recruits from other sources. Perhaps one could find signs of a feudal reaction in the history of the provincial estates during the eighteenth century,[16] but evidence seems to indicate that the estates did not increase in power and prestige as political bodies, but solely as financial and credit granting agencies. Members of the *Stände* grumbled under Frederick William I, under Frederick II, and

14. (Cambridge, Mass., 1958); Rosenberg, *Bureaucracy*, pp. 88–175.

15. (Berlin, 1962), pp. 71–74. See also pp. 90–93, 103–5, 139–43.

16. See Peter Baumgart, "Zur Geschichte der kurmärkischen Stände im 17. und 18. Jahrhundert," Dietrich Gerhard, ed., *Ständische Vertretungen in Europa im 17 und 18. Jahrhundert* (Göttingen, 1969), pp. 131–61, and the literature cited in his notes.

under the later Hohenzollern rulers; this bickering revealed frustration, not a growing sense of triumph. The judiciary, manned for the most part by bourgeois jurists, became the protector of the aristocracy because the *Adelschaft* was denied political power, suffered economic and financial decline, and found itself more and more dependent upon the largess of the king. The dependent aristocracy was in no position to bite the niggardly hand that fed it.

Writers such as Epstein[17] and Koselleck[18] have provided some insights into the nature of Prussian society after 1750. Epstein concentrated, of course, on the conservatives, but his successor could well concentrate on the radicals, the innovators, and the discontented; a novel picture of Prussia might well emerge. Koselleck tried too hard to show that the *Allgemeine Landrecht* heralded something new rather than codified something old. It is a frustrating job to try to find rebels among the cautious, pedantic, and bureaucratic-minded jurists. Novelty can be found in the writings of sensitive Protestant clergymen such as Süssmilch and in the universities between 1770 and 1830, not in judicial antechambers. Brunschwig[19] provided a foundation for this post-1786 study; others can continue. Pioneering work on the social content of fiction written after 1770[20] can again provide new leads to understanding the radical tradition in German history.

17. Klaus Epstein, *The Genesis of German Conservatism* (Princeton, 1966), is a very valuable book, even if the weight of detail obscures analysis, but it focuses, perhaps, on a much overworked theme in German historiography.

18. Reinhard Koselleck, *Preussen zwischen Reform und Revolution* (Stuttgart, 1967). The criticism of this book extends only to 1806, and, particularly, is limited to Koselleck's discussion of the *Allgemeine Landrecht*.

19. Henry Brunschwig, *La Crise de L'État Prussien à la Fin du XVIIIe Siècle* (Paris, 1947). His discussion of *La Crise Bourgeoisie*, pp. 142–76, should provide a basis for future studies.

20. Ernest Baasch, "Der Kaufmann in der deutsche Romanliteratur des 18. Jr.," *Aus Sozial-und Wirtschaftsgeschichte* (Festschrift für Georg von Below), (Stuttgart, 1928), pp. 279 ff. See Brunschwig, *Crise*, pp. 166 ff. Walther Hubatsch, *Friedrich der Grosse und die preussische Verwaltung* (Cologne, 1973), is certainly not a radical departure. In fact this book is a nostalgic recapitulation of the Schmoller thesis, in which Frederick does everything and great progress is made on all fronts. It is also a poorly organized survey of the internal history of the Prussian state.

BIBLIOGRAPHY

Part I: Archival Sources

The author wishes to thank the archival staff of the *Deutsches Zentral-archiv, Abteilung Merseburg*, in the German Democratic Republic for its cooperation with him in the course of research. The specific files used in this study and previously cited include:

Rep. 9, *Allgemeine Verwaltung*   A, 20, Fasc. 4
   C, IB, 3, Fasc. 31
   L, 8, Fasc. 10, nos. 22, 23, 24, 25
   L, 8, Fasc. 11, Fasc. 6, Fasc. 9

Rep. 46B, No. 229
Rep. 92, *Cocceji*, no. 8, Vol. III
Rep. 96, *Geheimes Zivilkabinett, ältere Periode*. Brenckenhoff, 3

No. 410 e	No. 410 g
No. 410 N	No. 410 o
No. 410 p	No. 411 D
No. 412 C	No. 421 B
No. 423 A, Fol. 25	No. 410 T
No. 422 F, 4, Fol. 85	No. 426 M, Fol. 114

Rep. 120, *Ministerium für Handel und Gewerbe* I, Tit. III, no. 1
Rep. 121   Abt. A, Tit. III, Sect. 4, no. 1
   Abt. A, Tit. IV, Sect. 2, No. 2, Vol. I
   Abt. A, Tit. IV, Sect. 3, No. 104, Vol. I
   I: VI, 10
   Abt. A, Tit. X, Sect. I, No. 101, I
Rep. 121   Abt. A, Tit. IV, Sect. 4, No. 1
   Abt. A, Tit. IV, Sect. 3, No. 104, Vol. I
Rep. 121A, Tit. X, Sect. I,   No. 101, I
Gen. Dir., Gen. Kassen Dept.,   No. 24, and No. 49
Gen. Dir., Kurmark, Tit. XIX, No. 1, Fol. 20
   Tit. LXVII, Sect. B, No. 15
   Tit. CCXLVII, No. 5
Gen. Dir., Magdeburg. Tit. CLVII, I, II

Gen. Dir., Mil, Dept., No. 2
Gen. Dir., Ober Bau Dept., Tit. I, No. 2
Gen. Dir., Tabacks-Sachen, A, Tit. I, 1. and A, Tit. V, I
The author wishes to thank the archival staff of the *Staatsarchiv Potsdam,* "Orangerie," Potsdam, in the German Democratic Republic for its cooperation with him in the course of research. The specific files used in this study and previously cited include:
Pr. Br., Rep. II, A. Allgemeine Kammer –S. A 367
    Rep. II, I, Dom. Reg., A 11
    Rep. II, D 1801
    Rep. II, I, Dom. Reg., D 1819
    Rep. 30 A, 16
    Rep. 30, A, Tit. 39, no. 1, vol. IV
    Rep. 30, A, 16
    Rep. 30, Berlin, Tit. 23, no. 2
Finally the author wishes to thank the archival staff of the *Zentrales Archiv der Deutschen Akademie der Wissenschaften,* Berlin, in the German Democratic Republic for its cooperation with him in the course of research. The specific files incorporated in this study, and previously cited, are: [files of Akademie der Wissenschaften, Berlin]
        I: V, 15
        I: VI, 2, 80, 82, 142
        I: V, 10
        I: III, 84
        I: VI, 10

Part II: Published Primary Sources

Acta Borussica: Denkmäler der preussischen Staatsverwaltung im 18. Jr. Behördenorganisation. Ed. Royal Academy of Science, Berlin, 16 vols. (Berlin, 1892–1970).

Schmoller, Gustav, and Hintze, Otto, eds., *Die preussische Seidenindustrie im 18 Jr.,* 3 vols. (1892).

Schmoller, Gustav; Naude, W. and Skalweit, A., *Die Getreidehandelspolitik und Kriegsmagazinverwaltung Preussens 1740–1756.* Vol. 3 (Berlin, 1910), vol. 4 (Berlin, 1931).

Rachel, H., *Die Handels- Zoll- und Akzisepolitik Preussens 1713–1786,* Vols. 3 and 4. (Berlin, 1922–28).

Schrötter, F., *Die Münzpolitik Preussens.* 3 vols. (Berlin, 1900–1904).

Brenckenhoff, Franz Balthasar Schönberg von. "Brenckenhoff Berichte" *Schriften des Vereins für Geschichte der Neumark,* 10: 38–40.

Koser, Reinhold, ed., *Briefwechsel Friedrichs des Grossen mit Grumbkow und Maupertius. PKPA* (Leipzig, 1898).

Küntzel, Georg and Hass, Martin, *Die politischen Testaments der Hohenzollern* (Berlin, 1919), vol. 2.

Mylius, O., *Corpus Constitutionum Marchicarum*, Continuatio und Novum Corpus (Berlin, 1736–1800).

Oeuvres Posthumes de Frédéric II, Roi de Prusse, 13 vols. (Berlin, 1788).

Politische Correspondenz Friedrichs des Grossen, Volz, Gustav, *et al.*, eds., 36 vols. (Berlin, 1879–88).

Preuss, J., ed., *Frederick II Oeuvres*, 40 vols. (Berlin, 1847 ff).

Publicationen aus den Königlichen preussischen Staatsarchiven. Stadelmann, R., ed., vol. 11; pt. 2 (Berlin, 1882). Lehmann, ed., vol. 10 (Berlin, 1881), vol. 13 (Berlin, 1882), vol. 14 (1883).

Rehmann, E. "Kleine Beiträge zur Charakteristik Brenckenhoffs," *Schriften des Vereins für Geschichte der Neumark*, 22: 101 ff.

Part III: Select Bibliography of Secondary Works and of Contemporary Commentaries, Diaries, etc.

Aner, Karl, *Die Theologie der Lessingzeit* (Halle, 1929).

Arnim, *Über die Canton-Verfassung in den preussischen Staaten* (Frankfurt, 1788).

Aubin, Gustav, *Zur Geschichte des gutsherrlich-bäuerlichen Verhältnisses in Ostpreussen* (Leipzig, 1910).

Baasch, Ernst, "Der Kaufmann in der deutsche Romanliteratur des 18. Jr.," *Aus Sozial- und Wirtschaftsgeschichte: Gedächtnisschrift für Georg von Below* (Stuttgart, 1928), pp. 283–98.

Bassewitz, Magnus Friedrich von, *Die Kurmark Brandenburg: ihr Zustand und ihre Verwaltung. . . in 1806* (Leipzig, 1847).

Baumgart, Peter, "Zur Geschichte der kurmärkischen Stände in 17. und 18. Jahrhundert " Dietrich Gerhard ed. *Ständische Vertretungen in Europa im 17. und 18. Jahrhundert* (Göttingen 1969).

Becker, Erich, *Gemeindliche Selbstverwaltung* (Berlin 1941).

Beheim-Schwarzenbach, M., *Hohenzollernsche Kolonisationen* (Leipzig 1874).

Bennecke, W.G., *Stand und Stände in Preussen vor den Reformen* (Berlin 1935).

Berghoff-Ising, Franz, *Entwicklung des Landwirtschaftspachtwesens in Preussen* (Berlin n.d.).

Beutin, L., "Die Wirkungen des siebenjährigen Kreiges auf die Volkswirtschaft in Preussen " *Vierteljahrsschrift für Sozial- und Wirtschaftsgeschichte* 26 (1933): 209–43.

Bielfeld, Jacob Freiherr von, *Institutions Politiques* 2 vols. (Leiden 1760).

Bornhak, Conrad, *Geschichte des preussischen Verwaltungsrechts* (Berlin 1884–86) 3 vols.

Bornhak, Conrad, *Geschichte der preussischen Universitätsverwaltung bis 1810* (Berlin, 1900).

Bowden, Witt, *Industrial Society in England* (New York, 1925).

Brunschwig, Henri, *La Crise de l'état prussien à la Fin du XVIIIe Siècle* (Paris, 1947).

Buchsel, Hans, *Rechts- und Sozialgeschichte des oberschlesischen Berg- und Hüttenwesens, 1740–86* (Breslau, 1941).

Büsch, Otto, *Militärsystem und Sozialleben im alten Preussen: 1713–1807* (Berlin, 1962).

Carsten, F. L., "East Prussia," *History* 36 (1948): 241–46.

———, *The Origins of Prussia* (Oxford, 1954).

Catt, Henri de, *Memoirs*, tr. F.S. Flint (London, 1929).

Craig, Gordon A., *The Politics of the Prussian Army* (Oxford, 1956).

Darjes, Joachim Georg, *Erste Gründe der Cameral Wissenschaften* (June, 1756).

Der Grosse Generalstabe *Die Kriege Friedrichs des Grossen* (Berlin, 1900–), 3: 1.

Dessmann, Günther, *Geschichte der schlesischen Agrarverfassung* (Strassburg, 1904).

Detto, A., "Die Besiedlungen des Oderbruchs durch Friedrich den Grossen," *FBPG*, 16 (1903): 165–86.

Dilthey, Wilhelm, *Gesammelte Schriften* (Leipzig, 1927), vol. 3.

Dorn, Walter A., "The Prussian Bureaucracy in the Eighteenth Century," *Political Science Quarterly* 47 (1932): 75–77.

Dorwart, Reinhold A., *The Administrative Reforms of Frederick William I* (Cambridge, Mass., 1953).

Durichen, J., "Geheimes Kabinett und Geheimer Rat unter der Regierung Augusts des Stärken in den Jahren 1704–1720." *Neues Archiv für sächsische Geschichte und Altertumskunde* 51 (1930): 72–88.

Eichborn, K.F. von, *Das Soll und Haben von Eichborn und Co.* (Munich, 1928).

Eldon, C.W., *England's Subsidy Policy towards the Continent during the Seven Years War* (Philadelphia, 1938).

Epstein, Klaus, *Genesis of German Conservatism* (Princeton, 1966).

Erdmannsdörffer, Bernhard, *Deutsche Geschichte vom Westfälischen Frieden bis zum Regierungsantritt Friedrich des Grossen 1648–1740*, 2 vols. (Leipzig, 1932).

Fechner, H., "Die Königlichen Eisenhüttenwerke Malapane und Kreuz zu ihrer Übernahme durch das schlesiche Oberbergamt, 1753–1780," *Zeitschrift für Berg- Hütten- und Salinenwesen*, pp. 43, 81 ff.

Freymark, H., *Zur preussischen Handels- und Zollpolitik von 1648–1818* (Halle, 1897).

Gelpe, F., *Geschichtliche Entwicklung des Landratamts* (Berlin, 1902).

Gloger, Bruno, "Der Potsdamer Steuerrat" (Ph. D. dissertation, Humboldt Univ., Berlin, 1957).

Gooch, G.P., *Frederick the Great, the Ruler, the Writer, the Man* (London, 1947).

Gotskowsky, J.E., "Geschichte eines patriotischen Kaufmanns," *Schriften des Vereins für die Geschichte Berlins* 7 (Berlin, 1873): 12 ff.

Graumann, Johann, *Gesammelte Briefe von dem Gelde, von dem Wechsel und dessen Curs, von der Proportion zwischen Gold und Silber . . .* (Berlin, 1762).

Grünhagen, Colmar, "Die Entstehung eines schlesischen Sonderministeriums," *FBPG* 20 (1907): 107–9.

Grünhagen, Colmar, *Schlesien unter Friedrich dem Grossen*, 2 vols. (Breslau, 1890).

Hahlweg, Werner, "Die Grundzüge der Verfassung des sächsischen Geheimen Kabinetts 1763–1831," *Zeitschrift für die gesamte Staatswissenschaft* (Tübingen, 1943).

Hanus, Francis, *Church and State in Silesia 1740–1786* (Washington, D.C., 1944).

Harnack, Adolf von, *Geschichte der Königlich preussischen Akademie der Wissenschaften zu Berlin*, 3 vols. (Berlin, 1900).

Hartung, Fritz, *Das Reich und Europa* (Leipzig, 1941).

Hartung, Fritz, *Enlightened Despotism*, tr. H. Otto, Historical Association General Series No. 36 (London, 1957).

Hartung, Fritz, *Staatsbildende Kräfte der Neuzeit* (Berlin, 1961).

Hashagen, J., "Die preussische Herrschaft und die Stände am Niederrhein," *Westdeutsche Zeitschrift* 28 (1909): 17 ff.

Hass, Martin, "Friedrich der Grosse und seine Kammerpräsidenten," *Beiträge zur brandenburgischen und preussischen Geschichte: Festschrift zu Gustav Schmollers 70. Geburtstag* (Leipzig, 1908), pp. 210–19.

Hassenkamp, Xaver von, "Ostpreussen unter dem Doppelaar," *Neuen preussischen Provinzial-Blätter*, 3rd ser. 9 (1866).

Hassenstein, W., "Zur Geschichte der Könige Gewehrfabrik in Spandau," *Technik Geschichte* 4 (1912): 27–40.

Haussherr, Hans, *Verwaltungseinheit und Ressorttrennung* (Berlin, 1953).

Hegel, Georg Wilhelm Friedrich, *The Philosophy of History*, tr. J. Sibree (New York, 1944).

Henderson, W.O., *The State and the Industrial Revolution in Prussia, 1740–1870* (Liverpool, 1958).

Henderson, W.O., *Studies in the Economic Policy of Frederick the Great* (London, 1963).

Hess, Ulrich, *Geheimer Rat und Kabinett in den Ernestinischen Staaten Thüringens* (Weimar, 1962).

Hinrichs, Carl, "Der hallische Pietismus als politisch-soziale Reformbewegung des 18. Jahrhunderts," *Jahrbuch für die Geschichte Mittel- und Ostdeutschlands* 2 (1953): 177–89.

Hinrichs, Carl, "Hille und Reinhardt, zwei Wirtschafts- und Sozialpolitiker des preussischen Absolutismus," *Preussen als historisches Problem* (Berlin, 1964), pp. 161–71.

Hintze, Otto, "Einleitende Darstellung der Behördenorganisation und allgemeinen Verwaltung in Preussen beim Regierungsantritt Friedrich II," *Acta Borussica: Behördenorganisation*, vol.6, pt. 1 (Berlin, 1901).

Hintze, Otto, "Die Hohenzollern und der Adel," *Historische Zeitschrift* 112 (1914).

Hintze, Otto, *Die Hohenzollern und ihr Werk* (Berlin, 1915).

Hintze, Otto, "Johann Ernst Gotzkowsky," *Historische und politische Aufsätze* (Berlin, 1908) vol. 3.

Hintze, Otto, "Agrarpolitik Friedrichs des Grossen," *FBPG*, 10: 293 ff. (1898).

Hintze, Otto, "Der österreichische und der preussische Beamtenstaat im 17. und 18. Jahrhundert," *Historische Zeitschrift* 86 (1901) 402–44.

Hintze, Otto, *Staat und Verfassung* (Leipzig, 1941).

Hintze, Otto, "Der ursprung des preussischen Landratsamts in der Mark Brandenburg," *FBPG* 28 (1915): 357–80.

Hinze, K., *Die Arbeiterfrage zu Beginn des modernen Kapitalismus in Brandenburg-Preussen* (Berlin, 1927).

Holthausen, H., *Verwaltung und Stände des Herzogtums Geldern* (Bonn, 1916).

Holtze, Friedrich, *Geschichte der Stadt Berlin* (Tübingen, 1906).

Holtze, Friedrich, *Geschichte des Kammergerichts in Brandenburg-Preussen* (Berlin, 1890–1904).

Hubatsch, *Friedrich der Grosse und die preussische Verwaltung* (Cologne, 1973).

Isaacsohn, Siegfried, *Geschichte des preussischen Beamtenthums*, 3 vols. (Berlin, 1874–1884).

Jany, Curt, *Geschichte der Koniglichen preussischen Armee bis zum*

Jahre 1807 (Berlin, 1929), vol. 2.

Joachim, Erich, *Johann Friedrich von Domhardt* (Berlin, 1899).

Johnson, Hubert C., "Theory of Bureaucracy in Cameralism," *Political Science Quarterly* 79 (Sept. 1964): 378–402.

Juhr, Hannelore, *Die Verwaltung des Hauptamtes Brandenburg/Ostpreussen von 1713 bis 1751* (Berlin, 1967).

Justi, Johann H.G., *Policeywissenschaft.*

Justi, Johann H.G., *Staatswirtschaft*, 2 vols. (Leipzig, 1758).

Klavern, Jacob von, "Fiskalismus–Mercantilismus–Korruption," *VSWG* 47 (1960): 333–53.

Klein, Ernst, "Johann Heinrich Gottlob Justi und die preussische Staatswirtschaft," *VSWG* 48 (1961): 145–202.

Kosselleck, Reinhart, *Preussen zwischen Reform und Revolution* (Stuttgart, 1967).

Koser, Reinhold, *Geschichte Friedrichs des Grossen*, 4 vols. (Stuttgart, 1912).

Koser, Reinhold, "Die preussische Finanzen im siebenjährigen Kriege," *FBPG* 13 (1900): 340–51.

Krüger, Horst, *Zur Geschichte der Manufakturen und der Manufakturarbeiter in Preussen* (Berlin, 1958).

Leesch, Wolfgang, "Die Einführung der Commissarii Perpetue (Justizräte) in Schleisien im Zuge der Coccejischen Justizreform," *FBPG* 54 (1943): 382–90.

Lehmann, Max, *Freiherr von Stein*, 3 vols. (Leipzig, 1902).

Lehndorff, E.A.H. von, *Dreissig Jahre am Hofe Friedrichs des Grossen* (Gotha, 1907).

Lenz, Friedrich and Unholtz, Otto, *Die Geschichte des Bankhauses Gebrüder Schickler* (Berlin, 1912).

Loehr, A.O., "Die Finanzierueng des siebenjährigen Kreiges," *Numismatische Zeitschrift* 58 (1925): 95–110.

Martiny, F., *Die Adelsfrage in Preussen vor 1806 als politisches und soziales Problem* (Berlin, 1938).

Matschoff, Conrad, "Friedrich der Grosse als Beförderer des Gewerbefleisses," *Technik Geschichte* (1912).

Mehrig, Franz, *Historische Aufsätze zur Preussisch-Deutschen Geschichte* (Berlin, 1946).

Meinecke, Friedrich, *Machiavellism*, tr. D. Scott (New Haven, 1957).

Mertineit, Walter, *Die fridericianische Verwaltung in Ostpreussen, Studien zur Geschichte Preussens* 1 (Heidelberg, 1958).

Mirabeau, Honore G.V. Riquetti, Comte de, *De la Monarchie Prussienne sous Frédéric le Grand*, 4 vols. (London, 1788).

Moegelin, H., "Das Retablissement des adligen Grundbesitzes in der Neumark durch Friedrich den Grossen," *Forschungen zur brandenburgischen und preussischen Geschichte* 46 (1935): 233 ff.

Mylius, C.O., ed., *Corpus Constitutionum Marchicarum-Continuationes und Supplement* (Berlin, 1744–1751).

Notbohm, Hartwig, *Das evangelische Kirchen- und Schulwesen in Ostpreussen* (Heidelberg, 1959).

Pinson, Koppel S., *Pietism as a Factor in the Rise of German Nationalism* (New York, 1934).

Preuss, Hugo, *Die Entwicklung des deutschen Stadtwesens* (Leipzig, 1906).

Preuss, J.D.E., *Friedrich der Grosse*, 6 vols. (Berlin, 1833).

Rachel, H. and Wallich P., *Berliner Grosskaufleute und Kapitalisten* 2 (Berlin, 1938).

Rath, K.W., *Stadt und Kreis* (Berlin, 1926).

Reidel, A.F., *Der brandenburg-preussische Staatshaushalt in den beiden letzten Jahrhunderten* (Berlin, 1866).

Ring, W., "Kolonisationsbestrebungen Friedrich des Grossen am Niederrhein" (Ph.D. diss., Bonn, 1917).

Ritter, Gerhard, *Friedrich der Grosse: ein historisches Profil*, 3rd ed. (Heidelberg, 1954).

Rohde, Georg, *Die Reformen Friedrich des Grossen in . . . Geldern* (Göttingen, 1913).

Rohr, W., "Zur Geschichte des Landratsmats in der Altmark," *Sachsen und Anhalt* 4 (1927): 167–84.

Rosenberg, Hans, *Bureaucracy, Aristocracy, and Autocracy* (Cambridge, Mass., 1958).

Schill, F., "Der Landrat in Kleve-Mark" *FBPG* (1908): 326–27.

Schlechte, Horst, *Die Staatsreform in Kursachsen 1762–1763* (Berlin, 1958).

Schlenke Manfred, *England und das friderizianische Preussen, 1740–1763* (Munich, 1963).

Schmidt, Eberhard, *Fiskalat und Strafprozess* (Munich, 1929).

Schmoller, Gustav, *Deutsches Stadtewesen in älterer Zeit* (Bonn, 1922).

Schmoller, Gustav, "Die preussische Einwanderung und ländliche Kolonisation," *Umrisse und Untersuchungen* (Leipzig, 1898).

Schmoller, Gustav, "*Uber Behördenorganisation*," *AB*, vol. 1.

Schnee, Heinrich, *Die Hoffinanz und der moderne Staat* (Berlin, 1953), vol. 1.

Schön, P., "Die Organization der städtischen Verwaltung in Preussen," *Annalen des deutschen Reiches* (1891), pp. 707 846.

Schrader, Kurt, *Die Verwaltung Berlins* (Ph.D. diss., Humboldt Univ., Berlin, 1963).

Schultze, W., *Geschichte der preussischen Regieverwaltung von 1766–1786*, pt. 1 (Leipzig, 1888).

Schwarz, Franz, "Organisation und Verpflegung der preussischen Landmilizen im siebenjährigen Kriege," *Staats und sozialwissenschaftliche Forschungen* 7 (Leipzig, 1888).

Schwarz, Henry F., *The Imperial Privy Council in the Seventeenth Century* (Cambridge, Mass., 1943).

Schwarz, Paul, ed., "Berichte des neumarkischen Kammerpräsidenten über die Einäscherung Cüstrins durch die Russen in August, 1758," *Schriften des Vereins für Geschichte der Neumark* 25 (1910): 103 ff.

Schwenke, Elsbeth, *Friedrich der Grosse und der Adel* (Berlin, 1911).

Seckendorff, Veit Ludwig von, *Teutscher Fürstenstaat* (Frankfurt, 1700).

Seyffert, J.C., *Annalen der Stadt und Festung Küstrins* (Kustrin, 1801).

Skalweit, August, "Die Getreidehandelspolitik und Kriegsmagazine Verwaltung Preussens, 1756–1806," *AB Getreidehandelspolitik* 4 (1901–1910).

Skalweit, August, "Wieviel Kolonisten hat Friedrich der Grosse angesiedelt?" *FBPG* 24 (1911).

Skalweit, Stephan, *Die Berliner Wirtschaftskrise von 1763 und ihre Hintergründe* (Stuttgart, 1937).

Skalweit, Stephan, *Frankreich und Friedrich der Grosse* (Bonn, 1952).

Sommer, Louise, *Die österreichischen Kameralisten*, 2 vols. (Vienna, 1920–25).

Spiro, Edith, *Die Gravamina der ostpreussischen Stände auf den Huldigungslandtagen des 18. Jr.* (Breslau, 1929).

Stadelmann, Rudolph, "*Preussens Könige in ihrer Thätigkeit für die Landeskultur*, part 2, *Friedrich der Grosse*, "Publikationen aus den K. preussischen Staatsarchiven," vol. 11 (Berlin, 1882).

Stein, Robert, *Geschichte der ostpreussischen Agrarverfassung* (Jena, 1918).

Stölzel, Adolf, *Brandenburg-Preussens Rechtsverwaltung und Rechtsverfassung*, 2 vols. (Berlin, 1888).

Stölzel, Adolf, *Carl Gottlieb Svarez* (Berlin, 1885).

Süssmilch, J.P., *Die göttliche Ordnung in den Veränderungen des menschlichen Geschlechts*, 3 vols. (Berlin, 1765–1777).

Sulicki, Carl von, *Der siebenjährige Krieg in Pommern und in den benachbarten Marken* (Berlin, 1867).

Treue, Wilhelm, "David Splitgerber ein Unternehmer im Preussischen Merkantilstaat," *VSWG* 43 (1954): 253–67.

Tröger, H., *Die kurmärkischen Spinnerdörfer* (Leipzig, 1936).

Tümpel, Ludwig, *Die Entstehung des brandenburgisch-preussischen Einheitsstaates* (Breslau, 1915).

Volz, Gustav, *Friedrich der Grosse im Spiegel seiner Zeit*, 3 vols. (Berlin, 1901).

Walter, Friedrich, *Die Österreichische Zentralverwaltung* (Vienna, 1938), pt. 2, vol. I, 1.

Weber, Max, *Essays from Max Weber*, ed. and tr. H. Gerth and C. Mills (Glencoe, Ill., 1950).

Weill, Herman, *Frederick the Great and Samuel von Cocceji* (Madison, 1961).

Winter, E., "Die Wegelysche Porzellanfabrik in Berlin," *Schriften des Vereins für Geschichte der Stadt Berlin* 35 (1898): 14 ff.

Ziekursch, Johannes, *Beiträge zur Charakteristik der preussischen Verwaltungsbeamten in Schlesien bis zum Untergange des friderizianischen Staates* (Breslau, 1907).

Ziekursch, Johannes, *Das Ergebnis der friderizianischen Städterverwaltung* (Jena, 1908).

Ziekursch, Johannes, *Hundert Jahre schlesische Agrargeschichte* (Breslau, 1927).

Zottmann, A., *Die Wirtschaftspolitik Friedrichs des Grossen* (Leipzig, 1937).

INDEX